David Power Conyngham

The O'Donnells of Glen cottage

a tale of the famine years in Ireland

The O'Donnells of Glen cottage
a tale of the famine years in Ireland

ISBN/EAN: 9783741136894

Manufactured in Europe, USA, Canada, Australia, Japa

Cover: Foto ©Thomas Meinert / pixelio.de

Manufactured and distributed by brebook publishing software
(www.brebook.com)

David Power Conyngham

The O'Donnells of Glen cottage

THE O'DONNELLS

OF

GLEN COTTAGE.

A TALE OF

THE FAMINE YEARS IN IRELAND.

By D. P. CONYNGHAM, LL. D.,

AUTHOR OF "SHERMAN'S MARCH THROUGH THE SOUTH," "THE
IRISH BRIGADE AND ITS CAMPAIGNS," "SARSFIELD, OR
THE LAST GREAT STRUGGLE FOR IRELAND,"
"LIVES OF THE IRISH SAINTS AND
MARTYRS," ETC., ETC., ETC.

"Without or with offence to friends or foes,
I sketch the world exactly as it goes."—BYRON.

NEW YORK:

D. & J. SADLIER & CO., 31 BARCLAY STREET.

MONTREAL:
No. 275 NOTRE-DAME STREET.

1881.

PREFACE.

IRELAND is a fruitful theme for the poet, the novelist, the orator, and the historian. Her wrongs and her grievances have been, like a thrice-told tale, so often repeated in song and story, that it may appear difficult, indeed, to add anything new to the sad catalogue of oppression on the part of England and of suffering on the part of Ireland.

The English policy of coercing Ireland into English views and English ideas is neither a wise nor a statesman-like one.

The love and devotion of a nation, like that of an individual, are secured more by friendly concessions, and a desire to promote mutual interests and prosperity, than by oppressive laws and coercive measures. The Irish are a generous and chivalrous people, whose friendship can be won by kindness and justice; but they are, on the other hand, a jealous and resolute people—jealous of their liberty, jeal-

ous of their rights and privileges, and resolute
in the maintenance of them, even though they
had no other means to guard them but by band-
ing together in that wild spirit of revenge which
has been so fruitful of blood and misery.

For seven hundred years England has tried
a system of coercion on Ireland. It has
failed in pacifying her. She has followed up this
by maligning and slandering her before the
world by her subsidized writers, such as Cam-
brensis and Froude. What is the result to-day?
Trampled and despised Ireland is prouder and
more defiant than she was when the first Anglo-
Norman set foot on her soil ; and her long-cher-
ished inheritance—her Catholic faith—which
has cost centuries of persecution and oceans
of blood to wipe out, is to-day purer, stronger,
and more firmly rooted on her soil than ever.

Such an introduction as this may appear out
of place for a novel ; but then it must be recollected that this "o'er true tale" is founded
on the incidents arising from that most fearful
period of Irish history and Irish suffering—the
famine years. The unfeeling, unchristian spirit
displayed at that time both by English states-
men and the English press can never be forgotten. When the Irish were dying by thousands of actual starvation, and when the living
were scarcely able to bury the dead, the London

Times, in a fit of jubilation, cried out—"The Irish are gone, gone with a vengeance ; the Lord be praised !" In the same spirit English states-men prevented Turkey and other powers from sending relief to Ireland, as such generosity would look like a reflection on England. In fact, several steamers laden with grain had to return with their cargoes, and others were so hampered with red-tapeism that their cargoes rotted before they could be delivered. It is no wonder that starving Ireland became disaffected. It is no wonder, while, in the same spirit, the land-lords were wiping out the unfortunate peasan-try to make room for sheep and black cattle, that many of them were shot by the infuriated people. Such assassinations were followed by Special Commissions, and such men as Judge Keogh were instructed to do the work of the government, and to strike terror into the dis-affected—which simply meant to hang all they could muster up evidence enough against. The brothers Cormack, who were executed in Ne-nagh, County Tipperary, were victims of this decimating policy. The first jury that tried them (on which jury, by the way, were near relatives of the writer) disagreed and were discharged ; but Judge Keogh, fully resolved on doing the work of his masters, immediately empanneled a more obsequious one, and they were convicted and subsequently executed. The innocence of the Cormacks of the murder of Mr. Ellis was so generally known that His Grace the Most Rev. Dr. Leahy, Archbishop of Cashel, joined in a petition to the Lord Lieutenant, requesting a commutation of their sentence. But the fiat had gone forth; terror should be stricken into Tipperary, and two innocent young men were immolated in order that her Gracious Majesty might live in peace and reign in security.

The scene of "The O'Donnells of Glen Cottage" has been laid in Tipperary, and the plot chiefly turns on the sufferings of the people during the famine years and the execution of the Cormacks. The characters introduced are each and all real personages, many of whom are living to-day. The names of some few of them have been slightly changed, but the majority of them come before our readers under their real names.

The pictures of the sufferings of the poor starved peasantry during the famine, the heartless evictions of Lord Clearall, the treacherous, unprincipled conduct of his agent, Mr. Ellis, and his sanctimonious protege, the Rev. Mr. Sly, are no fancy sketches. They are unfortunately true pictures of the state of Ireland at the time.

Such are the scenes and incidents that go to make up our story; and if the author has but succeeded in laying before his readers a truthful picture of the state of Ireland, and of the wrongs and sufferings of the Irish people, during the famine years, he feels satisfied that his labor will be fruitful of good results.

D. P. CONYNGHAM, LL. D.

New York, *July, 1874.*

CONTENTS.

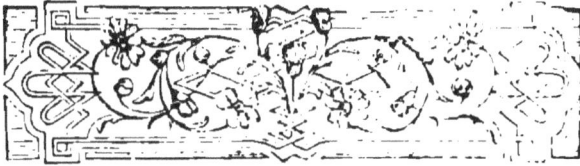

THE O'DONNELLS

OF

GLEN COTTAGE.

CHAPTER I.

FATHER O'DONNELL.—A STROLL THROUGH "THE BOOK OF CASHEL."

IT was an autumn eve; one of those beautiful evenings that seem to linger, as if loath to leave us to winter's chilly blasts.

In a cosy little parlor, in a comfortable cottage, near the village of Clerihan, sat an old gentleman, reading a large volume which lay on the table before him.

He was a stout, full man, with a good humored appearance, that told more forcibly than words could do that he was at peace with himself, and the world besides.

A crucifix stood on the chimney-piece before him, and several prints and pictures of Our Saviour and the Holy Family hung around the walls.

From these, and from his black dress, and closely shaven face, it was evident that he was a priest.

"*Deo gratias !*" said he, as he finished a chapter from his breviary.

Father O'Donnell closed the book, leant back in the arm-chair, and placed his feet on the fender, near the little fire that burned so brightly before him.

His little dog, Carlo, seemed to enjoy the quiet of the thing, too, for he dozed away upon the hearth-rug, occasionally opening his drowsy eyes, and taking a sly peep as he moved, to see would he be reprimanded for his rudeness.

At the other side of the fire, puss, rolled up in his sleek coat, and his lazy paws stretched out from him, purred a contented *cronaun* for himself, as a contented happy cat should do.

Having finished his office, the priest leant back in his chair, and fell asleep.

A graceful young girl, with a world of fun and mischief sparkling in her laughing blue eyes, stole along the hall; she peeped in at the door, and seeing the priest asleep, noiselessly slipped behind him, and clapped her hands upon his eyes.

"In God's name who is this ? who dare do it ?" exclaimed Father O'Donnell very indignantly, as he strove to pull off the hands.

"Ha! ha! ha!" rang a very musical voice behind him; "guess who's in it ?"

"Go along, you baggage, and take your hands;

isn't this a respectful way to treat an old priest, I ask you?"

"Now, don't get vexed with me, Father O'Donnell," said the young girl, flinging back the curls from her pretty face, with a toss of her head, "sure I was only joking."

"Well, well, sure I might easily know who it was, for none other but mad-cap Alice would do the like," said the priest, relaxing into good humour.

"That's it," said the other, playfully; "you now look like yourself; but you had such a cross look that time, you nearly frightened me; now, you look like a Christian, but these faces"—and she hung her brows, curled her lips, and pursed her mouth, in imitation of Father O'Donnell—"pooh! it frightens me."

Father O'Donnell leant back and laughed heartily at the caricature.

"Well, well, Miss Madcap, I can never make anything of you. The face certainly was a good one," and Father O'Donnell laughed heartily again.

"Well, then, Father O'Donnell, I have some news for you, so I came over all the way to tell it."

"And pray what is is it, Miss?"

"O! I am not going to tell it here, though. Come out in the garden, until we pluck the flowers and hear the birds singing, this beautiful evening. How do you live in this stifled room; it is as close as bee-hive; I couldn't live five minutes in it."

"Now, Alice, don't go on at such a rate; if you

were as tired as I am, after traveling through the
parish—really, I don't know how a poor old priest
like me can stand it. I first went———"

"That will do now; if you get into a history of
your day's adventures, I fear it would be night
when they'd be concluded. Now, I have but fifteen
minutes to honor you with my precious company, as
I have left my car at the village, and ran up to see
you and tell you the news."

"Well, then, let us have it, if you please; but I'd
much sooner you'd leave me here."

"Not a bit of it; here is your old hat; good gracious ! why don't you buy a new one; it is a regular
scare-crow; put the good side in front, though; now,
come out."

Father O'Donnell followed, greatly perplexed
as to what the important news was that should disturb him from his quiet nap—that should bring her
up from the village to tell him.

"Well now," said he, standing in the middle of
the walk, and facing Alice, " tell me what you have
to say ? " Alice looked at him with a rich humor
sparkling in her eyes. She then tossed her head to
fling back some straying curls that floated about her
face.

"I tell you what, Father O'Donnell," said she,
" you poor old priests, like old bachelors, don't know
how to address a lady. Just think of it, to tell me
I must do a thing; but then, poor creatures, ye
don't know better, ye don't know how to enjoy

life cosily and comfortably at all; not you, who could tell you; not a time I come but I find your books and glasses and other things in one rich state of confusion, whilst you think them all right, because Mrs. Hogan, who in your imagination is an immaculate house-keeper, placed them so."

"Do you know, Alice," said Father O'Donnell, striving to look as if such light conversation detracted from his dignity, "I often think that Lady Morgan must have met you somewhere, and taken you as her model for her 'Wild Irish Girl.' I need not read the work any more to learn all the pranks of her heroine, while I have such an original before me."

"There are more of your mistakes. Now, I believe I was scarcely born when the 'Wild Irish Girl' was written."

"Well, well! you're right, child; but now, out with your news?"

"I suppose I must; then, in the first place, I and papa will go to the races to-morrow, if you come with us."

"No, no, child; a race is no place for an old priest like me; I am become insensible to the sports of this life; besides——"

"Now, Father O'Donnell, I will not be let go unless you come, and I have set my heart on going, so do not disappoint me," said Alice, eagerly.

The priest looked at her, as a shade of sadness crossed her handsome sprightly face.

"I don't know, I don't know; I don't like to disappoint you, child, yet——."

" Do come, Father O'Donnell! " said she, plead·
ingly; besides, Frank O'Donnell, or as you call him,
' your child,' though he's a young man over twenty
years of age "——

" What about him ? " said the other, eagerly.

" He's to ride the Fawn for the Rock Stakes;
won't that induce you ? "

" Frank O'Donnell to ride a steeple-chase! " said
the priest, raising his eyes, and looking the very
picture of surprise.

" Now, if you put such a horrid phiz upon you
again you'll frighten me away. What ·is there
wrong in it; would you have him become a Tra·
pist, and not have a spark of life in him; as for my
part, I should like to see him riding, he will look so
grand when dressed."

" Child, child! you know not what you say; can
an O'Donnell descend to become a jockey ? "

" There you're wrong again; the best of gentlemen ride; look at Lord Waterford—but it's getting
late; will you come ? "

" Yes, I will go; I'll meet ye at the little gate in
the morning, so good-bye now."

" Good-bye, and don't fail," said Alice, as she
tripped away.

" I will be there, sure enough," said Father
O'Donnell to himself, " to prevent him from riding;
this racing brings on such habits of idleness and
dissipation, I must try and save him."

There is a splendid view from the picturesque and majestic Rock of Cashel.

Extending along beneath you, in one beautiful fertile plain, lies the golden vale, so called on account of the great fertility of its soil. Villages and the ruins of abbeys and castles dot the landscape, while here and there are gentlemen's seats and farm houses. The silvery Suir flows through this beautiful tract of country, and the stately Gaultees, Slievenamon, and Knoc-Mael-down, raise their towering heads in the distance. The city, with its ruins of abbeys and churches, lies in one panorama at your feet. What shall we say of the Rock itself ?—once the seat of kings, and even now bearing the impress of kingly grandeur upon its brow. Though the hand of time has pressed heavily upon it ; though the zeal of rude fanatics has pressed heavier still, yet there it stands, proud, stately, and majestic, even in its decay, a living monument of the zeal and power of Catholicity in the olden times.

On the day with which our tale commences, there was nothing of that sleepy indolence that too often characterizes our decaying towns and villages, about the city of kings ; no, the people appeared joyous and happy, for it was a races day.

On such occasions strangers and sightseers take a run through the Rock before the races ; you might see crowds of boys and poor men, who eagerly pay their penny, to run about its vast ruins, and to wonder and speculate for what it was built at all.

But look at these respectably dressed men, with their guide carefully explaining every part to them; they have paid their shilling and entered their names in the visitors' book, for the edification of future tourists. They nod an assent to everything the guide says, and he, honest man that he is, tells them a great deal, be it true or false ; no matter, he gives them the full value of their money.

Apart from the rest strolled two men ; one was our friend, Father O'Donnell, the other was a young man of about twenty ; he might be a few years older. He was of middle height, with a light, elastic step, and a pleasing appearance. His hair was dark, and clustered in thick curls about his ample forehead. His eyes were dark, but intelligent-looking ; and though a smile played occasionally around his handsome mouth, still, an air of sadness, that ill became one so young, overshadowed him by times.

The two stood for a time without speaking, for Father O'Donnell seemed to have something heavy upon his mind ; at length his young companion said : " I'm sure, uncle, it is not to see the races you came, for I think you were never an admirer of them."

" No, Frank, it is not ; what would a poor old priest like me want to races ? "

" Why, sir, the old require enjoyment as well as the young, and after your heavy duties a little relaxation would serve you ; for the mind requires rest as well as the body."

"True enough, child ; but when the mind grows old, and the body totters on the verge of the grave, all our amusements should consist in the performance of those duties we owe to God and man ; there is a terrible reckoning hereafter, Frank, moreover, for a poor old priest entrusted with the salvation of others."

Frank said nothing, but commenced an inspection of a stone effigy of St. Paul, that lay at his feet.

Father O'Donnell laid his hand upon Frank's shoulder, and then, after a few hems, said, " Tell me, Frank, are you going to ride to-day ? "

Frank held down his head, and seemed to commune with St. Paul.

"I know, Frank," continued the priest, " you won't tell me a lie. I see it is true, child. It is a poor ambition, Frank, for an O'Donnell ; I always thought that you would fill my place when I'd be in my grave. Despite your mother's solicitations, you have given up the Church, and now, you are going to descend so low as to become a jockey."

Frank still held down his head and was silent.

"Frank," said the priest, taking him tenderly by the hand ; " you know I love you, my dear child ; do this now to gladden the heart of your poor uncle; give up this racing ; nothing good can come of it ; I have come here on purpose to ask this favor of you."

The tears stood in Frank's eyes as he replied— " My dear uncle, I would do anything to please you, but I have promised to ride the Fawn to-day ; now you have always taught me to keep my word. Perhaps I was wrong in promising; I know I was, but, as I have, allow me to ride this time, it will be my last."

" Well, since you have promised, be it so, but never do it again."

" I pledge you I will not," said Frank.

" Well, then, go now, boy, I'll meet you in the evening ; but stop, we hav'nt seen much of the rock; that mad-cap, Alice Maher, that brought me here, Frank, you know her, don't you ? "

"Oh, yes, I have met her at your house."

"She is a wild girl, Frank, and after all, somehow I'm fond of her ; if you heard how she fought for you yesterday, I'm sure you'd be fond of her too."

All this time Frank was turning the unconscious saint over and over ; he examined it at all points ; in fact, he might become a statuary, and carve one for himself, so closely had he tried it in all its bearings. Father O'Donnell wondered at his silence, but like most old men, he loved to have all the talk to himself, so he did not mind. He did not know, so little was he versed in the intricacies of that strange thing, the human heart—he did not know, when he told Frank that he ought to be fond of Alice Maher, that Frank had dutifully anticipated his advice. Five years had passed since Frank had met Alice at his uncle's. Father O'Donnell fondly hoped that Frank would replace him in his house

and place, and as pastor and law-giver to the village
of Cleriban, and the adjacent parish. Frank's
mother, too, longed for the day that her son would
be a blessed *soggarth-aroon*, but, contrary to all their
expectations, Master Frank O'Donnell found that he
had no vocation for a clerical life. He made this
discovery about two years before we introduce him
to our readers ; some thought that the sparkling
eye and roguish ways of Alice Maher had a great
deal to do with it. Father O'Donnell—poor innocent man that he was—still persisted in looking upon
Alice and Frank as children. He little knew what
a deep passion was agitating their young bosoms.

" Come, now, let us have a look at the rock,
Frank ; I know it pretty well, so I'll be your guide.
See, Frank, see this magnificent cathedral, look at
these grand Gothic jointed arches, see how beautifully they are chiselled, how fine the tracery is ; it is
said to be founded about the year 1152, by Donald
O'Brien, king of Munster ; some think that it was
built by the celebrated Cormac M'Cuilenan, king of
Munster and bishop of Cashel. He was killed in the
year 908 ; be this as it may, it is a grand structure.
Look at all these old tombs, effigies, and monuments,
that lie scattered about. That old stone coffin beyond belonged to King Cormac. Look at that
richly carved tomb with the effigies of the twelve
Apostles near it. Of all these monuments, perhaps
that erected to Milor M'Grath is the most remarkable. He apostatized, and was translated from the

bishopric of Down to that of Cashel in 1570. This
is an effigy of him in a recumbent position with his
mitre on.

"The following is a translation of his quaint
epitaph, which he wrote himself:"—

*The verse of Milor McGrath, Archbishop of
Cashel, to the traveler. The most sanctified
Patrick, the great glory of our soil, first came into
Down. I was also in Down the first time; though
succeeding him in place, would I were as holy as he.
I served the English fifty years, and pleased the
princes in raging war.*

*Here, where I am placed I am not, I am not where
I am not, neither am I in both, but I am in both
places. He that judgeth me is the Lord. 1st Cor.
4 chap.*

"*Let him that standeth take heed lest he falleth.*"

Father O'Donnell mused, and looking about him
on the crumbling monuments, said,—"Kings, and
bishops, and lords lie mouldering beneath our feet;
how far does their pride or ambition avail them now,
Frank; one kind act, a cup of cold water given in
the name of the Lord, would smell sweeter before
heaven than all their vain pomp and parade. The
poor peasant that moulders in his humble grave beneath the canopy of heaven has a sweeter sleep than
these lordly ones in their storied urns."

They then passed into Cormac's Chapel.

"This," said Father O'Donnell, "was built by
Cormac M'Carthy, in the early part of the twelfth

century. It is cruciform, of the decorated Norman
style. All its capitals aud traceries are embellished
with grotesque heads of men and animals. Near it
is a fine round tower in a good state of preserva-
tion."

As they passed beneath the splendid arch which
springs from the centre of the cathedral, and is about
fifty feet high,

"Look," said Father O'Donnell, pointing upwards;
"this was the belfry; it was battered in 1647 by
Cromwell's troops under Murrogh O'Brien, Earl of.
Inchiquin. What a strange medley of good and
bad these O'Briens were. There was in the hall at
Dromoland a rough marble table, on which their
progenitors were wont to behead their refractory
subjects, but this was in accordance with the spirit
of the times, when, as their motto has it, *'lamh
laudhir amuaktha,'* or the strongest hand upper-
most."

" Here is the castle at the west end, the residence
of the ancient kings, where

" Stately the feast and high the cheer,

that echoed through its halls. Now let us pass out.
Beneath this rough stone cross the kings of Munster
were crowned. Look at all these abbeys around;
there is a whole host of legends about St. Patrick,
Ossian, an enchanted bull, and an enchanted lady,
that decoyed people to *Tir-ne-nogue;* but I must re-
serve them for another time. So, you see, Cashel
was a place of importance in its day.

2

"I know you are impatient to go now, Frank," continued Father O'Donnell to him, as he stood counting the chimes of a neighboring clock that struck eleven. "Well, go, child, and God bless you; and as for me, I'll return to commune with myself among these deserted halls and cloisters. It is pleasing to listen to the music and chirping of the little birds in these grey old ruins. They seem so happy amidst the surrounding desolation, none of our cares or troubles disturb their joyous existence. These sculptured walls and architraves do not recall any feeling of the past to them. These lonely graves do not speak to them of decay, nor can they conceive the desolation of the sublime spirit that makes us shudder at death; but, then, there is hope, for angel voices above us inspire us with the belief that God shall accept our good works, and hearken to our humble prayers.

"While you are enjoying yourself, Frank, I will people these ruins with mailed warriors and ladies fair; with thronging worshipers bowing before their prelate and their king; with priests and monks around the sacred shrines, chanting God's endless praise,

"———— in deep and measured flow,
Of psalmody and hymn!"

CHAPTER II.

As Frank returned to the city the streets were thronged with people; conveyances, too, of all kinds dashed rapidly on. There was the coach-and-four with its liveried servants and fair inmates; next came the tax-cart, with its dandy driver in white kids and immaculate tie: then the jaunting-car, laden with the wealthier class of farmers' sons and daughters; and lastly the Scotch car, with its rosy-cheeked laughing occupants, reclining upon trusses of hay or straw, and modestly blushing at the bantering jokes of happy swains, whose blarneyed tongues and good looks proved irresistible passports.

The hotels and shops were crowded with lounging squireens, smoking their cigars, sipping their brandy, and betting and speculating.

There were, too, plenty of wet souls fortifying themselves with spirituous comforts, and loving souls coaxing their sweethearts to take the least "tint of wine against the day; shure the dear creatures would want it."

Seldom did the old royal city of Cashel witness such a concourse of drinking jovial souls, bent on

fun and enjoyment; not, perhaps, since the shouts
of a quarter of a million human beings from the
priest hill startled the old rock and the quiet dead
therein reposing, with the glad tidings that Ireland
was to be free. O'Connell said so, and the people
hailed him with lusty lungs.

Strange, all this time pauperism was beginning to
overspread the land; the people were treading upon
a mine; they rushed on with light hearts, whilst
starvation was enfolding them with its sable wings.

As Frank approached the hotel, a most ludicrous
scene blocked his way. There, elbowing and crush-
ing one another, was collected a ragged group of
beggars. Some of them hobbled on crutches, others
on dishes, others had crying children in their arms
to create sympathy.

Jarvies, too, were vigorously whipping their jaded
rosinantes. " A seat, sir, only sixpence; a splendid
drive, sir," shouted a squat little fellow, with a red
handkerchief tied around his neck, to Frank.

"A beautiful drive, indeed; oh, musha, do you
hear that; into the pond, I suppose, where you are
after leaving Mrs. Parse and her family; the day is
fine enuff, glory be to God, to take a shwim; up
here, your honor; I have got the horse," shouted the
rival.

"Ay, barrin' the two spavins and the blind eye,"
retorted the other; " begorra, sir, it will be as good
as travellin' in a balloon; the beautiful way he has
of dashin' you up with the hind feet."

" Goin' out, sir, just goin', wants only one; jump up. Arragh hould your prate, every mother's sowl of yes; this is the horse that ran against the ' rock.' "

" No wonder," said another, " considering that he hasn't a sthem; shure he's always running against rocks and cars."

" I mean Captain Rock, your honor, he only won by a neck."

" Was it this races twelve months, Jim," enquired another, " that he broke Mr. Ryan's leg ? You see, your honor, when he heard the bugle, he ran away and upset the car upon the poor jintleman; shure we had a dacent berrin' upon him; the scarf I got made a shirt for my little boy."

There was au old gentleman settled very comfortably upon the car with his rug loosely about his feet, but the old gentleman became very pale and jumped off; the driver insisted that he should remain, but the old gentleman wisely paid his fare and decamped.

" This is the horse, your honor, that does the thing handsomely," shouted another, as he whipped up to the old gentleman.

" I think I won't go at all," said the old gentleman, doubtingly.

" Arragh do, your honor, he's as quiet as a lamb," and he drove up to him among the ragged group, whose devotions he disturbed.

" One penny for the good of your father's sowl."

" A weeny sixpence betune a lot of us, poor forlorn women; do, your honor, and God reward you."

The old gentleman looked bewildered among the group.

"Bad luck to you, do you mean to drive the horse on top of us?"

"Arragh, will you look before you, you *omadhawn*, and not rush on the top of the poor."

"Out in five minutes; lay the way, ye set."

"The curse of Cromwell attend you, Jack Lanty; who'd go upon yur broken-kneed, broken-winded garron?"

In truth, Jack's horse showed evident signs of being a pious horse, and also of a breaking constitution; the chief sign was a dry, asthmatic cough, that almost shook the driver from his perch.

Jack whipped the horse more fiercely among the group, which set crutches and dishes in active use. The old gentleman vowed that he wouldn't go at all, and succeeded in elbowing his way through the crowd.

"For God's sake, will you let me pass in?" said Frank.

"Throw a weeny sixpence betune us, your honor."

"Musha, faith, the young blood doesn't have much to spare now-a-days; God be wid ould times," said an old cynical beggar, with a short dudeen in his mouth.

"He has the good face, any way," said another.

"Mary's the good face carries an empty pocket, though," said the cynic, drawing out his dudeen to indulge in a good whiff.

"Here," said Frank, putting his hand in his pocket.

"Long life to your honor. Shure it's Mr. O'Donnell; it's kind for him to be good to the poor. Shure he's to ride the Fawn, and may he win; he's the handsome gentleman, God bless him."

"Whoop, tallyho there! lay the way for Mr. Frank," shouted a voice from behind.

Frank turned around and beheld a nondescript figure dressed in a red hunting frock and cap, and whirling a club that might do credit to a Cyclops.

"It's only *Shemus a Clough*, a poor simpleton, your honor," shouted the group.

"Ah! is this Shemus," said Frank, turning to him.

"Sarra anither, Misther Frank; whoop, tallyho."

"Shure you wont forget us, your honor," said the beggars.

Frank flung some coppers among them, and while the lame and blind and halt were mixed in one scramble, he got into the yard with Shemus, who, as was his habit, was all the time singing snatches of songs.

> "Some loves to kiss a pretty lass,
> Some loves to toss a flowing glass;
> But I loves a sporting pack
> A chasing reynard in their track.
> Tallyho, tallyho, in the morning."

"Isn't that beautiful, Misther Frank; hurra, I am glad to see you here, and you'll win, Misther Frank; shure I know it, for something here," and he placed

his hand over his heart, "tells me the good news
always, you know. I can sing and laugh then, and
I can sing and laugh now."

> "Some loves their horse and hounds,.
> Some loves their pleasure grounds ;
> But I loves a sporting pack
> A chasing reynard in their track.
>   Tallyho, tallyho, in the morning."

"And Shemus, poor fellow, you have come all the
ways to the races ? "

"Faith, in troth I have. Isn't it pleasant, Misther
Frank, though I was scarcely able to come, for I fell
into the big quarry of Garryleagh last week ; we
were in such a chase we never saw it until I rouled
head over heels into it, along with Spanker and
Dido ; wasn't it pleasant ? "

"Poor fellow, I think not. Why did you come
here, for really you look ill ?" said Frank, compas-
sionately.

"Misther Maher got me taken to his house, and
I'm there since with his colleen of a daughter ; I'm
fond of her, for she's good to poor Shemus. Well,
when I heard that you were to ride the Fawn,
whoops, I jumped out of bed this morning, for they
wouldn't show you fair play if I wasn't there ; well,
I stole away, and shure when they overtook me,
Miss Alice took me up beside her ; aye faith. I'm
fond of her ; she's a *colleen bawn.*"

> "Her cheeks are rosy, and her sparklin' eyes
> Are like two stars in the azure skies ;
> Her voice is sweet, and her golden hair
> Floats as soft and free as mountain air.
>   My colleen bawn dhas Machree."

" Isn't that purty, Misther Frank ? "

But Frank did not heed him, so occupied was he with his own thoughts.

" I'll sing the rest of it ; shure she desarves it."

" Not now, Shemus, not now. Here, take this to get your dinner, and meet me after the races."

Shemus' simple tribute of praise to the girl of his soul awoke a delicious feeling in his bosom; a chaste desire thrilled his heart, and suffused his cheeks with its warm glow. Frank, with a sigh, turned away, muttering to himself, " Alice, sweet Alice ! "

A number of gentlemen, jockeys, and other lovers of the turf were collected around the centre table in the parlor of the hotel. Some decanters of wine and whiskey were upon the table, and, from their consumptive state, it was evident that they were done ample justice to.

" Ah, here's O'Donnell," said one. " Come, my dear fellow ; where were you all day ? Try a drop of this, and let us be off."

Frank drank a glass of wine.

" Can I travel out with you, O'Ryan ? " said he to a young man near him.

" Certainly, my dear fellow ; I hope we won't be the worst friends by and by. You see, if I fall, O' Donnell, you must pick me up, and *vice-versa*."

" Nonsense, man, I wont kill you if I can avoid it."

" It will be, as the old saying is," said another,

"the devil take the hindmost." Ha, ha, ha, shouted the company.

"I fear, then, I will come in for his share, for I'm always looked upon as his child," said O'Ryan.

"Then you ought to have the devil's luck," said another; "however, I think we had better be moving now."

An Irish races, and, I suppose, an English one too, is a very important event; it affords a fire-side gossip to the peasantry for months previous. They speculate on the merits of the contending horses; they lay by their little savings for the grand occasion; even the young maidens look forward to it with the greatest anxiety, and no wonder, for many a colleen meets her sweetheart there, and arranges how some relentless father or guardian is to be propitiated; many a sedate father meets his neighbor to arrange that little affair between the colleen and his gorsoon.

An Irish peasant is a most incomprehensible being; though steeped in poverty, though, perhaps, the agent has distrained his last cow, still he will rush into the gayest scenes with a kind of reckless pleasure. This unaccountable levity after grief, like sunshine after a storm, is, as he says himself, "to kill grief, for an ounce of care never paid a pound of sorrow."

It is hard to fathom an Irish peasant's heart, agitated by all the feelings, passions, and virtues of other men; his unrequited labor, his unceasing

struggle for existence, his blighted prospects, too
often stir up the worst passions of his mercurial
nature, and fill his heart with that wild spirit of
revenge that too often brings desolation in its
track.

The day was fine, beautifully fine ; the roads were
crowded with masses of people, and cavalcades
moving towards the course, which was about a mile
from the city.   As Frank and his party reached the
showy stand-house upon the top of the hill, it was
crowded with gentlemen with their cards stuck
jauntingly under their hat-bands.   Some used opera-
glasses, which they invariably pointed towards the
long range of cars and carriages at the other
side.

Gallant cavaliers often rode up to the carriages,
trying to make themselves particularly agreeable to
their fascinating occupants.   There was occasionally
a hearty laugh at the expense of some dandy, whose
dusty coat showed that he had come to grief in try
ing his bit of blood at the hurls.

This scene was enlivened with the cries of

" The color of the rider, and the rider's name."

" Twenty fusees for a half-penny."

" Who rakes and sports again, who rakes and
sports again."

" Five to one on the Fawn, five to one on the
Fawn."

" Three to two on Harkaway."

" Three to five on Slinger."

"A cigar, sur, a cigar, sur; a light, sur, a light, sur."

"A card, sur, a card; a true and correct bill of the races."

"Three ballads for a half-penny; a full account of the execution of the Codys, and how they tried to kill the hangman, glory be to God! all for one half-penny!"

The weighing-ground was a walled-in space beside the stand-house, and after some minor races, the bell rang for the great event of the day—the steeple-chase for the Rock stakes.

Frank threw off his over-coat and stood in his green silk jacket and pink cap, a perfect type of a gentleman rider. His slight, graceful, and well-built frame looked to advantage in his picturesque dress. The riders now mounted and cantered their horses about the roped-in space to put them in move-ment.

As Frank passed on he cast a hurried glance at the cars; he was greeted with a friendly nod and kind smile.

They now returned as the last bell tolled and were formed into a rank. As the signal was given, away they dashed in beautiful style.

They took the small wall leading to the pond in a-breast, then swept over the pond, keeping well to-gether.

As they dashed up the hill in the heavy ground, Frank allowed the strong horses to lead him, for the

Fawn was a slight mare, highly bred, and possessed
of immense speed. Two rolled over at the kiln
fence, but Slinger, New Light, Harkaway, Fawn,
and a few more, kept their places well together.
As they turned the rise of ground, Fawn took the
lead at a fearful pace, but slackened against the hill
near the stand-house. Harkaway now dashed in
front, followed by New Light, Chance, and then the
Fawn. Frank noticed a white handkerchief waving
to him as he shot by. Now they were nearing the
pond again; down went New Light, and Chance.
Frank raised the mare and thought to jump her over
the sprawling horses and riders. As the Fawn dashed
over them with one fearful spring, she rolled heavily
abroad with Frank beneath her.

"There are two in the pond," shouted the spectators from the hill. "Whist, the Fawn is down,
he's killed, she's on top of him!"

Alice leant back pale as death.

"What's the matter, child?" said her father,
anxiously.

"Hurra! he's up again!" shouted the people.

"Nothing, papa, I'm well now," said Alice, as she
heard the shout.

The Fawn had scarcely rolled over, when Frank
was pulled up and flung upon her back; neither of
them was much hurt.

"Hoorrah! whip away, Misther Frank; you'll win
yet," shouted Shemus-a-Clough, as he flung him into
the saddle.

As Frank recovered himself, Harkaway and two
others were contending hard for the next fence.
They were about a hundred yards a-head.

Frank, depending upon the mare's breeding and
speed, gained upon them until he came up to the
kiln fence.   As they turned the fall, Fawn took the
lead, and they came nearly a-breast for the last jump.
The mare's high breeding and mettle now stood to
her, for, though hard pressed by Harkaway, she ran
in winner by a length.

" Come, my dear fellow," said Mr. Maher, taking
Frank by the arm, as he left the scale; " you got on
cleverly, we have a bit of lunch for you, so you must
come and join us."

Frank assented, and drew his top-coat over his
riding dress.

As they passed through the crowd, a wild chorus
of cheers and a flourish of alpeens greeted them; but
high above the rest Shemus' voice and cudgel were
equally prominent.

" Alice!" said Mr. Maher, to his daughter, " I have
caught the lion of the races for you, and I am sure
he wants some refreshment now; so I brought him
to you."

" You are always very kind, papa," said she, with
a sweet smile, as she reached her trembling hand to
Frank.

" Alice," whispered Frank, as he pressed that fair
hand.

There must be some electric power in the human

touch, for Frank's heart beat high, and Alice blushed and busied herself about the lunch.

"Frank, my boy, fill a glass of wine, you look pale and agitated; no wonder, it was fierce riding; my heart jumped to my mouth when you fell, and some imps, confound them, cried out that you were killed. I hadn't much time to see whether you were or not, for just then Alice took it into her head to get a weakness like; you can't know when these women will fall upon your hands; but why the deuce arn't you drinking your wine, man alive; you look as pale as a ghost," said Mr. Maher.

The glass trembled in Frank's hand, and Alice was very busy looking for something she couldn't find.

"Ha, O'Donnell! is it there you are, boy; right old fellow; remember the supper, the winner to stand all, you know; devilish nice swim I had in the pond," shouted a young man from the seat of a tax-cart.

"I shan't forget, O'Ryan," stammered Frank.

"Stop, though, will we take you in, a seat for one?" and O'Ryan pointed to the vacant place, and winked to his companions.

"You can travel with us," whispered Alice.

"No, O'Ryan; I'm too comfortable as I am to change."

"So I thought; good-bye until dinner," and O'Ryan whipped his steed.

CHAPTER III.

The dining-room of the hotel was quite crowded. The little front parlor was occupied with a roulette table, surrounded by a number of gentlemen, some betting, others reclining on sofas or chairs, taking a nap. A waiter, with a white apron before him, and flourishing a napkin, announced—" Dinner, gentlemen, dinner," and he gave another flourish to the napkin.

" I say, waiter, will you waken Mr. —— there ? "

" Yes, sir. Mr. —— come to dinner;" and the waiter pulled him gently by the coat.

"Yes, honey; sure it is that cursed O'Ryan, bad luck to the scamp, made me drink; aren't we better go to bed, love."

A general roar of laughter convulsed the company, which made Mr. —— open his eyes, yawn, and ask, " where am I ? "

"Here, sir, " said the waiter; "the company is going to dinner, wont you come ? "

" Oh, certainly," said the other, " go on, I'll follow you."

It would not be easy to meet a more gay or jolly company than crowded around that dinner table.

There is something peculiarly gay about the Irish people. This is evident, not only among the peasantry, but also among the higher classes of society. Whether this is owing to our nature, to our soil or climate, I cannot tell; but it is true, at least, and happy for us that it is so, for this pliant elasticity supports us through the many trying vicissitudes that have harassed our country. The passionate elements of our strong nature seem but ill adapted to the state of sufferance under which we live. How often will you see depicted on the face of the peasant that dogged indifference that tells of sufferings deep and deadly, sufferings that would steel the heart of any but an Irishman against all the finer feelings of human nature; yet express but one word of sympathy, do but one trifling act of kindness for him, and the haggard, death-like face will brighten up, and a tear of gratitude will glisten in the eye so dull and stupid with despair a moment before.

" Will you help me to some turkey, gentlemen ? " said a fat, puffy man, from the end of the table. This puffy one always ended his subject with a long " pooh."

" Certainly, Mr. Baker," said another. " Doctor, pray dissect that turkey near you."

" Ay do, doctor ; you ought to be good at dissection, you know. Pooh, pooh."

Mr. Baker pursed up his mouth, leant back in his chair, and indulged in a very long "pooh."

"I say, Mr. Baker," said O'Ryan, who sat near him, "would you give us a change of air?"

This created a general laugh.

"Hand it to the coroner; let him try it," said the doctor.

"Which?" said Coroner Mara—"the air or the turkey?"

"Both, Mr. Coroner, both; we want a *post mortem* examination."

The dishes were removed, and the drink circulated freely, enlivened with song, and jest, and story.

"Will you tell us, Burke," said one, "what Sergeant Purcel O'Gorman said to the priest?"

"Aye, faith, that was a good one," said Burke.

"I had some business to the session at Urlingford. After the court broke up, I called to see the sergeant about some special business."

"'Ah, glad to see you, Mr. Burke; just done dinner; will you have a glass of punch?'"

"'With pleasure, sir,' said I. So we got on from glass to glass, until we had a dozen each. 'Ring that bell, Mr. Burke, if you please.' I did so, and the servant shortly made his appearance. 'John,' said he, as John poked his head through the door, 'John, get a broil; I feel a little sick, and don't mean to retire until late.' 'Yis, sur,' says John, with a bow. So we were quietly brewing another

glass, and the grateful steam of the broil was
ascending, when we heard a rap at the door. John
soon made his appearance. 'Who the devil is that,
John?' said the sergeant. 'The priest, your worship; he wants to see you.' 'Show him up—and
John, take care of the broil.' 'Yis, your worship.'
Father —— was shown up. 'Ah, welcome, Father.
This is Mr. Burke. Will you have a glass?' 'With
much pleasure,' said the priest, who had a point to
carry. 'John, a glass for Father ——.' 'Yis, your
worship.' 'I have a case for your worship to-morrow,' said Father ——. 'Ah, now, justice must be
done you, of course.' 'In your hands I am confident of that,' said the priest, with something like a
sneer. 'It is a case of ejectment, in which I am
defendant. I go more on the principle of the thing,
as it is an important one, than on ——.' 'Oh, certainly, we will see all about it; now take your
punch. Your health, Father ——.' 'Good health,
sir.' Father —— rose to depart. John, show
Father —— down stairs.' 'Yis, your worship.'
They had scarcely gained the landing when he called
out—'John.' 'Yis, sir,' shouted John. Sergeant
O'Gorman was puffing and blowing all this time,
and now thinking the priest had left, he called out
'John.' 'Yis, your worship,' shouted John, from
the middle of the stairs. 'John, bring up the devil,
the priest is gone.'

"Father —— was all this time standing with the
door ajar, undecided whether he'd go, or return to

impress his case more forcibly; but when he heard of the devil, he made a hasty exit. I think it served his case, for, when it was called next day, the sergeant ordered it to be dismissed, giving as his reason, that the priest would not defend it if it were a just case."

" Faith, that was a novel reason," said one.

" Ah, you know little about the law, or you wouldn't say so," said Mr. Burke.

" O'Ryan, will you tell us how you killed the gauger ? " said another.

" Killed a gauger ! " said all the company, with surprise.

" Aye, faith," said O'Ryan, "and waked him too."

"Tell the story, anyway."

" Well, there was a gauger hunting for a still ; he called to me one evening just as I was going to dinner ; I was after a spree, and half-drunk. 'You didn't dine,' said I to the gauger. ' No, but ' —'Oh, now, no excuse, my dear sir ; we are just going to dinner, so you will take pot luck with us.' The gauger assented. After dinner we fell at the punch. I had a bottle of tincture of opium, and whatever devilment seized me, I let some of it spill into his punch. Bedad, he shortly fell off into a comfortable heavy doze. I had Ned Wright and a few more scamps with me ; what did we do but take the poor man and stretch him on a long table ; we then threw a sheet over him, and lit candles

around him. I rang the bell; 'Biddy,' said I to the
servant, 'the gauger is dead; don't make any noise
about it.' Biddy stood at the door almost petrified,
with her mouth and hands opened to their fullest
extent, and her eyes staring at the supposed corpse.
Biddy, like a good, dutiful girl, being told not to
make any noise, ran out into the street as soon as
she was able, and told it to every one. The people
crowded in, and before we could rouse up the gauger
the room was full. When he came to himself, I
never saw a man so angry; he told me that I would
never have a day's luck, and I believe he told the
truth. Here, shove round the bottle."

"It was a sporting trick," said O'Donnell.

"Faith, then, so it was. By-the-bye, who was
that fair one you were so engaged with, when I
accosted you on the course?" asked O'Ryan.

"Oh, she is a noted belle," said another. "She
wouldn't favor the races to-day but to see how a certain gentleman in green and pink would look."

Here he gave a wink at O'Donnell.

"Pooh! O'Donnell," said another, "don't blush
that way, man-alive, 'like a maiden with love over-
laden.' You see I am getting poetical. Here, man,
fill a bumper, and let us pledge this unknown goddess."

Frank smiled, and filled his glass.

"Now, all of you," and the glasses were emptied,
amidst a regular chorus of "hip, hip, hurrah!"—
"She is a right good fellow"—"To lady's eyes,

around, boys, we can't refuse, we can't refuse "—
* The glass of punch, the glass of punch."

"Fill again," said O'Ryan, "for another toast."

'Not after that ; I will not drink another to-
night," said Frank.

"Well, all right, boy," shouted the company.

CHAPTER IV..

THOUGH we have taken a hasty notice of Father O'Donnell in our opening chapter, we must now return to him more fully.

The little village of Clerihan, over which Father O'Donnell presided as priest and lawgiver, was, like most of our Irish villages, a straggling compound of shops—an apothecary's establishment, a church, a chapel, and then the suburbs were garnished with rows of filthy cabins. Irish landlords take little or no concern about improving the towns and villages on their estates ; and many, through a dogged spirit of non-interference with their rights, will not even give leases to the enterprising or industrious ; therefore, the good houses fast decay, whilst cabins of the most filthy kind spring into existence.

"Faith, sur, if he ejects us out of this aself, it is no great loss ! Shure, if we built a better one we should pay well for it," is the unavailing answer you will get if you ask why their houses are in such a wretched state.

Father O'Donnell's house, or cottage, was situated
at the end of the village. A small lawn extended
to the road. It was a comfortable thatched house.
Shrubs and trees were nicely ranged in front, whilst
the wall glistened with ivy and woodbine. Its interior was not less inviting. On one side of the hall,
which ran through the house, was the parlor, which
was contrived a triple debt to pay; for it answered
the purpose of drawing-room, parlor, and, on pressing occasions, bedroom. Father O'Donnell's parlor
was furnished in very respectable style. A nice
Turkey carpet concealed the cracks in the floor, an
easy-looking sofa occupied a niche in the side wall,
whilst a sideboard, glistening with glasses and some
real plate, stood opposite the window. But the seat
of honor, in which the good Father read his breviary,
heard the disputes of the parish and adjudicated on
them—in fact, ruled at once as the Law and the
Prophet; and there enjoyed a doze, was a fine old
arm-chair of ample proportions that occupied a place
near the fire. Now, if we add to this his little dog,
Carlo, which was stretched in the fullness of enjoyment on the hearthrug, and place Father O'Donnell
in his chair, we have a perfect picture of the good
priest after the labors of the day.

It is fair that we should take a look at the kitchen,
where Mrs. Hogan, the house-keeper, is enjoying
herself. Mrs. Hogan is seated in a corner beside a
blazing turf fire, with one foot thrown across the other,
her eyes turned up the chimney watching the lazy

ουιling smoke from the aforesaid fire. She looked a real picture of enjoyment, and no wonder, for the very tins glistened upon the dresser, and the flags were perfectly clean and smooth, and the flitches of bacon hung temptingly over her head.

"So, you expect Misther Frank, ma'am," said Neddy O'Brien, the boy of all work, as he sat at the other side of the fire enjoying its warmth.

" Yis, achora," said Mrs. Hogan, without lowering her eyes.

" Shure I am often wondering, Mrs. Hogan, why he did'nt become a priest."

" Well, asthore, as Father O'Donnell says, 'man proposes, but God disposes.' "

"True enuff for you, ma'am; oh, its you have the larnin' and scripture; faix, though what do you think of myself, but do be thinking that Miss Maher has something to do with it; begorra, ma'am, but I thinks they's courtin'." Neddy held down his head and blushed at the turpitude of his suggestion.

" May be so, achud; who knows; shure its natural; throw tow into the fire and it will burn."

"Thrue for you ma'am, but they say it is not lucky, when one is intended for the church to kick up; but Mrs. Hogan, I do be wondering that so fine a woman as you never married; shure Jack Grace, and you know he has a snug place, often ax's me would you marry; shure I don't know what to say."

"Git out of that now," said Mrs. Hogan, looking evidently well pleased.

8

" Sorra a word of a lie in it; faix he has me bothered."

" A good sensible man he is, and a snug little place he has.   I believe he milks two cows."

" Three, Mrs. Hogon," suggested Neddy.

" And what did you tell him ? "

" Faix I said I knew you would, that you had a handsome penny, and that there were many looking for you."

" That's a good boy, Neddy; shure it's a blessing for people to have their own house; you see, Neddy, if anything was to happen the poor old priest, God betune us and harm "—here Mrs. Hogan put the corner of her apron to the corner of her eye, and indulged in a little melancholy reflection; having composed her feelings, she continued—" if anything happened him, I would be badly off."

" That's what I does be saying myself, ma'am, in your absence.   I wish I had my dinner, for I feel hungry," said Neddy, breaking off with a yawn and stretching his hands.

" That's true, I was forgetting," said Mrs. Hogan, and she went and placed plenty of cold meat on the table, and fell at crisping the potatoes for Neddy.

" I will draw the table near the fire," said Neddy.

" Do, avic, and make yourself comfortable."

So he drew down the table, and made himself comfortable, all the time chuckling inwardly at how he " butthered " Mrs. Hogan; for Mrs. Hogan was remarkable for her miserly propensities, in fact for starving every person and thing she could, save and except herself.

"Neddy," said Mrs. Hogan, " maybe you'd like a glass of punch with that."

"If you please, ma'am, shure that's what would wash it down. I wish," and Neddy gave a sly look at her from under his brows, " I wish I had a house and a few acres of land, it's I wouldn't be long without a wife, and that's somebody I know." Here he gave another sly look.

" Who would she be, Neddy ?" said Mrs. Hogan, attempting a laugh, or rather a kind of chuckle.

" Faix, I needn't go outside the dure to find the best wife in the parish," and Neddy winked at Mrs Hogan, as much as to say, you know who I mean.

" Get out, you schemer," said Mrs. Hogan.

" Sorra a word o' lie in it, and that's what I do be telling Jack Grace." Here their *tete-a-tete* was disturbed by a ring from the bell.

Frank had driven over to Father O'Donnell's tnat evening, accompained by Uncle Corny.

As Uncle Conry is to be a remarkable personage in our story, it is fit that we should introduce him to our readers.

Corny O'Brien, or as he was more familiarly called, " Uncle Corny," had vegetated among the O'Donnells for the last forty years, and was now superintending the growth and military education of the third generation. Uncle Corny had been something of a Lothario in his youth; but at length he fell head

s in love with a pretty girl. Aileen was not
ile to his addresses, but, he being a younger
, with slender means, her father, who was a
old fellow, without a particle of romance in
position, took a common-sense view of things,
rried her to a wealthy farmer; who, if he had
e, had more wealth, which, according to her
notion of things, meant more happiness.
icle Corny must have been a fine man in his
even now, when his form was bent with age,
hair was grey, as also his moustache, which
ist reverenced, he was as fine a specimen of an
i, and an old soldier to boot, as you could see.
Corny, as I said, was deeply in love, and be-
ble to bear up against his affliction, thought
ld revenge himself on Aileen, and the world
eral, by getting himself knocked off the

ent and enlisted, and, in a fit of remorse, for
loved Aileen, he wrote to her not to take it
i too much if he should be killed.   Aileen
a happy mother, and laughed and sang, and
hought of Corny; whilst he, poor man, was
himself in a fair way of getting his brains
l out on her account.   But the fates were un-
ius, and Corny could not get himself killed
ie got some friendly hand to do the deed; so
rned home after the battle of Waterloo with
i.   Uncle Corny had obtained the rank of
.t, and felt highly flattered at being called

sergeant. After his return he lived with the O'Donnells, to whom he was distantly related, where his
chief occupations were smoking his pipe, relating his
military adventures, ard superintending the military
education of the lads of the neighborhood. It would
do your heart good to see Uncle Corny sitting on a
seat near the door, indolently watching for some
one idle enough to listen to his adventures, and complacently smoking his pipe. Even the pipe seemed
to enjoy this kind of somnolency, for its smoke
whiffed and curled in lazy wreaths around his moustache. He was occasionally visited by another
old soldier, called Shaun the Rover. The Rover
was a rambling, restless spirit; he was a man of
about fifty. Having lost the use of one of his eyes
a few years before in India, he was dismissed the
service. He traveled about from house to house,
where his fund of witticisms and conversational
tales gained him a welcome admittance and entertainment.

Uncle Corny occupied his seat earlier than usual
when he expected the Rover, for he seemed to know
the precise evening on which he would call. As
soon as the Rover came near enough, he shouldered
his stick, touched his hat. and saluted Uncle Corny
in the most approved military style, with "How do
you do, sergeant?" Uncle Corny took out his pipe,
gave a whiff of smoke, stood up, bowed, and generally replied: "Well, thank you, Delany," for that
was Shaun the Rover's name; "well, thank you

but this old stump of mine annoys me betimes;" and then he proudly looked at his arm.

"To win honor and glory we must suffer, sergeant," the Rover would reply, as he would take his seat beside Uncle Corny. Thus would they spend evenings together, fighting their battles over again, and winning renown and glory in the old seat near Mr. O'Donnell's door.

So great was their military mania, that one fine evening, in the absence of Father O'Donnell, they resolved to carry out their movements on a grand scale. They got a few boys from the village, and, having armed them with clubs, they resolved to celebrate the battle of Waterloo by a grand display in the priest's garden. Uncle Corny commanded the English, and took up his position in a small summer-house, as the farm-house of Fer La Hay.

The Rover, with his French troops, commenced an imaginary fire from behind a small hedge. This not dislodging them, the French leaped the hedge, and, with a shout, charged the enemy.

Whether it was that Uncle Corny thought his position not tenable, or that he thought it better to repulse the assailants before they attacked him in his stronghold, like all generals, he kept to himself; anyway, he gave the word to charge. Now, it happened that as they charged across a transverse walk, like many more soldiers, they did not well see what they were about; so, in the melee, they upset a hive of bees.

The bees took the war in earnest, and assailed
both parties. Never was a more beautiful retreat
effected than that of the French and English, with a
whole swarm of the enemy attacking them in front
and rear.

Hallowe'en happening the evening after Frank's
arrival at his uncle's, he promised to spend it at Mr.
Maher's, to enjoy the sports and play the usual
country tricks.

Mr. Maher was a free, easy, kind man, who yet
clung to the good old customs of the country. He
was as ready as the youngest of his family to burn
ruts, dive for apples, and the like pastimes. Though
belonging to that class called " gentlemen farmers,"
he was not above joining his servants in their innocent amusements. Mr. Maher, or as he was called
by the poor about, the " Masther," was a man,
indeed. If you doubt my word, you need only look
at the well-thatched rows of stacks and ricks that
filled the haggard. There was nothing of the
Paddy-go-easy way about Mr. Maher; none of your
windows stuffed with rags, nor your gaps with
ploughs—not a bit of it; everything bore an appearance of ease and opulence. Mr. Maher's house, too,
was altogether new; the parlor was tastefully furnished and carpeted, and a piano lay open near the
fire. And the kitchen—but here I must refer to
Mrs. Moran, Mr. Maher's house-keeper, for Mr.
Maher buried his wife a few years before, and Alice
being too young to manage so large an establish-

ment, he very wisely submitted it to the government
of the discreet Mrs. Moran. Mrs. Moran vowed "it
was the tidiest kitchen in all Ireland." And no
wonder, for it was well stocked with tins and china-
ware, and pans, and the like, all bearing shining
evidence to Mrs. Moran's cleanliness. Then the
tempting rows of sides and hams of bacon that hung
from the ceiling would make a hungry man's teeth
water with delight. Now, having said so much
about Mr. Maher's house, it is time that we should
say something about Mr. Maher's family, for Mr.
Maher's was a notable family. Mr. Maher had,
besides our heroine, two sons and a daughter, all
younger than Alice; and as Alice was but eighteen
they must be young.

As I merely introduce them to my readers for
acquaintance sake, we need say no more about
them.

As our friends joined the family circle, the sports
of the evening had already commenced. The
kitchen was swept clean, and the bright peat fire
threw its ruddy glow around the room.

The Rover and Shemus-a-Clough were quietly
ensconced beside the fire. As soon as Uncle Corny
appeared, the Rover did not forget his accustomed
salute of "How do you do, sergeant? glad to see
you;" nor Shemus-a-Clough his "Hurroo, Misther
Frank; arragh, didn't I do it well at the races—
flung you into the saddle while you'd be saying Jack
Robinson. Shure if I wasn't there you couldnt'

win; hurroo!" and he then performed his usual
gymnastics. After the usual greetings and welcomes
the party collected around the fire. The Rover
occupied the one corner, Uncle Corny the other,
superintending the sports. Uncle Corny seemed
superbly happy when he attracted the attention of
Alice Maher. When a child she would often spend
hours on the old man's knee, with her hands supporting her head and her earnest eyes drinking in
his strange words as he related his battles and
adventures.

Then a tear would often trickle from the old
man's eyes and moisten her little hands; and then
she would fondly look into his face and nestle on
his strong bosom, and ask, "What ails you, Uncle
Corny?"

Who can define the old man's feelings as he shed
these tears and pressed that nestling darling. Ah,
his good heart was not yet dried up—a balmy soft-
ness, like the manna of the desert, came to sweeten
its bitterness; for his feelings went back to the time
when he poured out the fullness of his gushing love
to her aunt—for Uncle Corny's first and only love
was Alice's aunt.

As Alice grew up she resembled her aunt; the
same mild expression, the same confiding look.
Uncle Corny, though an orthodox Catholic, was
something of a Pythagorean, for he firmly believed
that the spirit of the aunt had passed into the niece.
He spent much of his time at Father O'Donnell's, it

was thought for no other purpose than to be near Alice Maher.

The servant maids and boys were collected around a large kish or basket of potatoes on the middle of the floor, peeling them for the colcannon.* The maids took care to hang the first peel on the key of the kitchen door, for whoever came in first then was sure to be their sweetheart.

As I said before, the sports of the night had commenced. They all laughed immoderately at one young man who, in fishing for the apple, lost his balance and fell into the large vessel of water. He bore his misfortune very good humoredly, dried his neck and dripping hair. After several other games they placed clay, water, and a ring, on three different plates, then blindfolded the person trying his or her fortune. They all laughed or became grave as they laid their hands on the different plates, which betokened death, traveling, or marriage. So much importance do the peasantry attach to these rites, that they influence them very much. Even though free from these superstitious notions, Frank's heart beat heavily as he saw his Alice place her hand on

---

* As colcannon is a national dish, and as my American readers are fond of novelties, and good ones to boot, they might find this as agreeable as our beef and mutton, so I will give them the receipt. Peel and wash the potatoes, boil them, strain off the water, pound up the potatoes, then season with cream, onions, and parsley; pour it out on dishes, and place plenty of butter to dissolve in the centre; eat it then, and if you do not like it I cannot help you.

the water; and, on a second trial, on the fatal clay. Alice, too, looked sad, though she tried to smile away her fears. "Alice," said Frank, "let not such a trifle annoy you; you know these things are of no importance."

The large kitchen table was drawn near the glowing fire, and the punch was circulated freely among the elder members, whilst the younger collected closer around the fire, watching the burning of nuts that were to decide the issue of their love adventures. Frank sat on a small form, with Alice beside him, her hands resting upon his knee, both watching the progress of two nuts which were to represent themselves. There were a good many jokes and witticisms passed on them.

"They are burning smoothly enuff," said one.

"Not more than they ought,"

This allusion to their love, made Alice and Frank blush.

"I'll knock them down, if you don't hold your tongue," said Alice.

"Oh! you'd like it, Miss Alice," said one, "see how nicely they are kissing."

At length the small nut, which represented Alice, fluttered about, and flew off.

There was a general laugh and titter at this; some said, "she left him there;" others "they knew she'd do it."

"Faith, it was pleasant; ha! I knew you'd do it, ma Colleen Bawn!" said Shemus-a-Clough, rubbing his hands with delight; "that's the way the Fawn jumped over the ditch."

Frank was more than consoled for all this bartering by a soft whisper from Alice, saying:—

"Don't mind them, Frank; sure I couldn't help it; you know I wouldn't do it."

Frank squeezed her hand upon his breast.

Alice looked into his face, with all the love and milk of human kindness she possessed sparkling in her clear blue eyes.

And that look thrilled through Frank's heart, and spoke volumes of love.

The party at the table were getting very noisy. The Rover was fast beating the Sikhs at Chillinwallagh, and Uncle Corny in as hot pursuit of the French at Waterloo.

"War is a glorious profession," said Uncle Corny, warming to the subject; "if you were to see how we chased the French."

"Or the Sikhs at Chillinwallagh," cried the Rover.

"It is a curse," said Mr. Maher.

"How we formed into columns and lines, and charged," said Uncle Corny, not heeding the interruption.

"How we dashed into the streets, and—"

"How we mowed down the ciurassiers, although they were covered with steel;" interrupted Uncle Corny. "They came on us, the horses neighing and prancing, the bright steel glistening. 'On your

knees,' shouted our general—'present—fire.' They
dashed at us, but we met them with fixed bayonets;
the wounded horses turned and fled throwing the lines
into disorder."

As Uncle Corny was giving this glowing description of the battle, he had mechanically taken up the
very attitude, and converted a long pole into a musket. On the other hand, the Rover, all excited,
was charging across the table with a sweeping-brush,
to the no small danger of bottles and glasses.

"That was as hot work as our own," said the
Rover, shouldering his brush.

"Ay you may say that," said Uncle Corny,
grounding his pole.

" Many's the poor man it sent unprepared before
his God; many's the widow and orphan it left in
want; many's the broken-heart it has caused," said
Mr. Maher.

" We couldn't help that," said the Rover.

" We should do our duty," said Uncle Corny;
" besides it is a glorious thing to be praised."

" As for the praise," said Mr. Maher, " little of it
falls to the soldier's lot; his name may appear, with a
thousand others, in the *Gazette*, but then that's all
that's thought about him; and as to his gains, he has
a good chance, if, after getting a broken constitution
and a shattered body, he gets a few pence a day
pension. Look at our friend here, after endanger-
ing his life, he was dismissed with a trifle, and is
forced to go about for a living; what's glory, what's

honor to him? I want to know would they take thc hunger off him? wouldn't a snug cabin and a little garden be better for him?" ·

"It's true," said the Rover.

"He should get a pension, and he must," said Uncle Corny, with emphasis.

CHAPTER V.

A COUNTRY CHAPEL—A CONFESSION OF LOVE.

"First love! thou Eden of the youthful heart!
Of all earth's joys, the only priceless part."

THE little chapel of Clerihan was falling fast into
decay. Father O'Donnell was feeding himself with
the pious thought of building a new one; still, he
calculated the expense, and when he found that it
would press so heavily on his parishioners, he relin-
quished his darling scheme. The chapel was pretty
spacious, as it had, in addition to the long house, two
side ones, all which had galleries. The roof was
unceiled, except a part over the Sanctuary. This
was even cracked and broken, and a wing had fallen
off the dove that hung from it; even St. Peter had
lost his keys, and was getting grey with age. Here
Father O'Donnell inspired his humble hearers with
awe and reverence. He was, in truth, a fine specimen of a man and a priest. His flowing vestments added dignity to his person. An observer of Irish manners and customs must be struck with the deep devotion of the Irish peasant to his priest. If we consider that through all the vicissitudes of his wayward
life the priest has been his friend, has made himself
merry at his wedding, has repined at his troubles,

and stood by his sick bed to cheer and console him,
we should not wonder that this love should warm
into a kind of adoration.

Father O'Donnell was a fine specimen of the old
Irish priest. Simple in his habits and manners,
charitable to a fault, he was beloved by the people.
He knew every person in his parish, and he also knew
how to play upon their whims and foibles, so as to
create laughter and tears alternately.

Father O'Donnell belonged to the old school of
priests. Prejudiced writers have painted them as
rude and ignorant. It is too true, that, while a fine
was placed on an Irish priest's head, there could not
be that attention paid to their education that is in
the present liberal enlightened times. Thus school-
masters and persons of hurried education, but of
great zeal and devotion, had to be ordained to supply the great want. Writers are too apt to caricature the priest of the latter part of the past century
for those of the previous one.

As I said, Father O'Donnell had a good deal of
the old school about him. Though possessing the
polish and refinement of the priests of the present
day, still, he clung to old customs and habits, and
usually at the conclusion of the Mass, gave a lecture
on the state of his parish.

His exhortations, which, though homely, were always to the purpose, were received with evident
pleasure by the congregation, save and except those
at whom they were aimed. After Mass, Father

O'Donnell generally retired to the school-house to distribute the alms collected in the poor-box, and oftentimes to take his breakfast. The school was a neat comfortable room with a flight of stone steps leading up to it. Frank and Alice had retired there, for Alice was to spend the evening at the priest's house. Father O'Donnell had just done breakfast, and was bantering Alice about something, when a sturdy beggar poked in her head, which was illuminated with a broad grin.

" Well, Molly," said the priest, " what's the matter."

" Not much, your holy riverence," said Mólly, with a most submissive courtesy; " only, you know, I am in a bad way; I have myself and the two childers to support, and nothing in life to give them, but what we get from the neighbors, God reward them! "

" Molly, I thought you were in the poorhouse ? "

" Oh, the childers were, your riverence; but sure they couldn't live in it."

" Why, Molly ? "

" They were seeing nothing but the bad, one thing worse than another every day; they couldn't save their souls there at all, at all; Lord keep us from it your riverence, it's the sinful place."

Molly's sanctity was so shocked at the depravity of the poorhouse, that she raised her eyes in a pious attitude to the ceiling. Whilst doing so, Peg St. John, another sturdy vagrant, forced her head through the half-open doorway, and made good her

olaim with, "Don't forget me, your riverence, you
know the little girl is on the last legs, and ——"
Before she had time to proceed, Molly thrust her
back, telling her "not to be bothering his riverence;
shure one was enuff at a time."

Molly, having given this sage advice, fixed herself
firmly in the open space to prevent further intrusion.
Peg, indignant at such treatment, kept scolding and
remonstrating with her from behind, which Molly
answered by sundry back kicks and thrusts.

"I am sure, Molly," said the priest, who did not
seem to notice the struggle at the door, "I am sure,
Molly, if they satisfied you in eating and drinking,
you would not mind religion so much."

"Ah, throth, I would, sir, as you in your sarmon
—and it is you're able to give the fine one, that
makes us cry down tears from our eyes—but, as you
say, what's the world to one if they lose their mortal
sowls?"

"Molly, I didn't think you were so devout; do
you say the Rosary often?"

"We says it every day, and twice on Sundays."

"That's oftener than I say it myself; look at Peg,
how she grins at you, as much as to say, you don't
say it once in the fortnight."

Peg had contrived to fix her head in the opening,
and with a corner of her old apron stuck in her
mouth, she strove to conceal her laughter at Molly's
affected devotion; but when she came to how often
she prayed, Peg could contain herself no longer, but

burst out into a loud titter, which titter was taken
up by at least a dozen women and children that
lined the stairs outside. Molly was so enraged, that
she rudely shoved the other back, calling her the
greatest robber in the village.

"Don't mind a word she says, your riverence,"
said Peg, "shure I caught her last Monday stealing
a bag of praties. As for prayers, och mavrone !
sarra a one I believe she ever says."

"Oh, you villain," said the other; "shure I
wouldn't steal them but for you put me up to it;
you said you got a bag there yourself; the country
knows you well, Peg; never fear when they hear
that you are out, they'll run to take in their clothes,
and to have an eye to you; never fear they will,"
and Molly, in her indignation, shook her hand most
violently at the other. Peg looked up with pious
indignation at such an assertion, and then in the
depth of her humility, exclaimed: "Oh, did anyone
ever hear the likes; oh, oh, shure, if his riverence
goes to the pawn office, he will get more of the
neighbors' clothes there after her than "—Peg was
unable to finish, but looked for sympathy to the
priest. Molly, seeing no other means of redress for
her wounded honor, twined her hand most affectionately in Peg's hair, and applied the other to her
countenance.

"Stop there, the two of you, for one moment, until
I get a catechism, and I will see which of you have
your prayers the better. If you don't answer me,

maybe it is the whip you'll be getting," exclaimed the priest.

Father O'Donnell shut the door, and gave a wink to Frank, as much as to say, "I have got rid of them." Father O'Donnell was right, for when he came to divide the alms, both Peg and Molly had decamped.

Father O'Donnell, accompanied by Frank and Alice, returned to the cottage. After dinner he went to attend a sick call. On his return home he met the Rover trudging along.

"Ha, Shawn, is this you," said Father O'Donnell.

"Aye, indeed, your riverence," said Shawn, respectfully, doffing his caubeen.

"Where are you bound for now, Shawn?"

"I was thinking of going to Glen Cottage; but as the sergeant and Master Frank are with you, I was thinking of calling to see them."

"Why not, Shawn; sure you know you are welcome, while the poor priest has a bit or sup for you, or a bed for you to lie upon."

"I know that, Father O'Donnell; God bless you and give you a long life," and Shawn reverently took off his hat as he mumbled a Pater and Ave for the priest's especial benefit.

"That's a bad hat you have, Shawn," said the priest, remarking its broken state.

"It does for the fine weather well enough—shure it lets in the air."

"True enough; but when the rain comes, what will you do?"

"God is good," said Shawn, sententiously.

"Here, Shawn, poor fellow, this will buy a hat for you," and Father O'Donnell handed him two shillings.

Shawn hesitated. "It is too much—besides, I don't like to take it."

"Why so?"

"Maybe it's to drink it I'd do."

"Drink it! why, that would be a sin; and all the good it would do a poor person."

"That's what I was thinking myself; shure, you can give me an old hat, and that will do as well."

"Very well, Shawn; but why not buy it for the money?"

"It wouldn't have luck, sir," said Shawn, looking down; "it should go to feed the poor."

"Ha, ha!" laughed Father O'Donnell; "it is said so, Shawn, and I believe it's true. All we get belongs to the poor, Shawn, and to the poor we should give it. Money is a great evil, Shawn, when we place our affections upon it. St. Thomas Villanova ordered himself not to be buried in consecrated ground, if there should be a single chink found with him. A priest should never hoard up money, Shawn."

"So I does be always saying," said Shawn; "it would be a shame an' disgrace for them to do so."

" Well, Shawn, let us leave them to God; there
are some of them good and bad, like all men."

" The parson over there is a better man than many
of them.   God pardon me for comparing them,"
said Shawn.

Now, whether Shawn's dark side of the comparison was cast to the account of the priest's or the
parson's, I cannot say; I suspect the latter.

" Mr. Smith is a good, charitable man, no doubt,
and he shall have his reward.   I wish I could say as
much of these ranting preachers that are running
about the country sowing strife among Christian
people."

" Begor, they ought to be hunted like dogs."

" No, Shawn, no; God will take an account of
their doings.   Judgment belongs to God."

" Well, you know best,"'said Shawn.

Still he looked as if it would be a great deal
pleasanter to try a bit of rustic persuasion with
them.

"Shawn," said the priest, after a short silence.

" Well, sir."

"‑A hem—ha ! Shawn, I want to know how do
you live ? "

" Very well, sir," said Shawn, pretending to mis-
understand the priest; " very well, sir, the people
do be very good to me; I never want for anything,
glory·be to God ! "

" It's not that I mean, but do you go to your duty
—do you go to confession ? "

Shawn held down his head.

"Ay, Shawn, tell me now; you see, as a minister of God, it is my duty to look after you."

"Shure, I have no parish, Father O'Donnell; I am here to-day and away to-morrow."

"Oh, oh, you unfortunate man! is that the reason you would run headlong to perdition? is that the reason you would damn your immortal soul? is that the reason you would not go to confession—to the tribunal of penance? Oh, Shawn, I fear for you."

"I believe I am a wretched sinner," said Shawn, very humbly, "but not near as bad as you think."

"How is that?"

"Is what a man never did or never thought of doing, a sin?"

"Certainly not, Shawn."

"Well, then, when I found that I belonged to no parish, I thought that nobody had a right to me, so I never went near a priest nor to Mass, nor never thought of doing either. So I'm not as bad as you thought."

Despite Father O'Donnell's honest indignation at Shawn's want of religion, he had to smile at his nice distinction; so we will leave the worthy couple for the present.

After Father O'Donnell left, Alice and Frank walked into the little garden. There was a rustic arbor entwined with honeysuckles and hops in the corner of it. A green bank extended from it to a little rivulet that ran babbling and sporting along.

In this arbor Father O'Donnell was wont to read
his breviary on fine evenings, and here now our lovers
seated themselves. The little stream babbled on;
the merry voices of the lads and lasses of the village, as they passed along to the hurling green,
floating on the breeze. A thrush and blackbird,
from a thicket near, seemed to endeavor to tire each
other out. There was a delicious freshness in the
balmy air; it was an evening for lovers to breathe
forth their feelings of devotion. Though Frank
and Alice loved deeply, though they knew that they
were dear to one another, yet they never spoke of
love, but their eyes and hearts communed with each
other.

> "Oh, there are looks and tones that dart,
> An instant sunshine to the heart."

They were alone. As they sat side by side, how
sweet was the intoxicating draught of love that
agitated their young bosoms; you might hear the
ticking of their hearts. Her beauty, her wild, natural graces, joined with the unspeakable tenderness
of her affection, threw a charm around her that al
most hallowed her in the eyes of her young lover.
They remained some moments as if enraptured and
afraid to break the spell. True love is silent; the
heart is too full of a sweet thrilling sensation to find
vent in words. It is told by the furtive glance, the
suppressed sigh, the soft, low voice, and then, the
low, whispering words that tremble on the lips.
How sweet is this young love that brings the pearly

tear to trickle from the maiden's eye, like dew drops
from the morning flowers—this love that binds young
hearts with a mysterious feeling, with some strange
fascination, which is beyond the power of the writer's pen to portray. Love seems to be the great
inherent principle of our nature. In childhood the
lisping tongue breathes its little cares and hopes at
a mother's knees. Who can picture a mother's love
as she cherishes her first-born; as she fondles it with
enraptured gladness, her very heart throbs with
a delight unknown to all save a mother. Thus were
Frank and Alice insensibly drinking the delicious
poison.

"Alice," said Frank, as he pressed her little head
against his bosom. Alice looked into his face; there
was a beaming mildness in her eyes, and her rich
hair clustered around her face. "Alice, darling,
how wildly our hearts are beating; tell me, sweet
one, is this love?"

Alice hung down her head; a faint weakness came
over her, and she nestled on his breast.

"Oh, it is, it is! Alice, our hearts, our eyes, have
long been speaking what our lips now utter. Sweet
girl, say the blessed words, that you love me.

"Frank," said she, in a trembling voice, "sure you
know I do."

"Oh, Alice! Alice, my love, my life, I am happy.
I have lived and loved."

They spent some hours in the arbor settling their
little affairs, and gilding the future in pictures more

4

glowing than fairy visions. Who can blame them ?
We all know how sweet it is to sit beside the girl
we love, to look into her softly-beaming eyes, to feel
the pressure of that tiny hand, and the throbbing of
that fond heart, to feel her warm breath fanning our
cheek, and the rich luxuriance of silken hair floating around us. Oh, this is a feeling worth living
for, and so thought and felt Frank O'Donnell as
Alice Maher clung to him in all the confiding innocence of young love. As he looked upon that sweet
girl what visions of future happiness did he not
create. How he would labor and toil to win wealth
and a name for her; how he would make home
a paradise. The future was all bright and sunny to
his imagination. Dream on in your love; but, alas!
life has too may sad realities for dreamers. There are
few of us but have formed similar schemes of happiness for the girl of our heart. To-day, Frank, we
build gilded castles of hope to the goddess of fortune;
to-morrow, inexorable fate comes and levels them
to the ground, burying us, poor mortals, in the ruins.
It is truly said that youth is the season of love. It is
then our feelings gush forth in the most refined and
exalted character. It is then we feel the passion of
love in its purest and most delicate state. Our
views are free from any of the sordid selfishness of
maturer years. All the vivid impressions and associations of youth tend to the increase of this passion
'in its holiest and purest form. The energies of the

heart are vigorous and fresh; none of the vanities or petty pleasures, or selfishness that afterwards damp the warmth of our feelings, intervenes between the fond youth and the girl he loves.

CHAPTER VI.

FRANK and Alice were alone; they spoke little, but their hearts were full. The evening was calm and beautiful, and the sun was sinking fast, shedding its roseate hues o'er the neighboring hills. It was one of those calm, mellowy evenings so rare, and therefore so highly prized at that season of the year. The little stream babbled on, and the lovers from time to time threw fading flowers to float on its rippling current. At length they stood up, and Frank said,

"What a glorious evening, Alice; how calm; listen to the joyful laughter of the happy peasants, listen to the warbling of the birds. Oh, Alice love, everything seems in unison with our fond hearts."

"I often think, Frank, when we are happy ourselves, we picture the world bright and beautiful, but when unfortunate, we shadow it with clouds and darkness. I think we draw our images from our own feelings more than from exterior objects."

"It is true, love, to a certain extent; while the heart is full of a delicious feeling, as our's are now, we might indeed be excused in seeing nothing but ove and beauty in the world, but when the stern duties of life cross our paths, we will, indeed find much to make us look upon life as troublesome, and the world no better than it is."

"True, Frank. Do you know, but I often think, will our love remain through life as pure as now?"

"Why not, my love; though we should lose a great deal of the fervor a first passion creates, still, trust me, sweet one, our love will not be the less pure."

"But, Frank, will our parents consent? We are young, too young, perhaps, to settle in life."

"It is true, love, we are young, and our happiness will not be the less by remaining as we are for a few years; we can love each other, we can often see each other; in fact, we could not expect to be happier than we are. We will wait our opportunity. I don't see that our parents can have any objection, as we are equal in circumstances; I know, if any obstacles should occur, that my uncle will do his best for his poor children, as he calls us."

"What a good man he is, Frank; why, I often regret all my tricks; and yet, he is so simple-hearted, I cannot resist the temptation; you know, Frank, I am as playful as a young kid betimes."

"I know it, my little wife, that you are; he tells me all, and he told me how you defended me about the races."

"Stop, now," said she, blushing and smiling; 'now don't call me wife yet, don't be too sure of me, Frank; you know I am, as Father O'Donnell says, 'an arrant baggage,' so you couldn't know when I'd give you the slip."

And she looked with a playful, saucy smile into his face. Frank's answer was a kiss.

"There is more of it; I declare I'll run away from you, you schemer; look the way my hair is tossed."

"I'll settle it, love," and he commenced to braid her golden hair, and then tied it up.

I pity the man who can travel through life and call it a cold, barren journey; and so it is to the splenetic man, who will not cultivate its affections and cheerily collect the sweet fruit it offers. Such travelers mope wearily on, without looking to the right or left, to pluck one fair flower or cultivate one sweet sentiment. Their hearts are closed against the purer feelings of our nature; pride, avarice, or vanity button up their hearts and their pockets against love and charity. There are gentle spirits fanned by the wings of love that make this earth a paradise after all.

Frank's pleasing occupation was, however, interrupted by the appearance of Father O'Donnell, who was now nearing the little avenue. Father O'Donnell seemed to be in earnest conversation with the Rover, as no doubt he was.

"Now, Shawn I hope you won't forget all I have said to you; this world is nothing but vanity—here to-day, away to-morrow; vanity, vanity."

"Thrue for you, sir; the Lord be praised, it is a

a deceitful world; look at Mr. ——, after ating his fine dinner and drinking his punch, fell dead in a fit of plexy, or something they call it."

" Apoplexy, Shawn; it was a sudden death, no doubt, the Lord be praised. Run, Shawn, look at the pigs in the stacks, hunt them out, bad cess to them."

While Shawn was after the pigs, the priest rode leisurely towards the house.

Mrs. Hogan was quietly enjoying herself at the kitchen fire, listening to the feats of the hurlers discussed by Uncle Corny and Neddy O'Brien, who had just returned from the match.

" Arrah hadn't we fine devarshin ? " said Neddy.

" I enjoyed it very much," said Uncle Corny.

" Who was hurling ? " inquired Mrs. Hogan.

" The Fethard boys and us, ma'am; my soul, but we gave them the licking,"

" Neddy avick, you sthripped," said Mrs. Hogan, looking at him with an air of some contempt.

Neddy feared that Mrs. Hogan was going to open at him, for she entertained a great disregard for small men, and Neddy, though hardy and mettle-some, still came under her category of small men. Mrs. Hogan had read Jack the giant-kilier, the Seven Champions of Christendom, and, as I said before, held small men in superb contempt; so he thought it better, as he said himself, to mollify her.

" Arrah, Mrs. Hogan, why not ? shure it isn't the big men cut all the harvest."

" Dear me," said Mrs. Hogan; " dear me, I see ye had a fine hurlin' then."

" Sorra betther you ever laid your two purty eyes upon, Mrs. Hogan," said Neddy, not pretending to notice her allusion to himself.

" And ye say ye bet them, Neddy," and she gave a wink at Uncle Corny.

" Troth an' that we did, too; Jack Grace and I, and a few more of us wor on the sweep; it would do your heart good to see us cutting away with it; begorreys but Jack is as shmart as a hare, and faith I was close enuff to him; and whisper, Mrs. Hogan," and Neddy put his mouth close to her ear, " I have something to tell you in private that Jack said."

Whether it was the whisper, or Neddy's allusion to her purty eyes, or what it was, I cannot say, but Mrs. Hogan smiled and changed her tactics altogether.

" Shure, Neddy, I was only jokin'; I always heard that there wasn't a shmarter boy in the three parishes than yourself."

" The legs are purty supple with me, thanks be to God," said Neddy, looking down at his shanks, and then looking up. at Mrs. Hogan, evidently well pleased with the inspection.

" They are light enuff to carry you, anyway, Neddy."

" They are, Mrs. Hogan; and more betokens, as

you said, there isn't a man in the three parishes uble to run from me, except a certain Mr. Grace, that does be bothering me about some one."

Here Neddy gave a wink at Mrs. Hogan, and something like the ghost of a blush mantled on Mrs. Hogan's cheek for a moment only; for, then, as if ashamed of itself, it fled.

All this time Uncle Corny was laying the plan of an important battle, with the point of his stick in the ashes, but his grand operations were interrupted by the entrance of the Rover.

" How do you do, Sergeant ? " and the Rover touched his cap; "and you Mrs. Hogan, glad to see you looking so well; faith it's young and fat-looking you are getting. Run, Neddy, and take the priest's horse; shure the pigs have played the dickens with the stacks."

"Bad scran to ye, ye'll never be aisy," said Neddy, reluctantly leaving his warm corner.

" Neddy, you villian," said the priest, as soon as that functionary made his appearance, "I wonder but you could see the pigs in the stacks."

" Bad scran to them, but they are troublesome entirely; shure it's not five minutes since I put thim into the house."

" Well, put them in now again, and hasp the door; that old hog, I think, knows how to open it."

" Faith, thin, that she does, your riverence; shure I saw her myself and I after fastening the hasp with my two hands, and she tugging away from the inside at it; ay, faith, to see her catching it in her teeth."

" Catching the hasp in her teeth, Neddy; oh, the old thief ! "

A thousand of the most subtle syllogisms or a chapter of the most polished sentences could not say more for Father O'Donnell's easy innocent disposition than these words, " oh, the old thief," all the time forgetting that the door intervened between the pig and the hasp.

When Neddy returned to his corner near the fire, Mrs. Hogan, Uncle Corny and the Rover were in the midst of a very warm engagement.

" My artillery from this mound," said Uncle Corny, laying his cane on a heap of ashes, " would batter down the head of your column."

" What would my sharpshooters and cavalry be doing all the time; you see your left wing is unguarded, so I would silence you in less than no time."

" You see I have left a company here to provide against any surprise if —"

" Begor that's just like us with our party at the hurling," suggested Neddy, from the hob.

" If," continued Uncle Corny, not heeding the interruption, "if you should force my defiles, I have also placed some pieces along the slopes here of Mo'nt St. Jean."

" I would make a furious charge and throw your columns into disorder; then their retreat would be intercepted by the hill," and the Rover ran the poker with which he conducted the engagement along Uncle Corny's lines, thereby disordering them.

" Faith, it's hot work," said Mrs. Hogan, who was intently looking at the battle.

" You may say that," said Uncle Corny, drawing his sleeve across his forehead.

" That's the very way we were teeming hot when we drove in the ball," said Neddy.

There is no knowing how long the battle might have continued had not a pot of potatoes overflowed and deluged the works, and as it was too late to begin them anew, and as Mrs. Hogan hinted that it was time to get the supper, there was a general armistice. While the worthy trio are engaged discussing Mrs. Hogan's smoking potatoes and cold ham, we will try and give our readers a description of that truly national amusement in which Neddy seemed to take such peculiar delight—we mean hurling.

It is to be regretted that this fine manly sport should be fast passing away, giving place to the more fashionable game of cricket.

Among all the plays, games, and gymnastics of the ancient Greeks and Romans, there was none that called forth and developed the muscular action of the frame so much as hurling. Many's the Sunday and holiday evening I stole away with my hurly under my arm to join the invigorating game. Alas! for those happy days of boyhood, that morn of sunshine in a stormy, cloudy life; alas! for the past, with all its sweet and innocent joys. I then little thought that heavy clouds would darken the noon of life, and shadow its decline.

Now national pastimes are fast dying out; we seem to get ashamed of everything national. The famine years, no doubt, did away with a great deal of the elasticity and cheerfulness of character of the Irish peasant. They seem now as if doomed to serve but a probation in the land of their birth. They look to other lands as the land of promise where their toil is rewarded with peace and plenty. Despite of all the ties of home, so dear to an Irishman's heart, despite of all fond family associations, despite of his wish to sleep with the bones of his father in the old church yard, still he must move on. God's earth is wide and he must toil and live. Man has cursed his own green fertile land, so he must move on. On, on, to make room for the beasts of the field! Poor peasant, you and your cabin, and your fond wife, and your little prattling babes are in their way. Move on, I say! Such is the *ukase* that has gone forth from despotic landlords to their serfs! Such is the ukase that government has connived at, because the victims were aliens in blood and religion, and had the manliness to tug at the shackles that bound them. Ah! the millions of corpses that rot in pauper graves, that are tossed about by the ocean waves, or that sleep in far off lands, slain by the miasma of some pestilential swamp, will yet rise up in judgment. Well, well, let us draw a veil over this for the present, and as I am shortly going to describe all the horrors of the famine years, let us take a view of the merry green where the youths and maidens are dancing, hurling, playing hide and go seek, and the like pastimes. These arcadian scenes are now fast dying away; will some kind spirit rise up and revive them? Will you, good kind old priest, and fear not that you are infringing upon God's law? Will you, young man of influence and energy, and think not that it detracts from your dignity? Will you, maiden fair, with the soft beaming eye and light step, join our dance on the green, and listen to the music of the blind fiddler?

" It's not fashionable."

"Pooh! Who told you so?"

If laughing, gay, and merry hearts are not fashionable, then away with fashion for me, and let me rollick with that gay company of peasants yonder. Well, as I have said, I must describe a hurling match for you; for our exquisites of the present day dare not venture to one, lest they would injure their dignity or knock the polish from their boots. As I said before, let us take a peep at an Irish hurling. The place selected was generally some broad, level, green field.

Old and young, matrons and maidens, all brimful of anticipated enjoyment, collect to the trysting place.

The young men, in groups, collect from different parts of the country. They came on, leaping over hedges and ditches, laughing, shouting, and singing in reckless joviality.

All preliminaries being arranged by the elders, twenty-one young men at a side were selected. The spectators then retired to the ditches, and the ball was thrown up among the rival parties.

The ball was struck here and there, often pucked up in the air, then hit again before it reached the ground. Such lucky hits were acknowledged by cheers from the spectators. Then by tumbling, tossing, feint blows, and the like, at length one party succeeded in driving it to the goal, amidst a peal of shouts and hurras from the friends of the victors.

It was a glorious sight to see these fine athletic young fellows, stripped off in their linen, their damp hair floating around their faces, and a handkerchief, which they got from some colleen who wished them luck, bound around their waists—to see them thus, with flushed brows and kindling eyes, striving for victory.

All this time the old men and women were looking on, and encouraging the combatants, and prognosticating their future greatness from their feats. To hear their expression of natural pride out of . their own sons, and their encomiums on their neighbors. To hear one old man, with a sigh, regretting to his neighbor their young days.

"When the priest and the gintlemen used to head us, and we were all dressed out like jockeys in jackets and caps, and the green was all roped; thim were the times, Bill, when we used to have the fun."

"True for you, Jack; God be wid thim times."

And both sighed at the degeneracy of the days they had lived to see.

An Irish hurling was a glorious sight, no doubt; so think we, and so thought Louis XVI., when the young students from Munster and Leinster, dressed in green and white silk jackets and caps, amused his majesty and court by a game of Irish hurling match.

All Paris went to see them, and the strong athletic young fellows, fired with national pride, strove in glorious rivalry, until the king and court, and all Paris too, cried out that no exercise ever surpassed it.

When the hurlers have wiped their damp brows and hair, they retire to make a match of leaping, or of casting a stone; or more likely to join the girls, who are dressed out in all their finery, with their hair nicely combed behind their ears, and braided with the utmost elegance, and who are enjoying themselves at "drop the glove," "hide and go seek," or some other amusement equally innocent. There was an elegance in their fine natural movements, their light floating dresses, their blushing cheeks and smiling faces, which gave a fascinating beauty and picturesqueness to them.

Most likely the old traveling piper has set up his
stand in some corner, and is puffing away at the
" Humors of Glin," " Rory O'More," " The Fox-
hunter's Jig," or the like.   Then to see the boys and
girls twisting, capering, jumping, timing the music
with their heads, their hands, and feet; turning and
shuffling as if they were bit by a tarantula.   Oh! it
was grand! it showed the elasticity and exuberance
of spirit of the Irish peasant.   But now, what has
become of all this fine genuine feeling ?   Oh, the
famine years and a grasping landocracy have crushed
and broken all the finer feeling of their nature; have
made them what they wished them to be—helpless
slaves in their own green land.

Alice had the tea-things laid before Father O'Donnell.   The nice fresh cream, the yellow butter, the
hot smoking cakes, and the clean cups and saucers
looking so pleasant and tempting that he rubbed his
hands with delight, and wondered to himself how
Mrs. Hogan couldn't make things look so comfortable at all.   What made the fire burn so bright and
cheerily?   What made Father O'Donnell feel so
very happy as he reclined in his arm-chair, and
looked about him the perfect picture of content?
What made Carlo frisk and leap with joy as he did?
and what made puss purr his cronaun longer than
usual on the warm hearthrug?   As I am a bachelor
I cannot well answer the question myself; but this
I say, if I were in Frank O'Donnell's place, I would
think that Alice had lent some witchery to the whole.

"This is comfortable, my children," said Father O'Donnell, as he rubbed his hands again, and looked at the tea-table and then at Frank and Alice; "it is comfortable to have a home to cover one's head from the storms and sneers of the world—to have peace and plenty with all, and a few fond hearts to enjoy it with one; even for an old priest this is pleasant. O God, grant me these, and shower down riches upon the avaricious, and fame and glory upon the ambitious as Thou wilt!" When Father O'Donnell had lowered his eyes and hands, which he had raised in an attitude of prayer during his pious exclamation, he sat silent for a moment.

"Shall I get the tea, sir," said Alice.

"Yes, my child; yes, do."

Alice took her seat at the head of the table, and Frank and Father O'Donnell sat one at each side of her.

As she poured out the tea her hand trembled, and she sighed.

"What's the matter, Alice; your hand is trembling as if you had the ague, and you are sighing as —— I'm blest but there is another sigh. I hope, child, that your true love hasn't run away from you; but no, I'm sure, your little heart hasn't—heigh-ho, what's this they call him? ay, I have him, Cupid. Well, I hope Cupid hasn't seized on your little heart yet?"

"Who is he, Father?" said Alice, with an arch smile at Frank.

"Oh, you don't know, I suppose; but then you are too young. Wait a little, though, my little baggage, I warrant you that one of the first hearts he'll steal will be your own."

"Sure you would not let him, Father?"

"That's good, though--a poor old priest to prevent him; if Frank, there, had any pluck, he is a likely young fellow, he might take the start ——. Pooh, there is another sigh from Frank. I am blessed but it is infectious—but Alice; Alice, child! What the deuce—God forgive me; Alice, stop! don't you see that it is into the sugar-bowl you are pouring the tea?"

Both Alice and Frank blushed, and smiled alternately. Father O'Donnell looked at them and sighed too; and then mused and muttered—"Could it be?"

Now, we must try and make out what Father O'Donnell was hatching in his precious noddle when he muttered—"Could it be?"

"That will do, child; take away these things and bring us the makings of a glass of punch."

Alice did so, and then sat beside the fire playing with Carlo and puss. Carlo and puss received her attentions with evident pleasure; for Carlo frisked about and jumped into her lap, and puss purred and curled up his tail, and rolled on the rug, and then looked up as if envying Carlo his happiness, and then thinking that he had as good a right to be in her lap—he also jumped into it. Carlo, not liking

his company, grinned. " Now, Carlo, don't; you
naughty little dog, let pussy alone; do you be quiet
and sleep together, poor pusseen cat. I will tell you
something, pusseen cat; you ought to get in love
with Carlo, and then you will be quiet." Though
Alice said this in a whisper, Frank overheard it, and
blushed and looked into his glass, watching the dis-
solution of a lazy lump of sugar. Father O'Donnell,
too, overheard it, and stirred his punch, and took a
spoonful to see was it strong enough, and then, not
finding it exactly to his liking, he put a little more
whiskey into it, and again tasted it, and, not finding
it to suit, put another lump of sugar into it, and then
gave a " Pooh—can it be?"

Having finished his glass of punch, he leant back
in his chair and seemed to reflect.

He leant back in his chair and reflected for some
time, and then he slapped his thigh with his hands,
and exclaimed half aloud, " I will ask them!"

" Ask whom, Father O'Donnell?" said Alice.

"·Oh, nothing, love," said he.

" Now," said he, or rather thought he, to himself,
" what an ass I was near making of myself,—ask
them, indeed,—why that would be playing the
deuce with it entirely, but then it can't be,—in love,
in love! and they so young—two children, that used
to be climbing my knees a few years ago! no, it
cannot be; but then, sure I didn't feel them growing. Look at how big they are!" and he gave a side
look at Frank and Alice, as if to see how far they

had grown beyond the standard of children. "What
will I do with them? I'll tell you; I'll send Frank
home; I could not tell that laughing little baggage
to go;" here he gave another sly look at Alice, who
was busily engaged with Carlo and puss.

"Stop, Frank," said Alice, saucily; "stop, and
don't be pinching Carlo; look at the way they are
fighting, and as Frank had pushed near her to join
the fun, she saddled him with the grave offence, in
the priest's eyes, of pinching Carlo.

"Now, Frank, child, don't pinch the poor dog,
said Father O'Donnell.

"There again, Frank," said Alice, as Carlo gave
a squeel, and no wonder, for she had pinched puss,
and puss laying the charge to Carlo's account, stuck
his paw in his woolly ear.

"Come here, Carlo, from them," said the priest;
and Carlo jumped over to him, leaving puss in un-
disputed possession.

"Well, well; what will I do with her; and yet, I
cannot live without her," thought the priest. "I
don't blame the boy to be in love with her; look at
her, isn't she a noble-looking girl? I don't blame
him after all; sure it's natural, why wouldn't he love
her—she's so pleasant and winning, sure it's natural;
and if it makes the poor children happy, who would
grudge them their happiness? Not I, I'm sure. I
don't see what objection anyone could have to it;
they are a little young, to be sure; well, when they
got a little older, bedad I'll marry them myself—

why wouldn't they be happy?" Father O'Donnell rubbed his hands and looked at them and smiled, and rubbed his hands again, and exclaimed, "I will make you happy, my children. Come, Frank, what are you thinking about?"

"Not much, sir."

"Oh, no matter, boy, when you are a little older I will settle all, my children; sure you couldn't conceal it from me—but no matter, I will settle all, I will, Frank; give me your hand, and you, Alice, God bless you;" and he looked so happy; no wonder that he was, for the angel of goodness and mercy was fanning him with his wings.

Alice sat beside the good priest, and laid her hands upon his knee, and looked tenderly and confidingly into his face; a tear of joy and gratitude trembled on the lashes of her sparkling blue eyes. Father O'Donnell patted her cheek, and then threw back the golden hair that clustered around her brow.

"Alice, my child, believe me, there is a happy future in store for you; and now go and sing me one of your songs."

She did, and with a soft, silvery voice, trembling with emotion, she sang Davis' "Annie Dear."

"That is very sad, Alice; why didn't you sing something pleasant? No matter; Frank, sing Davis' Welcome.'"

Frank did so in a fine manly voice.

"Now, children, let us retire for the night.'

CHAPTER VII.

Mrs. INCHBALD says that "love, however rated by
many as the chief passion of the heart, is but a poor
dependent, a retainer on the other passions:—admiration, gratitude, respect, esteem, pride in the object. Divest the boasted sensation of these, and it
is no more than the impression of a twelvemonth, by
courtesy or vulgar error called love." Now, Mrs.
Inchbald, what do you mean by all this? If you
chance to be a crusty old maid I could forgive you;
but no, you are most likely a mother. I say then
that Mr. Inchbald must be a musty customer, without a particle of love to warm your heart and his,
or you never would write such nonsese. Love, a
vulgar error! a sentiment of courtesy! Hear this
ye love-sick swains and maidens! Hear this, Master Cupid! I tell you, madam, it is a passion, and
one of the deepest and strongest in our natures, too;
if not, why did many a poor d——l take it into his
head to drown himself for love. How would Alice
Maher define it that night as she retired to her
room? Would she call it a sentiment or passsion,
I wonder?

Alice sat beside her little bed, thinking about many things that had never come into her little head before.

There she sat, her slight graceful person leaning on the bed, and her head resting on her left hand, while her right played with her golden hair that fell about,

> " Showered in rippled ringlets to her knee."

Her thoughts must be sweet, for her breast heaved, and she smiled, and whispered to herself:—

"Frank, I love you!"

And then braided her hair and retired to her bed.

> " Nestling among the pillows soft,
> A dove, o'er wearied with its flight."

Sweet were Alice's dreams that night, for the passion, or sentiment if you will, of love had thrown its witchery around her heart.

Frank remained at Father O'Donnell's for a few weeks. He was a constant visitor at Mr. Maher's, where he made himself particularly agreeable to Alice's little brothers and sisters, by joining in all their childish amusements.

Mrs. Moran declared that "he was a nice young man," but she hoped he wouldn't be going on with his palavering on Miss Alice, and trying to coax her;" then giving a sly wink, as much as to say, "I know what's going on, don't I?"

Mr. Maher, too, felt a great interest in him, and

frequently took him about to see his stock and farms; if Mr. Maher noticed anything like what lovers call a mutual attachment springing up between him and Alice, he allowed it to take its course, for he looked upon Frank not only as a worthy young man, but also as a suitable match for his daughter. They spent the evenings in the parlor, sining, and chatting and romping about. Little Willy called him his brother, and often took him to ride, and hunt about with him. Alice, too, joined in some of their rambles, and then, mounted on Willy's pony, she rode around the fields, with Frank and Willy her escort.

It was in the evenings when collected around the parlor fire that they presented a true picture of domestic bliss. After tea, Mr. Maher and Frank took a quiet glass of punch, whilst Alice, seated at the piano, poured forth her mellowy, thrilling songs. Frank often sat beside her, and joined in the song. These were pleasant nights and as Frank rose to return to his uncle's, he felt happy, for there was one fond heart he could call his own. Alice called over to Father O'Donnell's on the day on which Frank was about returning home. They spent the morning rambling about their favorite walks, renewing their vows of love, and building fairy palaces for the future. Frank had sent home his horse, so he set out throught the country with his gun and dog, and Shemus-a-Clough as a companion.

After travelling a few miles, and meeting with

but little shooting, he sat down to refresh himself. Shemus, with his club, took his seat beside him. Shemus' feet were of immense size. This was owing, in a great measure, to the frost and cold, for Shemus never wore shoes but on one occasion.

" Don't your feet be sore, Shemus ?" said Frank, ₁ooking at his swollen cracked feet.

" Sometimes, sir; they are used to the road now though; use makes masther."

" Why wouldn't you get shoes, Shemus ! I'll get a pair made for you for the winter."

" No use, sir; Father O'Donnell gave me a pair once, and I couldn't wear thim."

" Why so, Shemus ? "

" I'll tell you all; shure I couldn't carry thim."

" Try another pair now; I'll get them for you."

" Divil a bit; it would be only throwing away money for nothing; for the priest said to me one day, ' Shemus, will you have shoes; if so, go down to Toomy, and tell him I sent you for thim; and be the same token, tell him, that it was yesterday he sold me boots,' so down I goes. The priest told me get a pair of shoes, says I. 'Did he?' says he. 'To be sure he did; so hurry out wid thim.' 'O, wait for your time,' says he, 'there is luck in leisure.' ' By my soukens, thin, I will go back and tell his riverence.' ' O, don't,' says he; ' come in and thry some.' So in I goes; phoo! I might as well go whistle jigs to a mile-stone. Shure divil a one would come near me at all. 'Now, go home and tell his

5

riverence to get a pair of lasts made for you, and I
will make the shoes.' So I did, and well be done of
him, but went out to the carpenters and tells thim
to make lasts for me; so they set to work, and when
they wor finished I set out wid one under each arm.
O, mustha, but they were as big as two rouling pins.
If you wor to see me wid me new shoes and a fine
bran new pair of stockings, that Mrs. Hogan made
for me out of an ould blanket, for any others would
not fit me, begor I was grand intirely, sir, and I had
a new hunting coat and cap.

" 'Shemus,' said the priest, 'you must run to Cashel
of a message for me, and dont let a blade of grass
grow under your feet, for I'm in a hurry.'

" Off I started like fun; after two or three miles
they began to shlap and clatter on my feet. Bad
scran to ye's, says I, shure ye are playing the dickens
wid me intirely. By and by I looked down, and
there was my heel all skhinned. I took and flung
the fellow in a field of wheat; after a short time
the other got as bad ; I flung him after his
brother."

" What did my uncle say ? "

" What did he say ? Shure he was mad; but how
could I help him; shure I could get thim for him
afterwards; for one day I went into a cabin and
there I saw my beautiful shoe turned into a cradle
for the baby."

"I believe I might as well not get any for you
so ? "

"Sarra use, thin."

" Is it long since ye had any hunt, Shemus ? "

"Last Tuesdy; begor we had the fun intirely.
Isn't it pleasant work, Misther Frank; shure we met
a fox at Grove, and thin to see all the jintlemen wid
their red coats and caps and they collected around
the cover, and the huntsmen bating the bushes this
way," and Shemus jumped up and struck a bush
with his cudgel; " and, thin, to see the hounds this
way," and he threw himself all fours, and ran along
the ground, crying "bow, wow, wow!" "and thin
to hear thim when the fox got up; begorra it was
as good as any music to hear the cry they set up,
and thin the jintlemen fell at cracking their whips
and shouting ' yoicks tallyho! yoicks tallyho!' and
away they dashed.   Shure I was houlding Mr.
Ryan's horse, and he gave me a shilling, and off wid
him.   To see them dashing over ditches and hedges,
and some of them rouling head over heels; wasn't it
pleasant ? "

"It was pleasant enough to be looking at, Shemus."

"They ran on for Kilcash, and I crossed the field.
I was going over a ditch where there was a big
boggy place, when I saw Lord Clearall riding
towards it, and he standing in his stirrups trying to
look over the ditch. ·'I say, fellow,' said he to me,
'is that place sound outside?' 'Oh, it's very sound
at the bottom,' says I, purtinding not to know him.
With that he jumps out, and to see himself and the

horse rouling and splashing in the bog hole. Begor,
they druv water up half a mile in the air—shure
myself couldn't help laughing at him.

"'You scoundrell' says he, looking up, 'why did
you tell me that this had a sound bottom?'

"'So it has,' says I; 'but you are not half there
yet.' I ran away and left him to get out as best he
could."

"Why did you do that?"

"Why did I do it!   Och! Misther Frank, shure
he is a bad man—he pulled the house down over me
aunt and she sick wid the fever, and the poor woman
died in the ditch side.   Oh, to hear her raving and
crying and calling her children; but you know they
wor all gone to Merika, and her husband was sick
too; and the neighbors were afeerd of the fever, so
they had no one but myself. I made a shed for
them in the ditch wud the thatch and sticks, and I
placed my coat around thim, for it was snowing and
very cowld. My aunt was talking about her children, and to take her home; but near day she said
she'd shleep, and I placed my coat and bundles of
straw about her; but whin we went to wakin her
she was dead."

"That was too bad, my poor fellow," said Frank,
with a sigh. And Frank thought on the contrast
between that proud aristocratic nobleman, that refined educated gentleman, the admired of gay
saloons and balls, that turned out that poor old
couple under frost and snow to die in the ditch side,

and that poor despised simpleton that acted the good Samaritan.

"But I had my revenge, though; hadn't I? Oh, to see him tossing in the mud, and his fine coat and cap all puddly; wasn't it funny?" and Shemus laughed and rubbed his hands with delight.

Shemus' simple narrative touched a tender chord. Lord Clearall was Frank's landlord; their fine farm would be out of lease in a few years, and what if he should carry his clearance system so far as to evict them; but, no, it could not be; and Frank banished the evil foreboding, and proceeded on his journey.

After Frank's departure, Father O'Donnell went to attend a sick call, and Alice, feeling the place too lonely, also set out for home, as it was only a pleasant walk across a few fields to her father's house. When passing out of the little lawn she was interrupted by a company of soldiers, who were on their march; so she leant on the wicket to let them pass. Captain Pry and Lieutenant Done, who were in command, saw her passing down the little avenue.

"By Jove, Pry, there is a divinity for you: look beyond!" and he pointed to Alice.

"Aye, faith, she looks a perfect Juno—how sylph-like! Isn't there grace and elegance in her movements?"

"There is. Do you know, but I am a fervent admirer of sylvan nymphs. Give me a graceful creature, with all the playful charms of a Ninon,

and I will leave your starched, staid votaries of
fashion to whom you please."

"Very fine, my dear fellow ; all very fine. She
might be just the thing for an arcadian life; but
introduce her into high life—heigh-ho! I think you
would wish your nymph at ——. No, I won't say
it ; but here she is at the gate—a perfect beauty."

"I say, we will have a lark with her. An oyster
and a champagne supper; but I will pick up an
acquaintance, and get an assignation." And the
handsome lieutenant stroked his moustache and
whiskers, as much as to say, "Let her resist these
if she can."

"Done, my dear fellow ; I would willingly pay
forfeit for an acquaintance."

As they came up to the gate, Lieutenant Done
doffed his cap in the most approved fashionable
style and bowed.

"May I take the liberty, miss, of asking you how
far is the town of Clonmel from us?"

"About ten miles, sir."

"A gay place, I suppose. We, officers, are such
votaries of fashion, that gaiety is necessary to our
existence."

"Well, I think you will find plenty of it there. '

The officers stared at her, and then exchanged
glances. Alice noticed this ; besides, she overheard
a part of their former conversation, so she resolved
on having her revenge, if they only gave her the
opportunity.

"What a quiet-looking little nest this is?" said
Done, looking at the priest's house. "I am sure
one should feel very happy here; if he only had
some loving spirit to share it with him, it would be
an Elysian."

And the lieutenant sighed, and looked at Alice.
Alice blushed and then smiled, and replied:

"I fear you would shortly grow tired of your
paradise; as soon as it would lose its novelty, it
would lose its charms."

"I vow not," and he made a most obsequious bow
to Alice. "I wish I were favored with the chance
of a trial."

"Well," said she, blushing, "as you seem to
admire the place so much, if you do not think the
journey too far, I am sure my father would be most
happy to see you at dinner in his humble cottage
any day."

"Bless my soul! you overpower us with kindness,
miss. We shall, then, with your kind permission,
do ourselves the favor of dining with you on Thurs-
day next. Now, may I ask to whom have we the
honor of speaking?"

"Miss O'Donnell."

"I am Lieutenant Done. This is my friend, Captain Pry; allow us to present our cards."

They then bowed most politely, and took their
leave.

"Well, Done, what do you mean to make of this!
You have the devil's lot of pluck. I dare say the

poor young thing is in love with you already; did
you see how she blushed?"

"Heigh-ho!" and he stroked his moustache again.
"Heigh-ho! you are in for the supper, boy."

"I confess it; but tell me, what do you mean to
make of it? That poor thing will jump into love,
as naturally as we would into a trench. Now, it
wouldn't be honorable to gain the innocent creature's
heart, and then leave her. She is handsome enough
to be a countess."

"Don't know—we'll think hereafter—carry on a
pleasant *liaison* at least—how your pretty country
nymphs fall into love, my dear fellow?"

Alice, on reflection, did not know whether she
had better cry or laugh at the joke. She was afraid
that she might offend Father O'Donnell. There
was no help for it now, so she left the good priest to
receive his unexpected guests as best he might.

According to promise the two officers drove up to
the priest's gate in a beautiful phæton. All the
dogs and idlers of the village were after them, but
they were above heeding such curiosity. They certainly were two fine-looking young men, dressed out
in spotless kids and ties, ready to besiege the heart
of any young lady, and sure of an easy conquest of
Miss O'Donnell.

They had laid wagers with their brother officers
as to the result, they betting largely on their success; one thing puzzled them—how none of their
acquaintances knew Miss O'Donnell, of Clerihan-

but then, she was young, and didn't make her *debut*
in society yet.

They drew up at the priest's door and rapped
very gently. Father O'Donnell was after enjoying
a beefsteak, when he heard the noise of the phæton,
and then the knock.

"Bless my soul! who is come now?" said he,
starting from his seat; "how will I stand it; a poor
priest cannot enjoy himself after his steak, ay, and
yesterday a fast day, and I after riding. Let me
see, from the widow Delany's; the poor woman is
very bad; I told the butcher to give her a pound of
fresh meat and a loaf of bread every day, until she is
well; she wants it poor woman—how would I feel
myself, if I were sick, to want it. I went from that
to Tom Casey's, and back to Harry St. John's, about
fifteen miles; I must get a curate, but then the
parish wouldn't afford to pay him; bless me, there's
the knock again; who' that, Mrs. Hogan?"

This was addressed to our old friend, Mrs. Hogan,
who poked her head through the door.

"Two jintlemen, your riverence, that wants to
see you; I think they are officers."

"Officers, Mrs. Hogan! in God's name, what do
they want me for?"

"Don't know, I am sure."

Now, it happened that Father O'Donnell had a
great dread of law, as he was once nearly ruined by
a heavy suit; so, being a simple kind of a man in

the ways of the world, he carried this dread to all officers in general.

He proceeded to the hall. As soon as he made his appearance the officers bowed most politely, and introduced themselves with, "I am Lieutenant Done; this is my friend, Captain Pry."

Father O'Donnell stood before them not well knowing what to say, whilst behind, at a safe distance, came Mrs. Hogan, and bringing up the rear, Neddy, ready to rescue the priest from the grasp of the law, if needed; for they all participated in Father O'Donnell's horror of law-officers, and feared a repetition of the old suit.

"Your humble servant, gentlemen," said Father O'Donnell; "to what do I owe the favor of this unexpected visit."

"You don't mean unexpected, sir; I presume your daughter has apprized you of the favor she has done us in asking us to dine with you to-day."

· "My daughter, gentlemen! There must be some mistake.

"Not the least, sir, not the least. Be good enough to inform her that we are waiting." The priest looked at Mrs. Hogan for advice.

The officers whispered—"Strange old cove this ·-devilish pretty daughter, though—will make amends for all."

Mrs. Hogan, not knowing what to make of it, only raised her eyes in bewilderment.

The priest turned to his guests. "Really, gentlemen, there must be some mistake. I am the parish priest. Oh, Alice, Alice! you mad-cap, this is all your doings; will you never rest!"

"The officers looked bewildered, and were proceeding—"Good sir, we met your daughter——"

"Arrah, hould your whist," said Mrs. Hogan, who, seeing that she had nothing to fear, stepped in to her master's assistance. Did any one ever hear the likes of it? Oh, holy Joseph! Out of the house wid ye,—to say the likes of that; ugh, ugh, out wid ye. O, blessed Saint Pathrick, if there was any one any good list'ning to yez, they would tach yez how to respect the clargy. Oh, Holy Mother!" and Mrs. Hogan raised her eyes to heaven, and then her apron to her eyes, and then began to sob.

Neddy O'Brien could not bear this appeal to his feelings, particularly from Mrs. Hogan. Her cold ham and turkeys, and the like, crossed his mind. In he bounced into the hall with a whoop, that would do credit to a red Indian, and cutting capers, and whirling a poker in a manner that might win him a civic crown at Astley's. Neddy also felt pretty certain that reinforcements were near, for he had very prudently sent a gorsoon to apprize the villagers of the priest's danger.

"Who dare insult his riverence now?" said Neddy, whirling the poker.

"Stop Neddy, you blockhead, stop," said Father

O'Donnell; "these gentlemen did not come here to insult me; they came here under a mistake, and as it happened so, I will feel favored if they take a beefsteak and a glass of punch with me."

"With pleasure, sir," said the officers, for to tell the truth they felt ashamed to return home without dinner to be bantered by their companions.

Father O'Donnell had to make a regular speech to disperse the motly group that had collected around the phæton. Mrs. Hogan dressed the beefsteak; though at first rather distant, she relaxed after a time, and when the officers slipped a piece of silver each into her hand at parting, she vowed that she never met the likes of them. Neddy O'Brien, too, as he jingled his two shillings, was of the same opinion. As for Lieutenant Done, and Captain Pry, they vowed that they never spent so jolly an evening. The old priest was so full of tales and anecdotes, that he kept them in roars. After a time, though, the whole joke leaked out; they were so quizzed about how they were done by an "innocent country girl," that they had to get themselves removed.

CHAPTER VIII.

THE village, which has been the scene of many of
the incidents narrated in this story, possessed many
other remarkable and interesting characters not introduced into this work. Our boyhood had been so
impressed with their originality and eccentricities
that we are resolved to give a few of the most prominent of them a separate chapter to themselves, feeling confident that our readers will not be displeased
at the digression.

Most readers of Carleton's humorous and graphic
sketches of Irish life would be inclined to think
that he drew largely on his imagination for his
leading characters, there is something so ludicrously
absurd in their bungling good-humored eccentricities
and oddities.

But to one brought up in the country, whose
young days have been spent among the gay, light
hearted Irish peasantry, each and every one of them
appear as natural as life. How often have I seen a
prototype of poor Neal Malone, who was "blue
moulded for the want of a beatin'," in some prim little

coxcomb, who strutted about with all the pride of a
bantam cock, until he was thoroughly sobered down
by a termagant wife. How many a Paddy-go-easy
is to be found, even to-day, smoking his dudeen in
the neighboring shebeen, complacently awaiting
some one to drop in either to give him a treat, or to
discuss politics and the affairs of the parish, while
his garden lay untilled—the rain poured down
through his cabin and his children ran about half
wild and naked.

As a specimen of the Neal Malone style of blatant
heroes, we remember a little hop-of-my thumb of a
tailor, who kept the village in which he resided, in a
continual broil by his bellicose, quarrelsome disposition. He strutted about like an inflated gobbler,
fuming in rage at the most trival reasons, and always
ready to fight with some one. He was so small in
appearance and so pugnacious in disposition that the
boys of the village treated him with that pitying
contempt a huge mastiff bestows upon a quarrelsome
cur. But they soon had their revenge for the tailor
got married, and his wife proved to be a perfect
vixen, the compound essence of vinegar and gall.
The poor fellow soon sobered down and insensibly
dwindled away almost to a shadow; yet, he occasionally made a show of authority; but the rebellion
was soon nipped in the bud, and Billy subsided into
a patient, submissive subject. Having broken out
on one occasion into a violent rebellion against the
ruling powers, he walked up and down the streets

flourishing a huge stick and shouting out, "There isn't a man in Ireland but what I'd lick, and some women too!"

Now, Billy was right in qualifying his notes of defiance, for he knew from bitter experience that one woman, at least, always came off best in the contest. With a crowd of urchins at his heels, who cheered him on, Billy paraded the streets with all the importance of a conqueror, and to prove that he was lord and master he stopped in front of his own house, or rather his wife's, and gave a rousing hurra, and a brilliant flourish of his stick, as he shouted out his war cry.

Scarcely had he given vent to his defiant whoop, when a woman was seen to rush from the cabin, and make for him. The poor tailor seemed paralyzed, the stick dropped from his hand, and he was unable to offer the least resistance as the Amazon seized him by the collar and flung him over her shoulder, as if he were a child, and as she pummelled his head with her right hand, she held him tight with the other, and thus bore him off in triumph, amidst the shouts of the assembled villagers.

Billy, though vanquished, was not conquered, for in a few hours afterwards a neighbor called to borrow a pot, to boil the goose that was killed in honor of St. Martin. "I have no pot," gruffly replied the tailor's wife. "You have!" shouted a voice from under the bed, where the poor tailor had to fly for refuge. The wife ran over and, kicking at him angr.ty said: "Hould your tongue there, you spris-saun."

"How can I?" exclaimed the poor, crestfallen tailor, "for I have too much of the man in me."

The neighbor shook his head, and walked out as he muttered : "However I'll manage to cook my goose, your goose is cooked for you, poor fellow."

It is true that such characters are fast disappearing, but yet enough of them remain to remind one of the good old times, of which we have heard so much.

There are few townlands in Ireland that do not still possess the traditional blind piper and his inseparable companion, the dancing-master. Though we must confess that the race is pretty well thinned out, we have a vivid recollection of a wandering minstrel, who traveled from place to place as musician and kind of servitor to as odd, as humorous, and as eccentric a professor of the light fantastic art as has ever been painted by writer or artist.

We have often wondered to ourselves how it was that nearly all of these traveling musicians were blind, and in our youthful ignorance thought that they were either born so, or, as a part of the Orphean Mysteries, they had to be deprived of their sight.

The poor, meek-looking, old, blind piper, with a little boy as guide and prop, is familiar to most of our Irish readers, and they cannot forget with what thrilling joy and gladness they hailed his arrival, and how the neighbors collected to hear him play "The wind that shakes the barley," "Garryowen," "Patrick's Day," and other favorite tunes.

Ah! those were merry days and happy times; for the gay, light-hearted peasants passed good-natured jokes, told amusing stories, and danced to the music of the blind piper with an abandon and relish that was really as fascinating as it was natural.

The honest farmer's house was a palace the night the blind piper visited it, for a *cead mille failthe* sparkled in his good-natured face, and his laugh was the heartiest, and his shout the loudest to greet some funny story, or some ambitious pair of dancers who strove to tire each other down. When the dancing-master, Billy O'Carroll, was present "teaching the ignorant the art of dancing by grammar," much of this abandon and innocent hilarity had to be kept in check, for Billy had marshalled his pupils around the room with the regularity of a drill-sergeant, and if a luckless wight indulged even in a titter he was at once upbraided by the indignant dancing-master as "an ignoramush, who knew no betther; for, poor crathur, shure he never thravelled or mixed wid the quality."

It is said that Charles Dickens took a special delight in giving strange and sententious names to his characters, but, to his great surprise, he soon found out that not a single one of them but had living representatives; and, to crown the climax, he was one day passing a tailor's establishment in the environs of London, and, to his utter surprise, found the name of the firm was "Dombey & Son." So it is with writers of Irish stories, and of fiction in general; no matter how improbable the characters they create, they learn to realize the fact that the truth is stranger than fiction.

As the classic village which is the scene of our story has been famous for producing a strange compound of oddities, full of laughable eccentricities, whose extravagant actions and farcical behavior would make a hermit laugh, we will just notice a few of them before we proceed with the adventures of our leading characters.

A bridge crossed the little stream near the site of the old mill from which the village derived its name. This was, time out of mind, the headquarters of a boccagh or simpleton, and no sooner had one gone the way of all flesh, than another mysteriously appeared, to take possession of the boasted privilege.

As the Salic law was not in force in this Arcadian realm, the ruling sovereign was just as likely to be a woman as a man.

Biddy Mortimer, a strange, half-witted creature, was the last of a long line of ragged, besotted rulers. A more strange character than Biddy could not be conceived. She was always dressed in torn, filthy rags, while she carried under her arm a bundle of straw, wrapped up in a dirty counterpane. This was her bed and covering at night. In one hand le carried a tin-can, which received the indiscrimi·

nate contributions of potatoes, soup and meat the
shopkeepers and others contributed to her support,
while in the other she usually carried a lot of sauce-
pans, kettles, and tea-pots, strung together. Biddy's
head-dress was the crowning feature in her strange
attire. Like all her sex, she had a passionate liking
for bonnets, and every one she could find was trans-
ferred to her wardrobe, which was no other than her
head; so that it was no unusual thing to see her
with a pile of bonnets rising from her head like a
thatched steeple, while beneath them hung her
straggling locks and bunches of gray and faded
ribbons. When Biddy became too feeble to levy
contributions upon her subjects, she was carted to
the poor-house. But, bless your soul, she was not
there a day when she raised a perfect revolution,
and she had to be sent back to her filth and independence. It was equal to a repeal meeting when
Biddy was driven into the village. There she sat
on the jaunting car, with her bonnets bobbing up
and down upon her head, her kettles and pans jing-
ling, and she flourishing the straw bed in triumph,
while a crowd of her youthful subjects followed,
laughing and shouting in mad discord. Biddy was
not disturbed during the remainder of her reign,
and a few years since she was laid to rest with the
long line of rulers who had preceded her.

Another strange character was Shaun Hicks, the
peddler. Shaun was a withered-faced, puckered-eyed
looking creature, and might pass for a brother to

any decent monkey. Shaun flourished though, and waxed wealthy, for his wife kept a little huckster store, which added considerably to their income. She was a sharp-eyed, shrewd viper, and though she blinked fearfully, she always kept an eye open for business.

In one of poor Shaun's tramps through the country to sell his goods, death seized the old man, and he scarcely had time to reach home to prepare for the dread summons.

He took to the bed, and called for the priest, but his matter-of-fact wife first brought in the village school-master to make his will.

The poor man who never had a will while living, was now compelled to leave one when dying, so he meekly submitted and then began.

"Put down, Mr. —— owes me five pounds, which I leave to my dear wife."

"Ah," sobbed the heart-broken woman—"poor, dear Shaun is sensible to the last! "

"And Mrs. —— owes me three pounds two, which I will to my wife."

"Dear me, what a good memory and clear head he has," sobbed the bereaved woman.

After enumerating all that was due to him, which he left to his afflicted wife, amidst her frequent comments upon his virtues, he resumed.

"And now, put down six pounds, which I owe Mr. ——, and which I enjoin my wife to—"

"Stop, stop!" exclaimed the sobbing woman,

" stop, the poor man is raving. Oh, Shaun, I know I'm a widow at last—God help me! What will become of me, a poor lone widow? Let him sign his name to the will at once, for I know he is going, and it's a sin and shame to be distressing him, now that he is going fast, besides, I want to call in the priest—sign it, Shaun, achorra, at once!"

Poor Shaun was brow-beaten into affixing his signature to the will, and the afflicted woman had the consolation of finding that a nice sum was left her, while she had not a single shilling of debts to pay.

She went into mourning for Shaun, but in three weeks she had a much healthier and stronger man in partnership with her.

But of all the odd characters which the village produced, perhaps Billy O'Carroll, the hop merchant, was the most amusing and interesting. It was not because Billy dealt in hops, or malt, or anything of the kind, that he was called the hop merchant. Not at all, poor Billy was a dancing master, but thinking the name too vulgar, he dignified himself by the title of hop merchant, and his pupils, and the peasantry in general, humored the poor man's eccentricity to his unspeakable gratification.

Billy generally patronized the farmers for miles around the village, and instructed the younger members of their families in all the mysteries of heel and toe, cover the buckle, and Sir Roger de Coverly.

It was really amusing to see with what impor

tance he strutted around as he ranged his pupils in order before him, and gave them their instructions, not forgetting occasional advice to the blind piper, such as, "go easy, the colleens can't keep up wid you," or "strike up, man alive, faster, don't you see we're all fallin' ashleep wid your music."

Billy himself was the most remarkable figure of the whole group. His very dress indicated his importance. His white linen pants always looked as if they had only just come from the iron; his well-worn but clean dress coat, was adorned with shining brass buttons as large as a small plate, his vest and tie too, were immaculate in their way, and the shine of his slippers was only equaled by the polish of his hat. The clothes, like himself, seemed endowed with the power of always keeping from growing old; for though we knew him for years, we believe he never bought a new suit of clothes, nor grew a day older, at least in appearance.

It is no wonder that our hero should look upon himself as a person of no small importance, and on the poor, meek, blind piper, who squeezed all kinds of outlandish music out of his dirty bag-pipes, as a necessary appendage, merely to be tolerated.

Billy always marshalled out his pupils with the regularity of a general, and then with a smirk and a bow, would address them thus, "Miss Nelly Quin, what are we going to dance this evening?"

She most likely would reply, "A double jig."

"A double jig, anagh; would nothing else do

you? throth, you want to get into grammar before you're out of your al-phabat!" Billy would most likely reply, for a double jig was his master-piece, and was reserved for advanced or favorite pupils. If she persisted, Billy yielded with a very bad grace, and called on the old piper to strike up the Fox hunter's jig. If she did not dance it to his satisfaction he retaliated by sneeringly remarking, "So you wanted a double jig, anagh; well to be shure, how high you want to jump; faith in troth, the next thing you will be asking for is a husband!"

This sally, of course, set the audience in a roar of laughter, and the young girl blushed, and most likely, sat down to hide her confusion. When a favorite pupil was dancing Billy ducked and bobbed around like a jack in the box, flinging out his arms and feet as if they were attached to his body by some mechanical contrivances, in his eagerness to teach her his steps; and if her dancing was to his satisfaction, he cried out in ectacies, "That's it, stick to that, ma colleen! four times that—raise off and double there! that's it—stick to that; that's none of your common dance—I have grammar home in the box for that—throth, you'll soon be as good as meself; maybe you wont astonish them at the crass of Cappanagraun a Sunday; faith, Mrs. O'Flyn, your darther is a prodigy, and you'll soon have to be lookin' out for the colleen, for somebody will be stalin' her heart."

Poor Billy, like the "good old Irish jintleman,"

outlived his time, and when quadrilles and other fancy
dances began to supersede the good old Irish dances,
he could not patiently submit to his fate, so he
moved around from farm-house to farm-house, railing
against the degeneracy of the times, and as he re-
peatedly shook his head, he emphatically exclaimed,
"Well, well, this new fangled dance is like everything else that comes over from England, there is not
much good in it, and it makes the colleens as proud
as peacocks, and as stuck up as a trussed turkey, to
think that they can dance like the quality!"

Thus the poor hop merchant lingered on, reviling
at the changed times, and shaking his head
until he, at length, gave it the final shake and
dropped off the stage.

CHAPTER IX.

MRS. BUTLER'S ESTABLISHMENT—WILLY SHEA—FRANK
AT HOME—WILLY'S HISTORY.

FRANK was amused by Shemus' conversational powers, as they proceeded in their journey. The mind of the latter seemed a regular fund of stories, songs, and legends; and as Frank's fowling operations were a sinecure, he had the more time to listen to him.

It was evening when they came in sight of Mr. O'Donnell's house, which was appropriately called, Glen Cottage.

" Begor, there's the house beyond, and here is Mrs. Butler's sheebeen; will we go in? Maybe any of the boys wud be there."

" And maybe you'd like a glass after your walk, Shemus; so we will go in."

Mrs. Butler's house was rather comfortable of its kind; it was well thatched, and the walls plastered; it had also two glass windows in front. In one of the windows a few loaves of bread, some candles and pipes, displayed themselves most conspicuously; behind these stood a broken glass and a jug, as much as to say you can get something else here besides bread and candles.

6

In such a sense did the initiated read it, for they knew well that there was some secret chamber or corner in Mrs. Butler's establishment as hard to be made out as the labyrinth of Crete, which was accessible to Mrs. Butler alone; for she presided as priestess over it, and discovered in its hidden womb nothing less than an Irishman's glory—the real potteen. Mrs. Butler's house had an exterior air of comfort; the interior of it also was clean and orderly. The little kitchen, with an attempt at a counter in one corner, and its rows of pints and tins in another, and its clean mortar floor and white-washed walls, bore strong evidence to Mrs. Butler's taste and cleanliness. The little room inside was equally neat; it had a bed hung with cotton curtains in one corner, and a kind of little closet behind among the mysteries of which she concealed her "muntain dew." Indeed, I must say, that the excise officers connived at it a good deal, for she was a poor struggling widow, trying to support herself and her only daughter. Mr. O'Donnell, too, for he was her landlord, left her the house and haggard free. So she was, as she said herself, "able to live purty well, glory be to God."

"Arrah, welcome, Mr. Frank; where have you been this week of Sundays? sit down." She ran over and dusted a chair for him, and then placed it near the fire. This was Mrs. Butler's salutation to our travelers as they entered her domicile. Mrs. Butler, though a large, corpulent woman, was still a

bus
lin

in
m
w
th

w
t

h

B
g
it
c

m
gr
str
est
for
It t
N
very
cent
wood

As Frank neared this retreat, for he met no birds in the grove, he thought that he heard the sound of music proceeding from it.

" Whist," said Shemus; " may I never sin but that is music."

" I think so, too, Shemus; let us go nearer.

As they neared the arbor they distinctly heard the sounds of a flute mingling with the soft drippling of the falling stream.

" Isn't it pleasant," said Shemus, evidently delighted; " listen to the murmuring of the water and the sound of the music sighing together."

Frank leant on his gun until the music ceased; he then went up to the arbor and was about to enter, when he heard a clear plaintive voice chanting the following song:—

> Oh! fair is the brow
>   Of Cathleen, dear,
> And mild is the glance
>   Of Cathleen, dear,
> And raven is her hair,
> And her skin is so fair
> That none can compare
>   With Cathleen, dear.
>
> Oh! light is the step
>   Of Cathleen, dear,
> And graceful the mien
>   Of Cathleen, dear,
> I am wild with delight,
> My heart is so light
> If I met but the sight
>   Of Cathleen, dear.

There is love in the eye
  Of Cathleen, dear,
There is balm in the sigh
  Of Cathleen, dear,
Soft and fair is her hand,
And her voice is as bland,
As breath of Araby's land,
  My Cathleen, dear.

Brighter than the day
  Is Cathleen, dear,
Purer than the spray
  Is Cathleen, dear,
Oh! I never will rove,
But true as the dove
I'll cling to the love
  Of Cathleen, dear.

My heart it is thine,
  My Cathleen, dear,
Then, will you be mine?
  My Cathleen, dear,
And our lives, well I know,
Will so lovingly flow
We'll have heaven below,
  My Cathleen, dear.

After the song there was a silence of some time.

"I declare," thought Frank, "'tis no other but my friend, Willy Shea; could that song be addressed to my sister Kate? I never heard it before, and he writes poetry. Well, I shouldn't wonder if he were in love with her, for she is a noble girl. I declare, if they made a confidant of me I would do my best for them, for I would not ask a nobler husband for my fair sister than Willy Shea."

The rustling of the trees near them disturbed the

party in the arbor, and Frank neared them, and
grasping his friend by the hand, exclaimed,

"Willy, my dear fellow, I am glad to see you;
when did you come? this is a pleasure I did not expect; and Kate, my sister dear, how are you since?
why, you look pale,—and my little Bessy," and he
kissed his young sister.

"Now, Frank," said Kate, recovering her composure, "sit down, you have asked so many questions
in a minute that I am sure you did not give us time
to answer half of them."

"Oh, I believe I must answer the first," said
Willy; "in the first place, I am here three days; I
was getting weary of the city, and, in truth, my
health wasn't too good, so I took a run to see my
kind friends."

"Welcome, my dear friend; and you strolled up
to my nest, as I call it; up here; here is where I sit
and think and dream over life's vicissitudes; isn't it
a wild retreat, Willy? just suited for a poet like
you."

"It is, indeed, a retired nook, separated from the
world; here you would hear no voice but that little
stream babbling its own discordant music; here the
soul could commune with itself."

"True, but I interrupted your music; you were
at some song I never heard before; I suppose one of
your own composition."

A slight blush tinged the student's pale cheek,
and a sympathetic one mounted on Kate's. Frank

did not pretend to notice it, though he was too well
schooled in the ways of love not to set down these
indications for their worth.

"Come, Willy, play something, and I will take
Bessy on my knee, and as our house is too small,
Shemus, you must remain at the door."

Shemus was fatigued, and stretched outside the
door; Bessy climbed to her brother's knee, and
nestled in his bosom, and Willy resumed his flute.

Though it was the month of November, still the
evening was calm and still; the weather was very
dry for the season, so there was but little water in
the stream. The birds were chirping their farewell
songs to autumn, the little rivulet fell with a gurg-
ling noise over the fall, and the soft sounds of the
flute floated on the evening breeze.

"Music has wonderful charms for me," said Frank.
"I think there is a great deal of truth in the fabled
lyre of Orpheus; it is a mere allegory, showing the
power music possesses of fascinating the most rugged
natures."

"True," said Willy: "the snake-charmers use it
in their incantations; why, it has a soothing influence on most animals, not to speak of man; the poet
has well said,—

> "Is there a heart that music cannot melt
> Alas! how is that rugged heart forlorn"

And yet, some of the finest minds had no taste for
music; let us take Dr. Johnson and Sir Walter Scott,
for instances."

"Few have that nice discriminating taste to observe a slight error in musical notes. If a single wrong syllable introduced itself into a verse, either of these great scholars would at once see the limping of the verse, their very ear would detect it, and yet they were not sensible of the pure harmony of music; this makes me agree with the Latin quotation,—'Poeta nascitur non fit.' I think though, art can do a great deal to perfect it, still nature is the great architect of our tastes and talents."

"Do you know," said Frank, after a pause, "let modern writers say what they will to the contrary, I think that our old bardic order and traveling minstrels did a great deal of good in their way; they kept alive the spirit of romance and chivalry that tended to refine and ennoble the people."

"Oh! how I'd long to hear one of these 'sons of song, firing his hearers with martial pride; there was something so soul-stirring in the bard. His was glorious music; now haughty and inspiring, and then sad and pensive, as if weeping. I went a few years ago to hear an old wandering minstrel in Cork. I might say of him:—

> 'The last of all the bards was he,
> That sung of ancient chivalry.'

He was a fine type of the old Irish bards; his grey hair floated in wavey ringlets like the old Irish coulin. There was a touching sweetness in his wild effusions that made me long to see the bardic order restored. I often listen in imagination to our great national bard, Carolan—him over whom the genius of his country breathed the spirit of inspiration. Is there not a tender pathos, an impressive grandeur, a metrical simplicity in his compositions, and a sublime witchery in the wild effusions of his harp."

" What a pity," said Kate O'Donnell, " that our old Irish harp should give way to other and newer instruments."

" And yet Kate, our neighbors, the English, will not allow us the poor privilege of claiming the harp a national instrument."

" I always thought," said Frank, " that they left us this much of our nationality, at least; I should not wonder if the Scotch, as they have seized Ossian, took the harp also."

" Dr. Percy says," said Willy, " that 'the harp was the common musical instrument of the Anglo-Saxons;' but Dr. Beauford says, ' I cannot but think the *clarseach*, or Irish harp, one of the most ancient Irish instruments we have among us, and had, perhaps, its origin in remote periods of antiquity.' "

" The Irish tradition is, that we are indebted for this instrument to the first Milesian colony that settled in this country. The music of the harp was grand indeed, though inferior to the bagpipes, as soul-stirring, martial music in the field; it far surpassed it in sweetness and pensive grandeur. How gay and animating is the Irish jig, and what surpasses the renecafadha, or war dance, which corres-

ponds to the festal dance of the Greeks.   Previous
to the innovation of foreign dances, all our balls or
dancing parties concluded with the reneeafadha, as
they often do now with a country dance.   The last
time it had been danced in honor of a great national
event, was to welcome James the Second on his
arrival in Kinsale."

"You said something, Frank," said Kate, "about
Ossian being a Scotchman; do the modern Scotch
claim him as such ? "

"Certainly, sister mine; what is it the English
and Scotch don't claim?   I shouldn't wonder if
Carolan should become a Scotchman or an Englishman by and bye, and most likely, after a time, Tom
Moore too; but happily their claims to Ossian are
now exploded.   To Macpherson is undoubtedly due
the merit of collecting the scattered Ossianic
poems; but then he so changed names, or rather
Scotchafied them, as to give them something of a
Scotch smack."

Night was fast setting in, so they prepared to
leave for home.

"I tell you what," said Frank, as they left the
grove, "winter is now setting in; as soon as the
weather breaks we must leave our bower for the
season.   Now, I propose that we take a cold dinner
here to-morrow; and to make it a banquet worthy
of the gods, I will bring my clarionet, and you
your flute, Willy.   Now, who seconds the resolution ? "

" I do," said Willy, " provided Kate will be our fair hostess, and Bessy our guest."

" Agreed, agreed! "

" Do you know, Frank, whom we had at dinner, and is to stay to night with us ? "

" No, whom, pray ? "

" Your friend, Mr. Baker."

" Now, capital by Jove! Tell me, has he many on his list of killed and wounded? any new victims ? "

" Oh! I suppose he has; but then we did not wait to hear of all his bloody deeds, so we left himself and papa to settle about the killed and wounded over their punch, and strolled out here."

" Willy, my dear fellow," said Frank, " we must draw out old Baker; he is the oddest fish in the world, a regular Jack Falstaff; if you credit himself the county is trembling with the very dread of his name, while I must tell you there never breathed a more arrant coward."

Our party found the worthy couple enjoying their punch together, and Mrs. O'Donnell, seated on a settee near the fire, enjoying Mr. Baker's " hairbreadth escapes by flood and field."

" Ha! Frank--well, are ye come, ladies—is this you --where were you these seven weeks ?—devilish well you rode the Fawn, my boy—give me the hand."

This was Mr. Baker's salute to Frank, the moment he made his appearance.

"Well, are you come lad; I thought you weren't going to come home any more," said his father.

His mother kindly looked up, with his hand in hers, and gave it a kiss, and whispered:—

"Welcome, my dear boy."

"That will do, now," said Mr. Baker; "leave your gun there; a nice day for shooting this, though I think your bag isn't very heavy; when I was like you, a young strippling, I often had two men loaded coming home. Ay, upon my soul, often three, often three!"

"You must have shot a sheep, or a dog, or, perhaps, a lot of turkeys then, to load so many?" said Frank.

This was a sly hit at Mr. Baker, for it was said that he wasn't very particular whether it were wild or tame fowl he met; in fact perferred the latter, as being in the best condition, and the more easily got at.

"Devil a bit, devil a bit, all wild-fowl, game every mother's soul of them. Often Lord Clearall said to me:—'Baker, how the deuce do you bag so many.' His lordship and I you know, are particular friends; he was never a good shot though. You heard that I shot —hem, that his lordship though shot— this is between ourselves though, honor bright—this is how it happened. We were fowling, and a covey of partridge got up near the dogs; bang went his lordship and I; bedad, one of the birds fell, and there was Spanker tossing head over heels, I thought it was over-joyed he was; bedad, when I went up to him he was beautifully peppered. His lordship stormed and swore, and said it was I that shot him; devil a bit; I knew better, but I didn't like to contradict him, for his lordship is my particular friend. Come, Frank, boy, get your glass."

'I think I will get something to eat first," said Frank.

"That's it, Frank; a man can never drink unless he eats; 'eat, drink, and be merry,' as his lordship says, for we are particular friends. I think I will have another leg of that turkey, Miss Kate; I can drink the better for it. Just take what .you want off the bird for Frank, and leave the rest here on the table; we can be picking a snack by times; that will do, Miss Kate; a loaf of bread now. A man should always be eating and drinking together; 'eat, drink and be merry,' as his lordship says; his lordship and I, you know, are particular friends. That roast mutton was so nice I think I will have a cut along with the turkey; that will do now. This is your own mutton, Mr. O'Donnell? devilish fine it is; never got such mutton as yours, except his lordship's."

We will leave Mr. Baker, for the present, to enjoy his snack, which consisted, of the most part, of a turkey, and about two pounds of mutton; we will also leave Frank to take his dinner, for which he had a good relish, after a walk of about fourteen miles through the country; and Shemus, too, to do ample

justice to a dish of broken meat and crisped potatoes, in the kitchen, and while they are all enjoying
themselves, we will introduce our new acquaintances
to our readers.

Mr. O'Donnell was a man about fifty years of age
—perhaps something more. He was very handsome
in his youth, and was still a fine portly man. His
figure was erect, his large eye bright, and the ruddy
glow of health was still upon his cheek. There was
none of the sternness of age upon his brow; nor was
the smile of love and friendship banished from his
lips. He was warm-hearted and affectionate, and
with merry laugh and song he joined the plays and
pastimes of his children. His parental authority
did not chide their innocent amusements, so he was
to them the kind, loving father and playful friend.
He was a man of wealth and respectability, too. He
farmed large tracts of land, and had lately set up a
discount bank in the village. His wife was a pale,
tall woman. There was something subdued and
melancholy in her appearance. This was owing to
the death of most of her children, by that most in-
sidious of all diseases, consumption. She was a
woman of warm affections and deep love; and it is
no wonder, when she saw her darling children droop
and pine away one by one, that the rose fled her
cheeks and the smile her lips. Even now she sighs
as little Bessy sits beside her on the settee and
nestles her head in her lap, for there is something in
the fire that sparkles in the eye, and in the hectic

flush that mantles on the cheek, and then leaves it
deadly pale as before, that wrings the mother's heart
with anguish for her pretty darling. So frail, so
gentle and retiring was Bessy O'Donnell, that she
seemed some ethereal being embodied in a frame of
mortal mould. She was the only one of the family
that possessed the golden hair and light blue eye of
the mother. She was a frail, gentle, loving child,
Bessy O'Donnell was. Though twelve winters had
not passed over her head, yet she was tall—tall for
her years—for the fire was burning within, and
building its structure to consume it again. And
Kate O'Donnell; she was in herself a wealth of love
and beauty. Though she had imbibed from her
mother a tinge of her chaste sadness, still she was
betimes cheerful as a child, with all the devotional
nature of true piety.

Her's was that beautifully moulded character of
intellectual taste, rare enjoyments, and good sense,
seldom met with; but which is no ideal after all,
dear reader. How many a Kate O'Donnell have we
met with in life? But I must describe her more
minutely to you. Her beauty was of the highest
order; she was tall and stately, without a particle of
pride or affectation. Her beautiful oval, but rather
pale, face was enlivened by a slight blush, and en-
circled with long braids of raven hair. A broad
forehead, white as alabaster, a nose of extreme delicacy, but rather *retrousse*, dark blue eyes, bordered
with dark lashes —such was Kate O'Donnell.

There was an elegance of symmetry, a correctness of form about her, that I have seldom seen surpassed in statuary. How often, dear reader, do we see a living Venus, with life and animation, with the rich blood circling through her veins, with animated and sparkling features? What is all your soulless statuary, your dry Venus-de-Medici, to her? Nothing; it is merely a beautifully chiselled ideal when compared to the real. Such was Kate O'Donnell, as she moved around that tastefully furnished parlor, that black velvet riband around her neck, contrasting so finely with the purity of her skin, and that rose-bud braided in her dark hair, looking out so wantonly from beneath the folds.

We know little, as yet, of Willy Shea, but that he was an orphan; Frank had met him at College. There was something so retiring and gloomy about that poor student, that he won on Frank's good nature to seek his society and followship.

Willy Shea seemed to avoid associating with any of the students. He was dressed in black, with crape on his hat; all the others knew about him was that he had lately buried his father, and was now left alone to battle against a rough world.

Frank, after a time, gained his friendship and his confidence, and when the fatal disease of his family, —consumption,—threatened, and when recommended to go to the country, alas! he had no home, and Frank wrote to his father, and there came in reply a welcome invitation for the student to make his home of Mr. O'Donnell's house until his recovery; he hesitated, yet Frank pressed him, and said so much about the kindness of his dear mother and his fair sister, that at length he consented. For something said to him, "though death has left you without kith or kin, though you have no fond mother, or gentle sympathizing sister—no one to love you, no one to feel for you, there is no use in feeling dismal and weary; go, there are loving hearts in the world that will love you," and something within him whispered, "go, there are loving hearts in the world that will love you,"—and he did go.

Willy Shea was then about twenty. He was rather tall and gracefully formed. His studious, pale-looking face, shaded with dark curls, possessed almost a womanly delicacy. There was a mine of thought in his dark dreamy eye. As I said, he had neither kith nor kin, and he tried to forget the past in deep reflective study. His thoughts and life were pure and unsullied; his aspirations noble and lofty.

At length the poor suffering student accompanied his new friend to his home in the country. Here every comfort surrounded him; the nicest attention was paid him, until his improved health testified that the change was indeed beneficial.

Mrs. O'Donnell thought of her own dear children and sighed, and was a mother to the suffering orphan. He was so exhausted from his delicate state and the fatigue of traveling, that he was confined to bed for several days. Kate was his principal nurse, and her low soft voice, her gentle step, and the cheerfulness of her presence, were a balm to his weary spirit. How he did wait and listen and long for her coming; what sweet emotions danced in his dreamy dark eyes, as she quietly glided into his room.

One day in a feverish sleep, as dreams of the past flitted across his mind, he exclaimed, "Oh, mother dear! oh, sister sweet! will you not come to me? but alas! I have neither mother nor sister—no one to love me."

He thought he felt a tear trickle on his brow; he looked up, and Kate was standing over him, her large eyes dim with pity and compassion. "So you have neither mother nor sister, poor youth; I will be to you a sister."

"God bless you, God bless you, Miss O'Donnell, for these kind words, and he pressed his lips to her hand. She blushed and timidly withdrew her hand

"Forgive me, Miss O'Donnell——"

"Kate, if you please, as we are to be brother and sister."

"Well, Kate—how dear a name—I am grateful for that sympathy which called forth your devotion to a stranger; I had a sister like you; her name was Kate, also."

"And she is dead?" said Kate.

"Yes, Kate, yes! that fatal disease of our family did its work; she was older than I by a few years;

she was the playmate of my young days, and the guide of my boyhood. We loved one another dearly. At length, her laugh became less merry— her step less buoyant. She was declining; yes, she was, for that short dry cough, that hectic flush, and the tiny blue veins and wasting frame told us so. Doctors were called in; they watched her heavy breathing, felt her pulse, wisely shook their heads, took their fees, and left. They ordered her whatever she desired; ah we knew what this meant. At length she became too weak to remain up. I constantly watched and attended her sick bed, and often watered it with my tears. I can never forget the day our poor infirm father came to take his parting leave. He had to be helped up stairs; he tottered to the bed; though weak, she raised herself up, clasped her tiny hands around his neck; his tears bedewed her face. His long grey hair floated around, mingling with her soft ringlets. There he lay in her embrace, breathing blessings on that good dutiful daughter, that never vexed him; that cheered and consoled him in his declining health. It was a mute scene of heart-felt grief. Memory recalled the love and kindness of past years. All the tenderness of the fond father and dutiful daughter was aroused in that awful moment, when they were about to separate for ever. With swollen eyes and throbbing heart I witnessed this scene. My poor sobbing mother buried her face in the bedcovering. The domestics wept, and at length bore him away from

that child he dearly loved, but was never more to
to see on earth."

"And your father, too?" said Kate, as she rested
her head on her hand, and the tears trickled between
her fingers.

"Is dead! Oh! I can never forget my feelings,
as I knelt beside his death-bed. With a heart
bursting with grief I knelt to receive his final blessing."

"Ah! in that moment what feelings agitate a sensitive mind. Our past lives rise up in judgment
against us; our faults and transgressions appear
so heinous that we feel almost ashamed to crave a
blessing. Alas! if we could recall that good father
to life, how changed we would become. What a
lesson is there in that separation. As I paid nature
her tribute beside that death-bed, some one whispered
—'You have one comfort, you were a dutiful son.' I
might reply—' Alas, I thought so while he was alive;
but now that he is dead, I think otherwise.' These
tears, Kate, were not weakness; no, for they sprung
from that fount, the holiest in my nature, that stirred
up this mutiny of sobs and tears for that dear father
whose wise counsels and protecting hand steered me
through life."

"And so you are alone in the world?" sobbed
Kate.

"Alone, Kate, without a domestic tie, one to love
me, to fill up the yearnings of my loving heart, for
my kind, gentle, loving mother soon followed them,

Father, mother, and sister sleep in one grave. Oh, God! how soon shall I join them ?"

"Hush, hush," sobbed Kate; "don't say that, brother, it is sorrowful. God is good; sure we will love you and comfort you."

"You love me Kate! Oh, did you say that?" and he leant up in the bed. "Oh, Kate, if one so good and pure as you would love me, I could almost forget the misery of the past in the happiness of the present."

Kate blushed and smiled, and said—"You forget that we are brother and sister already. Now try and sleep, for you are fatigued."

And did he sleep? No; he dosed away, and visions of the past rose up before him. He was a child again, and played with his sister at his mother's knee; and now tired and wearied with play, they knelt beside her and nestled in her lap, and she kissed them and hushed them to sleep; and his dear papa had come home, and walked in on tip-toes lest he would disturb his little darlings' rest. When they awoke, he had brought with him a horse for Willy and a doll for Kate; and how he laughed and raced with his horse, and Kate fondled her doll, and then when they retired to rest, how his mother pressed her good-night kiss upon their little lips. And then came up his schoolboy days, with crowds of happy children at play; their laughing faces full of smiles, and they lustily shouting in the exuberance of their mirth; and then came up the mournful faces

of strange men crowding around their house; and
some, he thought, were eating and drinking and
laughing, whilst others were bearing away his dear
sister in a coffin, and then came his father and next his
mother. He wept and cried, but the heartless men
put him aside, and bore away the coffins; and as he
wept, an angel came to console him, and she wept
with him, and then dried his tears with her wings;
and he looked up, and the angel smiled and left her
wings aside, and said—" I am Kate O'Donnell."
The poor invalid awoke, his heart was full of a sweet
sensation, and the brightness returned to his eyes,
and the glow to his cheek, for the unerring penetra-
tion of the heart told him that Kate O'Donnell loved
him. What wonder that these young hearts folded
in their bosoms, like a morning flower dripping with
dew, that sweetest and holiest of sentiments—first
love—that sentiment that so gladdens and beautifies
human life as to make a paradise of earth. Willy
Shea grew strong day by day; Kate was his constant companion; they feared not the world's cen-
sure, for they had pledged their young love to one
another, and their hearts were full of joy. The
' Spectator' says that "solitude with the person beloved, even to a woman's mind, has a pleasure beyond all the pomp and splendor in the world." How
the hearts of Willy and Kate responded to this sentiment as they built their fairy castles of hope in
some retired place, with no other eye but those of
God and the angels upon them.

When he took his leave, to follow his studies, for he was a medical student, he promised to return each vacation, and faithfully did he keep that promise, for there were fond smiles from all, and one loving heart to hail his welcome to Glen Cottage.

CHAPTER X.

It is fit that we should return to our friend, Mr.
Baker, who by this time had finished his little snack.
Mr. Baker was an attorney of very limited practice
indeed. He preferred getting his living by pander-
ing to the tastes of Lord Clearall, and other gentlemen, than by perseverance in a lucrative profession.
He was a man of very poor abilities, and although
he was looked upon as Lord Clearall's law-agent,
still, any cases of importance or difficulty were
handed over to men better versed in their business.
In fact, he was merely tolerated as a kind of family
dependent or lumber, that could not be well thrown
away. His humorous eccentricities gained him a
ready introduction to the tables of the neighboring
gentry. Besides, it being known that he was the
guest and law-agent to Lord Clearall, was another
strong letter of recommendation. We are all fond
of basking in the shade of nobility. There are few
disciples of Diogenes now in existence, and so our
friend found. Mr. Baker was naturally indolent
and a sensualist, and therefore he thought it much
easier and pleasanter to eat a good dinner with his

neighbor, than to go to the trouble of providing one himself. Mr. Baker seldom condescended to dine with farmers; so, after dining with Lord Clearall and Sir —— and Mr. ——, he could not infringe so far on his dignity; however, he relaxed a little on behalf of Mr. O'Donnell, for, as he said, Mr. O'Donnell had the right blood in him, and was a respectable man; the truth is, Mr. O'Donnell kept a good table, and gave him some legal employment connected with his bank, that added to his slender income.

As I have remarked, Mr. Baker had peculiarities and eccentricities; though a noted coward, still, he would keep his hearers in roars with all his encounters with robbers and murderers. He had a powerful constitution, or rather appetite, for he was able to eat and drink as much as four moderate men. He possessed a good deal of the narrow-minded bigotry of the old school, and it was laughable to witness his endeavors at trying not to damn the papists or send the Pope to hell, when in company with Catholics. Not if he had the power would he do one or other, for I really think, if Saint Peter gave him the keys of heaven, and that the Pope sought admittance, Mr. Baker would, after regaling him with a few good curses, let him in unknown to his friends; for, on the whole, this Mr. Baker was not a bad kind of man; he was, in fact, more a fool than a knave.

Mr. Baker had finished his little lunch, and then

7

carefully drew his seat near the fire, and mixed his
punch, taking care to put two glasses of whiskey
into each tumbler, for he vowed that weak punch
never agreed with him.

Frank and Willy Shea joined the party at the
table. Kate O'Donnell sat in an easy chair reading
a book, and her mother and Bessy were seated on
the sofa near her.

"This is comfortable, ay, comfortable, by Jove,"
and Mr. Baker looked from the bright fire, over
which he held his hands a few seconds, into his glass
of sparkling punch; so it was hard to say which he
pronounced comfortable; perhaps the two; or perhaps he was taking in the whole in his mind's eye,
and thinking what a happy man Mr. O'Donnell was,
with his kind wife and fair children, as they sat
around that cheerful fire, and that table sparkling
with glasses and decanters and streaming lights.

Mr. Baker was an old bachelor—and strange
things do run in old bachelor's heads; for, when
they enter a little Eden of domestic bliss, they wonder why they were born to mope alone through life,
without one tendril to keep alive the affections, or
one green vine to cling to them for support.

"Heigh ho! Devilish comfortable!" said Mr.
Baker, and he rubbed his hands and looked around
again.

"Yes," said Mr. O'Donnell; "a bright fire of a
chilly evening, a pleasant glass of punch, with your
family around you, telling some innocent stories, or

singing some pretty little songs, are comfortable things, no doubt, Mr. Baker."

"Devilish comfortable, though!" and Mr. Baker sighed.

"I wonder you never married, Mr. Baker," said Mrs. O'Donnell."

"Never, ma'am; never. Begad, I once thought of it when young; something or another knocked it up--I should tell you, the match was made, ay, made. I was so fond of that pretty little girl. I was devilish fond—I—oh, I see, I am making a fool of myself; and "—here he wiped his eyes and blew his nose very strongly—"that snuff makes a person sneeze so. Well, as I said before, she took the fever—devil take the fever!—God forgive me for cursing—bad luck to it!—What's that I said? Yes, she died, and I never minded marrying since."

After all, there were fine feelings lurking in that blustering rough man's heart.

"Never married, Mrs. O'Donnell; though Lord Clearall, for we are particular friends, says to me, 'Baker, travel where you will, there is no place so pleasant as home.'"

"Well, Mr. Baker," said Frank, "I didn't see you since the races of Cashel; how did you get home?"

"Capitally, boy, capitally. You rode devilish well, though; d——n me, but you did. A pleasant night we had at the hotel; pooh, hah, pooh!" and Mr. Baker leaned back in his chair, and then indulged in a pinch of snuff and a pooh. "That Mr. B—— said something to me; didn't he? They know the lion is getting old, Frank, so they do. Pooh!—God be with the good old times, when, if a man said anything to you, you need but send a friend to him and appoint a nice cosy corner of a field, and there quietly settle the affair. Now the law won't allow that satisfaction. Did you see that little affair between Cooke and myself how it was prevented? The police got the scent and dogged us. I always think that Cooke sold the pass, and sent word of the whole affair; for you know he was a stag, Frank—a stag; and knew well that I'd shoot him."

"The worst of it is, Mr. Baker, Mr. Cooke's friends gave out that it was you who forewarned the police."

"Oh! of course, Frank, of course, trying to shift the blame off themselves; he was a stag, sir, a stag —pooh;" and Mr. Baker proceeded with another glass of punch. "Good spirits this, Mr. O'Donnell; I generally put three glasses to my punch, but only two of yours; for, as Lord Clearall says—you know we are particular friends—well, as he says, 'Baker, never drink weak punch—never drink weak punch; it will sicken you, man; it is as bad as pope and——' hem, ha, I mean—oh, to hell!——; yet, it's devilish stuff."

"Mr. Baker," said Mr. O'Donnell, who could scarce conceal a smile at the blundering of his guest; "Mr. Baker, I am told our worthy agent is about resigning, as he does not wish to carry out his lordship's orders about clearing the Lisduff property; do you know is it true?"

"Yes, I think he will; devilish good man he was; he and the old lord pulled well together; tender old man that old lord was; never tossed anyone out, but supported widows and orphans, or, as the present lord calls them, idlers and stragglers—ay, faith, that's it. I don't see why he should resign. All poor people on that Lisduff. What loss are their wretched cabins? Besides, his lordship wants to make one sheep-walk of the whole, or to let it to large tenants. Fine farm-houses are more comfortable and tasty than poor cabins; and, as his lordship says, 'Why the devil shouldn't he do as he likes with his own?' And why not, Mr. O'Donnell? Miss Kate, this water is getting cold, I fear. Cold water never makes good punch; hot, sparkling, and plenty of whiskey, and there it is for you."

"Is it possible, Mr. Baker," said Frank, "that his lordship means to turn all the small farmers off the Lisduff property? Sure their little farms and cabins are as dear to them as is his palace to his lordship."

"Well, well; that may be, Frank——that may be; but then you know they belong to his lordship, and why not do as he pleases with them?"

"And what will become of the poor people, Mr Baker?" said Kate.

" Can't say, Miss Kate, can't say; I suppose they
. will go to America, or do the best they can.   They
are a lot of poor wretches, poor d—— P——, hem,
hem, ha! poor creatures, I mean.''

Kate sighed, and Frank held down his head, for
he did not wish to argue the matter further with
Mr. Baker, knowing his prattling propensities, and
fearing that his lordship would fee. offended at any
strictures on the management of his property from a
tenant.

"It is known who will replace him?" said Mr.
O'Donnell.

"You see how it is, Mr. O'Donnell; of course I
will get a preference, as his lordship and I are
particular friends; but then I won't take it, d——n
me if I do; I am now getting too old; besides, I
don't like hunting out poor devils,—I am d——d if
I do; so I suppose Mr. Ellis, our worthy Scotch
friend, will come in."

" Now, he has feathered his nest pretty well under
his lordship."

" Devlish well; ay, that is it; I will tell—but this
is between ourselves, honor bright—as I was saying,
he came there a poor steward, let me see, about
twenty years ago.   He didn't make much hand of
the old lord, but he picked up some nice farms for
himself and his friends; according as the young lord
wanted money, he supplied him with hundreds and
thousands; so, when the old man died, he became a
right-hand man with the son.   He supplies him with

money at his calls. His lordship finds him very
easy in his terms. He sometimes takes a mortgage
upon this farm or that, merely for forms sake, Mr.
O'Donnnell but he is sure that it is on some property
nearly out of lease; so in order to improve the land,
and carry out a system of high farming, he ejects the
tenants, builds houses, and improves the land, and
then brings over his friends from Scotland, who get
the land at about half what the poor popish devils
—— I beg pardon, Mr. O'Donnell, I mean no offence; as I was saying, they take the land for about
half the rent the damned pa—— O yes! the old
tenants I mean, paid for it, Mr. Ellis taking care to
be well paid by the new comers; but all this *sub
rosa*, you see, *sub rosa;* so Mr. Ellis is getting rich
every day, while his lordship is getting poor; and
the poor devils of pa—— tenants, I mean, are sent
about their business, to beg, or starve, or die, as
they please."

"Good God!" cried Willy Shea, "can this be
true; Where is that Constitution that boasts of being the protection of the weak against the strong?
The slave is fed and cared by his master, he is property; but the Irish slave cannot be bought or sold,
therefore he has no value as property; it is true, he
is the slave of circumstances, and his master is generally a tyrant that crushes him. Why does not the
law protect the weak?"

"Pooh! all nonsense, young man; pooh! I fancy
I know something about the law; don't I, Mr. O'Donnell?"

"Certainly, Mr. Baker."

"Yes, sir, I do. Frank, hand over the decanter while water is hot. So I do know something about it; now, will you tell me who makes the laws? Don't the landlords? a pity they wouldn't make laws against themselves, ay, young man?"

"But haven't we representatives, sir; what are they about?"

"Granted, granted, my young friend; who are your representatives but your landlords or their nominees; all a set of place-hunting schemers, who bamboozle the people and then laugh at them; no wonder, faith."

"God help the poor tenants," said Mr. O'Donnell; they are the worst off."

"To be sure, man, to be sure; between the priests, and landlords, and members, the poor are tossed about like a shuttle-cock."

"It is a strange country, indeed," said Willy Shea, "where men cannot live on the fruits of a soil so fertile—a soil literally teeming with milk and honey—a soil blessed by God but cursed by man. What have we gained by our modern civilization? —what by our connexion with England? Why, in the feudal times there was a kind of tie of clanship, and a rough, but social intercourse between the country gentlemen and their tenants, or retainers, that made them feel that they were bound by a kind of family bond; but now the tenants are not needed as a display or protection to the landlord;

they are, therefore, retained or dismissed at his whim or option. Is it a wonder, then, with so many and such wholesale evictions staring us in the face, that there should be agrarian discontent too often breaking forth in wild jus'ice of self-defence or banded violence?"

"That is, that they would murder us is it?" said Mr. Baker; for Mr. Baker always took care to identify himself with the higher class, though on account of his harmless blustering disposition he often, unconsciously, told bitter truths against them."

"That they would murder us, is it? ay, the damned pa—— hem, ha! yes, they would if they could; but you see I don't care that about them," and Mr. Baker held up a small teaspoonful of punch for inspection, and then drank it off. "Not that, faith! Hand the decanter down, Frank, my boy; that will do. Why, you are taking nothing. I would recommend it to you; nothing like a good glass of punch to keep up the spirits; I could never have done all I did but for it."

"There is no danger, Mr. Baker, that any one will attack you; you have given them too many wholesome lessons to mind you now," said Kate raising her eyes from the book, and looking smilingly at Mr. Baker.

As I said before, or, as I should have said, if I did not say it, Mr. Baker was a great admirer of the fair sex and though a heavy-looking man, never missed acknowleiging a compliment from a lady, so

he got up to make a bow, but in attempting to do so
he upset his glass of punch, and walked on Fid.   It
happened that Fid and the cat were enjoying themselves most comfortably on the hearth-rug, so when
Mr. Baker disturbed their tete-a-tete, Fid protested
against it in sundry angry yelps.

"Choke that dog!" said Mr. O'Donnell.

"Poor little Fid; come here, poor thing.   Where
are you hurt?   There now, don't cry, and I'll cure
you.   Sure, he couldn't help it," said Bessy, and
Bessy took Fid to nestle in her mamma's lap with
her.   Fid felt that he fell into kind hands, for he
only whined a little, and then laid his little silky
head to rest beside Bessy's.

"No, Miss, no, I couldn't help him—I'm d——d
if I could, for I could not; see, I spilt all the punch.
I beg your pardon, Miss Kate."

"Don't mind, Mr. Baker, no harm done," and she
wiped away the streaming liquid, and placed a clean
glass for Mr. Baker.

"I think, Mr. Baker, you were going to tell us
about some fellows that attacked you, or something
of that kind."

"Oh, yes; did I ever tell you, Mr. ——?" and
he nodded at Willy.

"Mr. Shea," suggested Willy.

"Well, Mr. Shea—devilish good name, too—where
is this I was?"

"Some adventure you were going to relate," said
Willy.

"Oh, yes; you see, I was coming from Cashel one night, and I had a large sum of money about me. Just as I was coming by the grove I saw two men, and they slunk into the ditch as soon as they saw me. Begad, something struck me, so I out with my pistols. When I came up one of them jumped out and seized the reins. 'Out with your arms and money, or you a are dead man,' he shouted; the other fellow was standing beside me with a gun presented. 'Here,' said I, putting my hand in, as if for them, but before he had time to look about him I out with the pistol and blazed at him. He turned about like a top and fell dead. My horse jumped with the fright and that saved me, for the other fellow missed me with his shot; I turned at him, but he jumped over the ditch. Just as he was going out I picked him behind."

"That was well done," said Willy; "did you bury the dead man?"

"No, the d——d pa——, rascals, 1 mean, took him away; at least he was never got."

"You had more adventures than that, though," said Frank.

"More! it would keep us till morning to tell you, by jove; but the villains are now so much afraid, they are shunning me. I suppose I shot about a dozen in all!"

"A dozen! really the government ought to pension you."

"So they ought, boy; so they ought; that's what

I do be telling Lord Clearall, for we are particular friends. Shove over the decanter; I hadn't a glass of punch this two hours."

Mr. Baker's measure of time must have been guided by no chronometer but his own, for the hand of Mr. O'Donnell's clock had not revolved over ten minutes since he had filled his last glass.

"I suppose you will not go home to night, Mr. Baker," said Frank.

"Certainly, boy, Certainly; why not?"

"It is rather late and the roads are said not to be too honest."

"Ha, ha, ha! no fear of that; they know old Jack Baker too well for that; many a one of their skins I tickled."

"Won't you be afraid, Mr. Baker?" said Kate.

"Afraid! ha, ha, ha, afraid—Jack Baker—afraid! by jove that is a good one! I assure you, Miss Kate, it would not be well for a man that would tax Jack Baker, old as he is, with cowardice; ha, ha, ha, ha! Jack Baker afraid! look at these bull dogs, Frank; need a man be afraid having them?"

Frank took the pistols to the side table, and under pretence of examining them, he extracted the balls, no doubt with the charitable intention of preventing Mr. Baker from committing murder; he then went into the kitchen. While Frank was in the kitchen, Mr. O'Donnell was taking a doze, and Willy being engaged in a cosy chat with Kate and Mrs. O'Donnell, and Bessy and puss. and Fid, held a council on the Sofa, so Mr. Baker thought the best thing he could do was to take a nap; and in order to make his doze comfortable, he first emptied his glass. Certain sonorous sounds emitted from Mr. Baker's nasal organs betokened plainly as words could that he was enjoying rather a heavy doze.

"Come, Bessy, child," said Mrs. O'Donnell, "let us leave Fid and puss now to sleep for themselves, and say your prayers."

The pretty little thing knelt at her mother's knee and rested her closed hands upon her lap. As she finished her little prayers she naively asked—"'Our Father, who art in heaven!' what does that mean, mamma? is it that God is our father?"

"Certainly, my dear child. He is the father of the fatherless, and he has called little children to him, for of such, he says, is the kingdom of heaven." Bessy was silent for some time, then she said:—

"Mamma, is heaven a beautiful place?"

"Yes, my love; no words could paint its beauty, for ears have not heard, nor eyes seen, nor has it entered into the heart of man to conceive the glory of heaven."

"Mamma, I would like to go to heaven; would you like me to go?"

"Mrs. O'Donnell looked at that quiet, ethereal-looking child, with her pale cheeks and bright eyes, and a pang of anguish struck her heart at these words, and she thought what would she do if she lost her darling child, and a tear trickled and fell on Bessy's little hand.

" What ails you, mamma? sure you would not grudge me to go to heaven; if so, mamma, and if you'd be very sorry, I will pray to the good God not to take me, and I know as He is so good He will not refuse me."

" No, child, no! do not; God will take you in His own wise time; but not now, Bessy; what darling would I do after you," and she pressed her to her bosom.

Bessy remained silent for some time, and then looked up and said:—

"Mamma, are Richard and Ellen in heaven; but I know they are."

" They are, child."

" Why, then, do you be crying for them if they are so happy in such a beautiful place?"

"I don't know, pet; I feel lonesome after them, and yet I know they are with God."

" ' Our Father who art in Heaven.' Oh, how good God is mamma, and how grand heaven is, when it is the kingdom of God's glory and of His angels and saints."

While this conversation was going on between Bessy and her mamma, and while Kate and Willy held an equally interesting conversation at the other side—a conversation which seemed to please them both very much, for they often smiled, and looked at each other and then at the book, for I am sure there was something very interesting in that book, we will take a look into the kitchen to see what Frank was about.

A farmer of the wealthier class must have a large establishment of servants in order to cultivate his farms and to collect in his crops. Besides the regular staff he generally hires additional hands, while cutting and saving his corn and hay, and digging his potatoes. Mr. O'Donnell had not all his potatoes dug as yet, and therefore was not able to dispense with his additional hands. When Frank went into the kitchen, most of the servants were collected around a large table playing cards. A few were sitting at the fire enjoying a comfortable shanachus with the housemaids.

"Arrah, sthop, James Cormack, and don't be going on with your pallavering," said a roguish, funny-eyed damsel to a good-looking young fellow, that seemed to be making love to her by the process of teazing her as much as possible.

"Sarra a haporth I'm doin' to you, Mary; you are only dramin', achorra."

"Well, sthop now, and let me doze away; you know how early I was up to-day, or faix if you don't, maybe it's the mishtress I will be calling down."

"You'd like it, indeed, Mary," said the other, with a most provoking look. Mary threw her arm carelessly over the back of the chair and leant her head upon it, and closed her two roguish eyes as if to sleep. James had a feather, with which he tickled her face and nose, which, of course, set her sneezing. James turned towards the table and asked, "how is the play going, boys ?"

"Och ! only middling," said a fellow, who had just turned his hat inside out to bring him luck. "Divil a haporth we are getting; Bill is winning all before him; some of the colleens must have sthuck a comb or needle in his clothes."

"I have the five," said another fellow, hitting a thump upon the table; "that's our game."

"Ye needn't laugh so," said Mary to the company at the fire, who were enjoying her bewilderment.

"Faith it is pleasant," said Shemus a Clough. "Begor, Mary, if you were to see the purty faces you were makin' you'd laugh yourself—turning up your nose this way, just like the hounds when they'd get the scent."

Shemus cocked up his big nose, and made some ludicrous faces for Mary's special enlightenment. Mary didn't seem to know well whether she were better laugh or cry at Shemus' rude comparison; however, she compromised the thing by moving up from the fire and placing her apron to her face.

"Ye think I didn't know who did it. That I may never sin, but if I were shure it was you that did it, James Cormack, I never would speak another word to you."

"Mary, alanna," said James, "don't blame me, now; that's a good girl; shure I was looking at the card players."

"Git out; maybe I di ln't see you," said Mary; giving him a slight kick with her little foot.

"Och, murther, Mary," said he, rubbing his leg, though the kick would not hurt Uncle Toby's fly, "sarra a one but you blackened my leg. If you do be as crass as that when you are married, God help the man that gets you. Och, I am sure when you have a couple of childers, there will be no sthanding you."

"There is more of it," said Mary; though from the little laugh she gave, and the slight red that gleamed on her cheek, it was evident she was well pleased.

"Whisper, Mary," said James, after a pause.

Mary held down her little head towards him, and James whispered something into her ear, and in doing so, her face came so near his, that he could not resist the temptation of trying a kiss. Whether it was the kiss or the whisper, I can't say, but Mary blushed up and struck him a slap on the cheek that might frighten a fly, and then bounced away, vowing that "nobody could live near the schemer, at all at all."

James rubbed his face, exclaiming, "See now a body's thanks for telling a purty little girl the truth; and as for the kiss, upon my souckens, if we were in the dark, it is dozens of them she'd give me."

"Sorra a one at all, though; and I hope you will never have the impudence to try another; shure it was only my hand you kissed."

"O never mind, I'll do better the next time."

"Arrah, maybe you'd thry; I'd advise you to look to your ears, then, James, and not be trying your comehether upon me. Shure maybe I didn't see you wid somebody at Mrs. Butler's last Sunday; take that, now, James."

"Phew! Upon my varacity, Mary, I am afered you are getting in a little fit of jellessy; shure, sorra one was wid me but my own first cousin."

"Ha, ha, James; maybe I didn't know who was in it; if you think it shutable to be in consate wid Miss O'Brien, that's nothing to me," and Mary looked as if it were everything in life to her.

"Oh, wurrah, do hear that; there's no coming up to yez for girls; what differs there be betune the hearts an' tongues of some people, and the way they speaks behind other's backs; shure you know that Miss O'Brien is going to be married, and I was only wishing her joy. Faix I know a nice, plump little girl, wid two roguish eyes like two shinin' stars, that's not a hundred miles from me this minute, I'd rather than Miss O'Brien, or any other miss any day ov my life."

He looked at Mary with a soft, smiling kind of look that told as plainly as words—it's your own darling self I mean. Mary blushed again, and found something astray with her apron-string.

"Faith it's pleasant," said Shemus-a-Clough; "ye are like two that wud be courting, going on wid ye'r droll ways; ay, my purty little Colleen, it's thrue for me."

This address of Shemus' created a roar of laughter.

"What will they do, Shemus?" said one of the party.

"Faix, they knows themself; my purty Colleen here, with her roguish eyes; aye, alanna, may be ye won't do it."

While these amatory scenes were going on near the fire, the players were not idle either, for they enlivened their games with snatches, songs, and stories; their leading spirit was Shaun the Rover.

"Mind your play there, and hould your whist, Shaun, will ye, bad's grant from you, why didn't you stick your king in there," said one of his partners, towards the end of the game.

"Whist," said another, "here is Masther Frank comming."

CHAPTER XI.

FRANK found the party in the kitchen in the height of their enjoyment; the laugh, and jest, and voice of the players rose from the table, while high above the rest rose Shemus-a-Clough's voice chanting one of his hunting songs. Frank beheld all this from the hall, where he stood a moment to listen to the merry voices of the party.

"Poor souls!" thought he; "one would think that they never knew care nor sorrow, so gay and light-hearted are they. There are some of these poor fellows, now, under notice to quit their happy homes, and yet they can laugh and sing, as if they were secure from landlord power. How would I feel I were to be turned out of my fine house and place; and, who knows, in this land of uncertainties! Good God! I fear I could not bear it so quietly. Yet it is hard to know them; there is within them a deep current of underfeeling; they could be gay and light-hearted as now, and in an hour again they could band together in the wild spirit of self-revenge. High ho! I pity the poor fellows if they should be turned out; and the Cormacks, my foster-brothers, what would become of them, and of their poor mother, my old nurse, and their fair sister; well, they shan't want while I am alive, anyway." So saying, Frank opened the door, and passed into the kitchen.

"Arrah! welcome, Misther Frank, welcome," was the exclamation that greeted him on his entrance.

"Thank you, boys, thank you, how are you?" said he, shaking hands with the brothers, James and John Cormack.

It is necessary that we should give some account of the relationship, if I may so call it, that existed between Frank and the Cormacks. This might be inferred from Frank's soliloquy at the door.

The tie of fostership is, or at least was, held as sacred as that of natural brothers. We have several instances of foster-brothers exposing, in fact losing their lives, in order to protect their wealthier relations.

In some work on '98 I have read a very feeling account of how a young insurgent gentleman was taken prisoner, and brought before the next magistrage; of course his committal was at once made out, but, it being too late--it was, on account of the disturbed state of the country, and the small force at the magistrate's disposal—thought better to detain him closely guarded, until morning.

The prisoner recognized in the butler his foster-brother. The latter did not pretend to notice him.

"Alas!" thought he, as he stretched in his little

prison, " I am forsaken by the world; come death I am ready for you!"

He heard singing and revelry going on through the house all night.

" These can laugh and be merry, while they hold revel over a poor wretch that is to die on the gallows," said he to himself.

At length the butler came in with something for him to eat. He looked at him—

" And have you too, brother, forsaken me ?" said he.

The other placed his fingers on his lips, in token of silence.

" Sthrip off smart," whispered he; " I have drugged their drink; the guards are all drunk or sleeping; put on my clothes, and act as butler; the hall-door is open, and pass out."

" No," said the other; " it would endanger you; they might make a victim of you."

" Not at all, man; here, I have them off; what would they do with me; they will treat it as a good joke when you are gone. Come, off smart; on wid them; there is not a moment to be lost! "

They exchanged clothes, and as he passed out with the dishes, he wrung the brave fellows hand, exclaiming:—

" God bless you! I'll reward you well."

" Pooh," said the other, " that will do, pass on now, and don't appear concerned."

He was challenged by the sentinel, and even by

the party in the parlor; yet, he stood the test. As soon as the butler heard the hall-door close after him, he breathed freely.

"Thank God! he is safe! I might as well say my prayers now; for I know the men I have to deal with too well to expect mercy; no matter, he's saved!"

When the magistrate discovered the trick that had been played upon him, there was no end to his anger; he at once ordered the poor fellow to execution. When going to the gallows, the magistrate asked him—

"Why did you do it?"

"Sir," said he, "I am his foster-brother!"

His death did not pass unavenged; for, after some years, the young gentleman returned from the continent; he challenged the magistrate to a duel. They had selected a retired part, near a plantation. They took their positions on two mounds. The magistrate was shot through the breast. After falling, the young man walked over to him, and whispered into his ears—

"You recollect John Mahon, he was my foster-brother; his grave is now drinking your blood; you murdered him, you did; but he is avenged. I have nursed my vengeance for years; I have practised until I could put a ball where I like; now, I have sweet revenge upon his murderer. And, if there be any one here," looking fiercely around him, "that says he was not murdered, let him take your place, you dog.'

Such was the affection existing between foster-brothers. Whether it is so fervid now or not, I cannot say ; perhaps, like a good many of our old Irish customs and habits, our very impulsive affections have given way to the cold, soulless philosophy of English innovators.

This was the kind of relationship that existed between Frank and the Cormacks. The Cormacks held a small farm of about ten acres ; they never worked for hire, as their little farm gave them sufficient employment ; they helped Mr. O'Donnell during his busy season, for which they received more than an equivalent in various ways—such as a plough to till their garden, a present of a cow, a few lambs or pigs, as they wanted them. With all O'Donnell's kindness, it is no wonder that the Cormacks were what is called well to do in the world ; besides, they were sober, industrious young men.

After some commonplace conversation with those in the kitchen, Frank remarked :

" We have old Mr. Baker above half-drunk. He is as usual killing every one. I was thinking it would be a good joke if two of you would meet him when going home, and take his pistols and money from him ; we would have such a good laugh at him."   *

" I and Neddy Burkem will go," said James Cormack.

" Well, I don't care," said Burkem.   " But he

does be so often at Mr. Ellis's that he might know me; besides he might fire."

"No danger of that," said Frank; "I have drawn the balls from his pistols; besides, he will be so much frightened I am sure he won't know any one."

"Let another of the boys go with you, James," said Burkem.

"Burkem is afeerd. I'll go, Misther Frank," said another.

"Oh, divil afeerd," said Burkem; "but you know, if he should chance to know me, I was undone."

"A four year old child needn't be afeerd of Slob Baker," said the Rover. "Did you ever hear what they did to him at Mr. Lanes?"

"Shure young Mr. Lane vexed him one night until they got him up to fight a duel. Well becomes Mr. Lane, he loaded his pistol with blood, and put nothing but powder in Mr. Baker's. They fired acrass the table. When Baker saw himself all covered with blood, he kicked, and tumbled, and swore he was shot. 'Oh, Lane,' says he, 'you have me murthered. God have marcy on me a poor sinner.' They all laughed at him. 'Oh! laugh and be damn'd' said he. 'You can easily laugh at a dead man,' 'Ha! ha! ha! You're not dead at all man,' said Mr. Lane; 'get up, man alive.' 'Dead—as dead as a door nail, man; if I weren't, I'd have you shot for laughing at a poor devil you are after murthering.' 'Ha! ha! ha! Where do you feel the

8

pain?' 'Where do I feel the pain? Shure a man
never feels pain after being shot until he's dead.
Shure I am all covered wid blood—isn't that enuff?
You kilt me; for you hadn't any ball in my pistol;
for if you had you were shot.' 'No, nor in mine
either; there was only blood in it.' Do you say so?
Gog! maybe I'm not dead affther all.' 'Divil a
dead.   Get up to a glass of punch.'   'Well, well;
did any one ever hear the likes! When I saw the
blood I thought I was done for.   Down wid the de-
canthur!' They then set him drunk, and rubbed
his face with lamp-black; so they took him up to the
drawing-room to dance wid the ladies.   Shure if
if they didn't laugh at him, nabocklish."

The parlor bell was rung.

"Run, Mary Cahill; and none of your sly ways
there with James; and bring them up more water.
I know that is what they want. And, Cormack, let
you and another of the boys get two peeled cabbage
stumps, and meet him at the gate. I'll go up to
hurry him off."

When Frank returned to the parlor he found his
father and Mr. Baker taking a parting glass.

"Come, Frank, boy, take a *doch a durris*."

"You don't mean to go home, Mr. Baker? it is
rather late and not too safe to travel."

"Safe! boy, safe! That's what makes me go, to
show you and the damned pa——, robbers, I mean,
that I'm not afraid; order my horse, Frank, order
my horse."

"Mary," said Frank to Mary Cahill, who had brought in the hot water, "Mary, tell one of the boys to bring out Mr. Baker's horse.

"Yes, sir."

As Mr. Baker rode from the house he held the following bit of conversation with himself.

I think I was a deuce of a fool, an ass, to say the least of it, to leave to-night; but then they'd say I was afraid; ay, afraid, and that wouldn't do, Mr. Baker. Afraid! who said I was afraid; who dare say it, I want to know? God protect me! what the devil is that though? Oh! only an ass—ha! out of my way. Well, if I meet any fellows will I shoot them? Sure they'd shoot me, but then I'd be a deuce of a fool to lose my life on account of two pistols and a few pounds. No, I am at the gate now, I ——"

"Deliver your arms and money or you're a dead man!" was shouted from behind the piers, and two wicked looking things, guns no doubt, looked out at him as if they would take great pleasure in cracking at him.

"Ye-ye-yes! gentlemen, fo-fo-for the love of God, don't shoot me! here they are," and he handed out his pistols and money.

"Ride back again now."

"Ye-ye-yes! gentlemen; Lord spare your lives for sparing me."

Mr. Baker thundered up to the hall door, and knocked fiercely; Frank made his appearance.

"O, Frank, Frank, for the love of God, hurry! Call out the men! I was robbed; about twenty men attacked me. I shot two, anyway; I think three; two for certain; then they overpowered me, but I made my escape from the damned pa——, robbers, I mean, robbers, Frank, robbers. There are four shot, anyway; four of the bloody pa——, robbers, I mean. The government will hear all this in the morning. I will have them taken like the bloody pa——, robbers, I mean, I shot coming from Cashel."

Right, Mr. Baker," said Frank, "I am sure you will get a pension; come in, anyway; you won't go home to-night, now?"

"No, Frank; no, boy."

"Come in, sir."

"What the devil are these?" said Mr. Baker, as he saw his purse and pistols on the parlor table.

"I think you ought to know them," said Frank. "Ha, ha, ha, two of the boys got cabbage stumps, it appears, and robbed you, ha! ha! ha!"

Gog! I have my purse and pistols anyway; you think I didn't know them Frank, right well; a good joke, by Jove; ha! ha! ha! I'd like to shoot your servants, wouldn't I; catch me at that, boy; ha! ha! ha! well for them it wasn't any one else was in it; ha! ha! ha! here, get up the decanter, and some hot water; ring the bell Frank!"

Mary Cahill made her appearance.

"More hot water, Mary," said Frank.

"See, Mary, try is there any cold meat for a snack," said Mr. Baker. "Ha ! ha ! ha ! faith, it was a good joke. Give me the hand, Frank, they may thank being your servants for having whole skins, that's a good girl, Mary; is that hot ? it is; now; Mary, what about the meat ?"

" I fear there is none done, sir."

"No matter, get a chop—devilish fine mutton! Nothing makes a man drink but to eat enough, ' eat, drink, and be merry,' as his lordship says; you know, Frank, we are particular friends."

Perhaps we have devoted too much of our space to Mr. Baker; moreover, as he belonged to a class, now nearly, if not altogether, extinct. Many of my readers, will, no doubt, feel surprised that the craft of his profession did not, like magic tricks, change his very nature, and make something of him; all I can say to this is, that he was not fit for his profession, nor his profession for him.

Like most, I might say nearly all, of my characters, Mr. Baker is no ideal being, created to heighten the plot; no, I give him in *propria persona.*

"I think, Kate," said Frank, at the breakfast table next morning, "as we had some rain last night, we must give up our little pic-nic to Glenbower!"

" I fear so," said Kate, looking disappointed.

"I will tell you what we will do; Willy and I will go shooting until dinner-time, and then we will spend the evening in the summer-house."

" Very well," said Kate."

So Frank and Willy set out, with their dogs and guns.

"I must pass by Ballybruff, to see my poor nurse, Willy," said Frank.

Mrs. Cormack's house was a nice clean one. It was surrounded with larch and poplar trees. The walls were rough-cast, and three real glass windows gave light and air to the interior. The yard was gravelled, and free from sink holes, or any nuisance of the kind. Nelly Cormack was very busy in the yard, feeding a whole regiment of poultry, that clattered and cackled about her.

"Good morning, Mary," said Frank; "old nurse doesn't see me yet, she is so busy at her stocking. How are you?" said he, coming up, and blocking up the door near her. Mrs. Cormack raised her head, and pulled her specks over her nose:—

"Arrah! is this Misther Frank?"

"It is, ma'am; and this is my young friend, Mr. Shea."

"Shure ye're welcome; sit down, gintlemen; Mary, get thim chairs."

Mary dusted two suggawn-bottomed chairs, and placed them near the fire. Willy cast his eyes about the clean, tidy kitchen, with its rows of tins, and plates, and noggins, all as bright and clean as sand could make them.

"This is a comfortable house you have, Mrs. Cormack," said Willy.

"It is, indeed, sir," said she; "but what good is

that; shure we are sarved wid an ejeotment," and Mrs. Cormack sighed, and wiped her eyes.

"Do you owe much rent ?" said he.

"Only a year's and I have it all barrin three pounds; but what good is that; I fear they won't take it; it is said that they mean to throw us all out, for to make large farms, as they did to the Crogh-lawn tenants."

"I hope not," said Frank; "they oannot be so cruel as that, to toss out a poor widow, that pays her rent."

"I hope not, sir, I hope not; but they have done as bad. If they were to throw me out I would not live long; mavrone, it would be the heart-break, where my father and mother, and my poor man all died, i. I don't be allowed to close my eyes there."

Mrs. Cormack wiped her eyes, for a mournful tear rose from the heart to them, and from them along her withered cheeks.

"Oh! offer them the rent nurse," said Frank; "I will see if I can do anything for you; they cannot refuse it

"I will, alanna, as soon as we sell the slip of a pig, to make up the three pounds, and may God soften their hearts to take it."

"Don't sell your pig, Mrs. Cormack," said Frank; "I will be your creditor, until you get richer," and he placed three pounds in her lap.

"I won't take it, Misther Frank; it is too good you are."

"No, now, you must keep it; it is my Christmas present to my old nurse; and God knows, Mrs. Cormack, I would not have a happy Christmas if you were disturbed."

"God bless you! Misther Frank; it's you have the good heart; God will reward you, Frank, for happy are they who feel for the widow and the orphan."

"Well, Mary," said Frank, in order to change the conversation, "I hope you don't be courting the boys yet."

"A little, sir," said Mary, looking most coquettishly at Frank, and then tossing back her hair with a shake of her head.

Mary was evidently a coquette; it was in the sparkle of her eye, it was in the toss of her head, it was in her pretty dimpled face, it was in every braid of her auburn hair.

"I fear, Mary, you are a coquette; take care that you don't burn your wings like the moth," said Frank.

"O! sorra fear of that, Misther Frank; I only pay back the boys wid their own coin; they think, wid their palavering, they have nothing to do but coax poor innocent colleens; faith, they'll have two dishes to wash wid me, I am thinkin'."

"Take care, Mary, take care; we are often caught when we least expect it; it is time for us to go now, Willy; good-bye, Mary, and take care of the boys," said Frank, extending his hand with a smile to her, "and you, nurse, good-bye."

"Take care, yourself," said Mary, with a sly wink at him. "I don't know is it devotion takes you to see your uncle so often; ha! ha! ha! take that."

Frank blushed up.

"Ha! Mary, you are too many for me, I see."

"Don't mind that helther-skelther, Misther Frank," said Mrs. Cormack.

"I believe you are right, ma'am," said Frank, "so good day."

"Good-day, and God bless ye!" replied Mrs. Cormack.

"Go to Clerihan on Sunday; there does be some one in a front pew there, looking out for Misther Frank," said Mary.

"She is a pretty girl, Frank, and can banter well," said Willy.

"She is," said Frank, with a sigh.

"I think there were some grains of truth in her bantering though," said Willy with a smile; "at least, Frank, you got very red in a minute."

"Hem! maybe so," said Frank; "I didn't turn poet yet though, Willy, and begin to make songs, and call her 'Cathleen dear.'"

It was Willy's turn now to blush.

"Oh! don't change colors that way, man," said Frank; "you see we both have our secrets; and, Willy, my dear fellow," said Frank taking him by the hand, "if I have judged your secret rightly, I will respect it, and be your friend, too."

"'God bless you! Frank, God bless you! it is just

like your noble, generous nature. I see there is no use or need to conceal it from you.   I love her dearly, Frank; she has been an angel to me; she has rescued me from the grave; she——"

" That will do now, Willy; we all think the woman we love an angel, at least until we get married; but married men say that there are no such things as human angels at all, and they ought to know best; but she is a noble girl no doubt, Willy.   Get on as well as you can, my dear fellow, and you will find a firm friend in me," and he squeezed the student's hand in his.

" When must you return, Willy ? " said Frank.

" To-morrow ! "

" To-morrow!   Will you promise to spend the Christmas with us ?   I will then introduce you to my lady-love."

"I shall feel most happy, Frank."

After crossing several fields, and meeting with but little game Frank stopped :—

" Willy," said he, " I must pay a visit of charity to a poor widow here below.   Kate told me that she is very ill, and as her poor children must be badly off, I will just call and see them."

" Why, Frank, will you not allow me to act the good Samaritan too ?"

" As you please; here is the cabin below."

There was nothing peculiar about Nelly Sullivan's cabin; it was like Irish cabins in general, low, smoky, and badly ventilated.   Small bundles of straw, stuffed into holes in the wall, answered the double purpose of keeping out the air, and keeping in the smoke; or rather, as Nelly herself said, " of keeping the cabin warm."

"There is some one inside, Frank; I hear them speaking," said Willy, as they reached the door.

" We'll shortly see, Willy."

They had to stoop to enter the low doorway. In one corner, upon a bed of straw, lay the invalid, Nelly Sullivan; beside her, with her feverish hand in hers, sat Kate O'Donnell. Three or four wretched children were collected around some bread and broken meat, near the fire; beside Kate was a basket, in which she had brought some nourishment for the sick woman and her wretched orphans.

"Ha! Kate, is this you? So you have fore-stalled me," said Frank.

Kate looked up and blushed; for true charity, like true piety, seeks no other applause than the consciousness of having done right.

"It is she, Misther Frank Lord bless her! only for her I was dead long ago."

" Good-bye, Nelly, I must go; I will call to-morrow," and she rose to depart.

" Can I do anything for you?" said Frank.

" Could you bring her the doctor, Frank?" said Kate.

" Certainly, I will have him come at once; poor woman, you should not be so long without him

rake this now," and he slipped a piece of silver into
her hand.

Willy remained after them, and gave his mite to
the widow.

"Don't tell any one," said he, as he went out.

"I think, Willy," said Frank, as the latter came
up, "I will go over by the glen; there ought to be
some game in it; you can see Kate home."

"With pleasure," said Willy, "and I wish you'
success."

"Oh, as successful as yourself, boy, I expect,"
said he with a careless air, and whistling to his dogs,
stepped over the ditch.

Kate and Willy walked on in silence for some
time.

"Kate," said he, "isn't there a great deal of
misery in the world."

"Yes, Willy; the poor are afflicted sorely here;
their reward, indeed, must be great hereafter."

"To feed the hungry is one of the works of
mercy, and our Saviour says, what we give to these
poor forlorn outcasts, we give to Himself."

"It's true, Willy, 'Charity covers a multitude of
sins.' "

"And shows the true Christian, Kate; why, love,
if you were adorned with precious stones and
jewels, you would not appear so charming to me as
you did beside that wretched bed."

Kate blushed.

"I have only done my duty, Willy. God does

not give us riches to close our hearts upon them;
no, Willy, but to relieve His little ones."

"There would be less misery here, Kate, if we
had fewer proud Pharisees, who wallow in the
luxuries of wealth, and forget that the poor are
their brothers."

"God help them! I fear they will have a black
account to settle."

"I fear so too, Kate."

"Kate," said Willy, and he took her hand in his.

'What, Willy?"

"Frank knows our love."

Kate blushed and held down her head.

"You needn't feel so, Kate, love; he promises
to be our friend."

Kate brightened up.

"Does he? Frank, noble, generous brother! but
how did he know it?"

"I think he heard me singing the song in the
bower yesterday evening; besides, Kate, he has, I
know, some love secrets of his own, and the heart
that once loves sees its workings in another as if by
intuition."

When they reached home Frank was before them,
and dinner ready. After dinner they retired to the
garden. The drizzling rain had ceased, and the
heavy clouds had passed away, leaving the evening
fine and calm. The garden was behind the house ;
a French window opened from a small parlour into
it. The little garden was tastefully arranged, and

nicely interspersed with gravel walks bordered with box, sweet-william, forget-me-not, bachelors' buttons, and the like. In a corner was a small summer-house, made of young larch trees, cut into various shapes; beside it was a little rivulet, over which was built a rockery of curious and grotesque stones, honey-suckles, sweet-brier, rose trees, and other parasitical plants and shrubs. There was a rustic seat around the interior; here they agreed to have tea. With light hearts and smiling faces; our party sat down to their delicious beverage, sweetened by the perfume of the aromatic shrubs, plants, and flowers that yet remained as if loth to fade away, and above all, by contentment—that inward balm, that sweetens the humble fare of the peasant, and often makes it more delicious than the sumptuous dishes of the peer.

Bessy strayed about the garden to pick the few flowers that were, like the last rose of summer, " left blooming alone." She then after presenting a bonquet to Kate, gave another to Frank and Willy.

" Thank you, Bessy," said Willy; " these flowers are like yourself, the emblem of innocence and purity."

" You're fond of flowers then, Willy," said Kate.

" Oh, yes, Kate; there is a dazzling joy about flowers that thrill through us like loving words; they speak to the heart of man. Look at a neat parterre when in bloom; how beautiful, how gorgeous they look. Are they not a type of all that is

grand and fair? God has made them the purest
language of nature—they speak to the soul. The
Persian revels in their perfume, and woos his mis-
tress in their language. He tells his tale of love in
a rose-bud or pansy. Thus he speaks to her of his
hopes and fears. They deck the marriage couch
and the bridal feast; they crown the youthful bride,
and twine her brow; they strew the warrior's path
—a nation's mute but grateful tribute; they garland
the lonely tomb, as a symbol of the decay of life;
they festoon the altar, mingling their odor with the
soft incense that ascends in grateful worship to the
Most High—such are flowers."

"Yes, indeed," said Kate, "flowers are beautiful;
they are nature's own painting; a skilful artist
may paint them to some perfection, and heighten
their gaudy colors, still, they want the fragrance,
the perfume, the reality of nature. Can the pencil
of a Rubens or an Angelo paint the rainbow, or take
off the varying colors of the sky? As well might
they attempt to give its true and natural life to a
rose."

"Are you as fond of music as of flowers, Willy?"
said Kate, after a moment's silence.

"I cannot say I am; still I love music very much;
though I must say, I have not a very fine ear for it;
still, I love its sweet sounds and soft influence over
the senses; I always like the soft and melancholy;
I believe it is more in accordance with my own
temperament."

"As for me," said Kate, "I think I could not live without music; when I feel heavy or lonely, or when anything displeases me, I play a few lively tunes, sing a few songs, and in a moment I forget that the world has either care or sorrow. I am, as Richard says, 'myself again.' But come, I think the genius of melancholy is stealing over us; get your flute, Willy, and Frank, your clarionet, and let us set up a perfect oratorio. Come now, I will sing with you."

The soft notes of the lute, the sweet, low, impassioned voice, the still silence around, gave it something of the air of those fabled bowers into which Sylvian nymphs decoy mortals. The evening was beginning to get chilly, and a low, fitful breeze was moaning among the trees.

"I think," said Frank, as he looked at little Bessy nestling under his coat, "the evening is chill; we have better go in."

"I think so, too," said Kate.

CHAPTER XII.

IT must be recollected that we are writing of a state of things that existed before the famine years. We are, so far, painting the peasantry in their gay, light-hearted, holiday enjoyment. Even then there were cruel, heartless task-masters, like Mr. Ellis, who hardened the hearts of the landlords, and pointed with the finger of scorn at the poor straggling farmhouses and cabins of the tenantry, and then with an air of triumph pointed out his own comfortable house and offices, his well-tilled, well-sheltered fields, his trim hedges, his model farm, as much as to say, see what industry, skill, and perseverance can do. Who would be looking at such wretched hovels, such abject misery as we see around us, when he could delight his eyes with indications of taste and luxury? Who would tolerate such a lazy, indolent people to incumber the soil?—people on whom precept and example are lost—people who will not be taught, but persist in their own barbarous, ignorant ways. He did not tell the landlord that he had a long lease of his holdings at a moderate rent, and therefore felt secure in his outlay; he did not tell the landlord that these poor tenants had neither lease nor protection; that they were living merely in a state of sufferance; that if they built houses or improved the land, they should pay an increased rent; that by his artful contrivances, notices to quit, and the daily fear of eviction and the like, he has damped their energies, and made toil without a prospect of gain hopeless; and that he has made them bend their necks to their servile state with apathy and indifference. The tenants must then naturally regard the landlord as a cold, unfeeling tyrant, incapable of pity or remorse, whose sole object is to crush and grind them down, until chance gives him an opportunity of exterminating them.

As I said before, I have, up to this, been describing a state of things existing previous to the famine years. The population had increased in rapid proportion. This was owing to the great facility there existed of procuring the necessaries of life. Parents felt no uneasiness about the support of, their offspring when food was so easily procured. The potato was the manna of heaven to the Irish peasant; it supported him in ease and plenty at least.

The potato grew almost spontaneously; it grew luxuriantly, placing abundance within the reach of the poorest; their moderate wants were amply satisfied. A peasant and his family, collected around a dish of mealy potatoes—if they had the addition of a sup of milk—felt that they were happy in their frugal enjoyment.

They then clung too closely to the land of their fathers, the land of their hope and love, to seek wealth or distinctions elsewhere.

The Indian does not leave his hunting ground or the bones of his fathers with more reluctance than does the Irish peasant his humble cabin, and the grave-yard, where rest the bones of those he holds dear. He will suffer persecutions in order to cling to the green fields of his youth, to the home of his affections. There was a charm for him besides in the light rolicsome humor, the merry dance and play, the kind and social intercourse that characterize our peasantry.

The famine came and changed all this. The heartless indifference, the experimental philosophy of the English Government, the cruel, unchristian conduct of Irish landlords, in laying waste the country, in levelling the poor man's cabin, and sending him and his family to a pauper's grave, have wonderfully changed this state of things.

It is true, that in the autumn of '45, the time of which I am now writing, there was a partial blight of the potato crop; and as all other crops were luxuriant, the people did not bring home to their minds the dreadful chances of famine arising from a more general failure.

It is time that we say something about Mr. Ellis. Beyond the few hints thrown out already concerning him, there is little to tell our readers.

He was a Scotchman, and had come over some

twenty years before as a steward and agriculturist
to the late Lord Clearall.   With the canny foresight
of his race, he improved his position, until he was
able to lend large sums to the young lord, whose
traveling and expensive habits forced him to make
frequent calls on Mr. Ellis's purse.   After the death
of his father, young Lord Clearall settled on his
fine property, and was guided in its management by
the sagacious Mr. Ellis.   On account of the large
sums he had advanced, Mr. Ellis came in for farm
after farm, agency after agency, until the exclusive
management of the property remained in his hands.
Mr. Ellis had his own ends in view; he was a deep
thinker, and for near twenty years his heart was set
on becoming proprietor of at least a part of the
estate.   All his plots, all his schemes, had this grand
object in view.   He impressed the landlord with the
benefit of improvement, for improvement with him
meant eviction first, and then to enrich himself and
his friends upon the spoil.   He drew the attention
of the landlord to his house and farms; nothing
could be better managed, nothing could be neater;
then he pointed out the rudely-tilled fields of the
tenants, whose weedy corn was evidence of their
laziness and improvidence.   Thus did he school up the
landlord with the spirit of improvement, until farm
after farm, estate after estate, were cleared off their
hard-working, but oppressed tenantry, and then
handed over to Mr. Ellis's reforming care.   When
this was done, Mr. Ellis was sure to recommend some

of his Scotch friends as tenants. The landlord took this very kindly of him, thinking that he was, in his zeal for his service, providing for him industrious, enterprising tenants.

It is true that large sums had been expended on the improvement of the land and in building houses, and after all, the so-called lazy Irish were paying as high, if not a higher rent, but then, there was such an appearance of neatness and improvement about the estate. Had Lord Clearall but given leases, or afforded protection to the old tenants, he need not expend these large sums that were sinking him in debt; his property would be well managed, and he would have raised about him a grateful and happy tenantry. Lord Clearall did not know that Mr. Ellis had got large sums from his Scotch friends for his kind offices in their behalf. Thus is the spirit of the people broken down, and their hearts demoralized by a system of cruelty and oppression peculiar to unfortunate Ireland,--a system which has poisoned the deeply reflective and imaginative minds of our peasantry, and has perverted their gay, light hearts, sparkling with wit and humor, into morose sullen spirits, thirsting for vengeance upon their oppressors*

It is better that we should let the reader see the subtle machinery used for regenerating the unfortunate tenantry.

* Whether tenant right has altered this state of things in Ireland we are not aware, but to judge from the numerous evictions and agrarian crimes still perpetrated there, we fear not.

The Lodge, as Mr. Ellis's residence was called, was situated about two miles from Mr. O'Donnell's. It was formerly the residence of some unfortunate farmer; it was repaired and ornamented, and some new wings built to it by its present occupier. It was converted into a very tasty-looking residence outside, and a very comfortable one within doors. It commanded an extensive view of a broad, fertile valley thickly dotted with trees, with their green foliage waving in the breeze. About a mile further down the glen, seated on a rising ground, stood the proud residence of Lord Clearall, or, as it was styled, the Castle. This, with its surrounding groves of shady trees, added to the picturesqueness of the view from the lodge. Behind the cottage was an extensive range of farm–houses, and a large haggard of hay and corn, well thatched and secured. Care and wealth marked everything, from the tasty dwelling, down to the humblest shed. If, without all were gay and well cared, within the appearance was not less pleasing. The large flagged kitchen, was well lit with a huge peat fire, and well stored with tins, pans, pots, and all the accessories of kitchen use, not forgetting several flitches of bacon, that hung from the ceiling. A hall, with stone steps reaching it from the outside, ran through the centre of the house. Off this hall branched a drawing-room and parlor. At the end of the hall, with a passage leading to it from the kitchen, was an office, where Mr. Ellis transacted his business with the tenants and servants. As we have no business there for the present, we will just walk into the parlor.

This was a comfortable room, covered with a Brussels carpet. Its furniture consisted of an elegant oval table in the centre of the floor, two lounges, some easy chairs, a side-board, and a piano. A large gilt mirror was suspended over the chimney-piece; whilst on the latter were placed a few pretty vases filled with flowers, and some rare china ornaments. In an arm-chair, to the right of the blazing coal fire, sat Mr. Ellis. He was a man of about fifty years of age. His dark hair was streaked with grey, and deep lines of care, that betokened his plotting nature, ran across his forehead. He was of middle size, and spare in flesh. His eyes were grey and penetrating. His lips were compressed about the angles of the mouth. On the whole, there was an expression of deep cunning and acuteness in every feature of his rather sinister-looking face. His dress was of the costume of the present day, to wit, a frock coat, tweed trousers and vest. At the other side of the fire, deeply engaged with some papers, sat a young man of about twenty-five. He bore evident likeness to the other. This was Hugh Pembert, nephew to Mr. Ellis.

There was a cunningness about the small grey eye, about his narrow wrinkled brow, and coarse, sensual-looking face, that made you feel not at ease in his company. He pored over his papers with a certain air of half assurance and uneasy diffidence, that ill became one so nearly related to Mr. Ellis. At the end of the table, with her head resting on her left hand, sat a young girl reading a book that lay open before her. She was about eighteen; her figure, of middle size, was gracefully moulded. Her face was rather long and fair. So delicate did she appear, that you might easily see the net-work of blue veins that traversed her forehead and hands. There was in her countenance, though, something of a dreamy listlessness, that gave her an air of childish dependence. Such was Lizzy Ellis, the daughter and only child of Mr. Ellis. There was nothing of the crafty cunningness of the father about her; she must have inherited her pale face and gentle, unassuming manner from her mother. Lizzy was alone, her mother had died a few years before, and as she had no society, for her father was seldom at home, she spent her time reading novels and religious tracts without due regard to their merits. Perhaps to this excessive, and I must say, unnatural study for one so young and susceptible, was owing her inactive listlessness of character.

" Well, Hugh, my boy," said Mr. Ellis " have you made it out yet?"

" Na, sir," said Hugh; for Hugh being but a few years from Scotland had not yet got rid of its dialect.

" Well, then, let them alone until to-morrow; we will have a glass of punch, for I have good news—ring the bell, Hugh."

Hugh did so, and a servant shortly made her appearance.

" Get some hot water and spirits," said Mr. Ellis.

" I must tell you, Hugh," said he when the servant disappeared, " that his lordship has appointed me agent over the Ballybrack property."

" Na, indeed," said Hugh: that is muckle kind of his lardship."

The servant had now laid the glasses and decanters. "That will do; you may go," said Mr. Ellis. "Come Hugh, lad, fill a glass and let us drink a health to his lordship."

" With muckle pleasure," said Hugh; and they emptied their glasses to the toast.

" How long do you think am I living with his lordship?"

" Five years, I ken," said Hugh; " counting from the death of the present lard's father."

" No, no, that's not what I mean. How long am I in this county altogether?"

" I dinna ken, I'm sure," said Hugh.

" Let me see —— " and Mr. Ellis leant back in

9

his chair in a state of deep reflection; "yes, that's it ! exactly twenty-five years next March, Hugh. I had three pounds in my pocket when I commenced as steward under his lordship. I am now worth, in cash alone, Hugh, about ten thousand, which is in his lordship's hands, so you see I got on well, and Lizzy here," said he, looking at his daughter, "will have a nice fortune."

"Ay, indeed, sir," said Hugh; "land and stock and all will make a pretty penny for a braw little lassy as Missy is"

"You are right, Hugh, you are right; of course she'll have all—and I think that his lordship will make over the fee-simple of this house and land on me shortly for a handsome consideration."

Lizzy looked up from her book and smiled at her papa. Hugh knit his dark brows, and a frown clouded his face, and he muttered to himself, "she will na have all if I can prevent her."

"You must give notice to the Ballybruff tenants to come over in a few days, say Wednesday next," said Mr. Ellis.

"I dinna ken the use, sir," said Hugh, submissively; "ain't they noticed?"

"They are, they are," said Mr. Ellis; "but when they come over, they will think it is to get a settlement, so they will bring what money they can; and as there is a year's running gale, which answers a year's rent, we can put them out afterwards."

Hugh smiled the smile of a demon.

" Let us soak them as dry as a sponge before
we throw them away."

" What of the Ballybrack tenants?" said Hugh.

" They are safe just now, safe just now; they
have leases, but they will be up in a few years,
and then let them look to themselves ; you may
be living in that cosy nest of the O'Donnell's yet,
Hugh."

Hugh gave a grim smile of satisfaction, and
Lizzy raised her heavy eyes from the book and
said :—

" Papa, isn't it wrong to turn people out of their
houses; now the O'Donnells are good kind people;
isn't it a pity to turn them out?"

" No, child; the people are lazy and indolent,
and it is better for them to be earning their day's
hire, or to go to some foreign country, where they
can live better than here, than be spoiling the
land. Look at the difference of my farm here,
that was all waste when I got it, full of furze,
gardens, and useless fences, that the wretched
tenants had made. It was then as bad as any of
the places you see around; look at it now, pet."

" I see, papa; it is a beautiful place, indeed; but
sure the O'Donnells have a nice place, and you
need not turn them out; besides, papa, it must be
a terrible thing to be turned out of one's house."

" It must, child, for persons having a comfortable house like ours," and he looked about the

warm, tasteful room; "but for those poor cabins, I'm sure it's a blessing to knock them down."

It is hard to say from what motive Lizzy's advocacy of the O'Donnells proceeded, as she seldom interfered in her father's business. She had been lately reading some romantic novels; and as she was walking through one of the fields, a few weeks previous, she became very much alarmed at the appearance of a young bull that bellowed at a good distance from her. She screamed, and might have fainted, had not Frank O'Donnell jumped over the fence, with his gun on his shoulder, and escorted her home.

He was courteous and gentlemanly, and as it generally is in some way of this sort romantic ladies meet with their lovers, there is no telling what notions crossed her precious little head.

CHAPTER XIII.

THE rent day is a very important day to Irish tenants in general. Those who have the rent must wear a look of grateful complacency, and those who have not, of abject dependence. They know that their fate lies in the hands of the great man, whose bad report to the landlord is as sure destruction to them as the ukase of the Emperor of Russia to his serfs; therefore the Irish serfs must study the humor of their lord and master, and adapt their line of policy accordingly. It is a nice point of dispute who will go in first, but the decree generally falls upon some one able to meet his rent in full. As soon as he comes out, he has to answer a regular fire of questions in Irish, such as:—

"What humor is his honor in, Bill?" says a poor fellow who, perhaps, is back a few pounds.

"Will he allow half the poor rates, Bill?" says another, who has scraped his up to that point.

"I don't know will he take my cow at a valuation; it is better to be widout the sup of milk itself than the cabin, God help us?" says another poor fellow.

Even their appearances must be adapted to their circumstances, or rather to the circumstances in which they would wish to appear,

The poor man that wants time, until he sells his cow, or his slip of a pig, generally borrows a good coat from a neighbour to let the agent see that he is well dressed; and that a little time with him is only a matter of convenience; while the comparatively rich man, with his rent in his pocket, appears in his every-day garb, lest his wealth would draw down upon him the cupidity of the agent.

It must be recollected that I am painting the dark side of the picture. It is true that there are many such men as Mr. Ellis in Ireland; but it is equally true, on the other hand, that there are landlords who would be ashamed to acknowledge such a man as their agent—men of honorable and Christian feelings, who treat their tenants with kindness and consideration—who take a pride in their welfare.

It is said, in defence of slavery, that slave masters were generally kind to their slaves; but there are some masters who use the power of life and death, with which they are vested, with a vengeance—who gloat over the sufferings of their victims, as they writhe with the torture of the lash and the stake—who laugh at their frantic cries, as the flame fattens on their flesh. Yes, there are such demons on earth; for when man's heart becomes hardened, there is no demon in hell more cruel.

Is it a sufficient plea for slavery that there are

some good, kind masters, such as St. Clair? Certainly not! Well, then, is it a sufficient plea for leaving the white slaves of Ireland at the mercy of men
as cruel and hardened as the brutal planter, Legree?
Certainly not. But then you'll tell me the law protects the Irish peasant; he cannot be whipped or
scourged—he is a freeman. ·Ha! it is true they
manage these things better in Ireland than they did
in Kentucky. They have a keen, systematic way
of doing things, less savage in its executions, but
not less sure in its results. They manage to kill the
body by a slow process of petty persecution, by
energies crushed, by the fluctuations of fear and
hope deferred, to end in ruin; after which they too
often try to kill the soul, by holding out the bribes
of Judas to their victims. Believe me, we are drawing no ideal picture, dear reader. The enlightened
statesmen of Europe wonder why the boasted,
humane laws of England would not step in between
the Irish Legrees and their victims. The attention
of Europe is turning more and more every day to
this anomaly. They know it is impossible for a
country to progress and gian material wealth where
power is used to crush, in the hearts of millions, all
those feelings, impulses, and incentives to industry
that beget a nation's wealth; for a nation cannot be
advanced by destroying in the hearts of the· many
the motives of industry. Lord Brougham, one of
England's greatest statesmen, talking of the vested
interests of slave-owners, says:—" . . . I deny

the right, I acknowledge not the property. The
principles—the feelings of our common nature rise
in rebellion against it. . . . In vain you tell me
of the laws which sanction such a claim. There is a
law above all the enactments of human codes—the
same throughout the world, the same in all times.
. . . . It is the law written by the finger of
God upon the heart of man; and by that law, un-
changeable and eternal, while men despise fraud,
and loathe rapine, and abhor blood, they will reject
with indignation the wild and guilty phantasy, that
man can hold property in man."

How applicable to the white slaves of Ireland and
their masters!

Mr. Ellis sat at his desk with a ledger before him;
Hugh Pembert was writing near him.

" Are the Ballybruff tenants collected yet, Hugh?"

" I dinna ken; I shall see, sir," said Hugh.

" No, no; go on with your accounts, I will call
Burkem," and he rang the hand-bell.

" Tell Burkem," said he, to the servant maid, " to
come up, I want him,"

" Yes, sir."

Burkem made his appearance with an air of the
greatest deference. He held his hat in his hand,
and bowed to the great man.

It is necessary that we should say a few words
about Burkem, whom we have seen before at Mr.
O'Donnell's. He was for some time in the police
force, but discharged for some good reasons. He

then got into Mr. Ellis' employment, where he acted as bailiff, doing all the dirty work for him. The scoundrel was so keen, and had such a consummate address, that he passed off among the people as a good kind of person, forced to act contrary to his wishes, in order to keep his place. He took care to impress this very slyly upon them. So that he was more pitied than hated.

Mr. Ellis raised his head from the ledger.

" Well, Ned, are the Ballybruff tenants outside?"

" They are, your honor."

" Have they much money, do you think ?"

" Sorra much; I'm sure I don't know where the lazy set would get it; one or two of them druv cows to see would your honor take them at a valuation."

" I suppose, Hugh, we had better; there is no use in letting anything back."

" Ya'as sir," said Hugh, looking up from his accounts.

" Burkem, show them in."

The tenants were collected in groups about the yard, discussing their position with the gusto of American politicians. There was in one corner three or four cows, with as many men sitting near them, keeping guard, with the most abject misery depicted on their countenances; near these was a woman with ten geese, to make up her little rent.

" God help us," said one of the men; "I dunna what the childers will do, the cratures, widout the sup of milk, and sure the praties are no great things this year; that blackguard blight has made them black and soft."

"I fear we are near hard times," said another, "though what harm if we could keep the cabin over . us."

"Sorra harm, Jem; there is no fear of a man wid a house over his head; it's bad enuff to want the bit or sup, but when a man wants the roof to cover him, och, mavrone, he's done entirely."

"I dunna what is his honor going to do wid us; shure if he were going to put us out he wouldn't send us word to make up a year's rint."

"That's thrue, he wouldn't," said another; "Mr. Burkem tould me that he only served the notices to hurry us in."

"I hope so," said the woman, with a sigh; "God help us, we are bad enuff as it is, widout being worse; see, I have brought these ten geese to make up the last pound; I'm sure he won't refuse them from the poor widow."

"And it's you had the nice job to drive them too, Mrs. Dunne; begor, you'd think the cratures knew where they were goin' to, they cackled and flew at such a rate."

A large group was all this time collected near the kitchen door, some thumbing old receipts, some looking over their little money, some in deep abstraction.

As soon as Mr. Burkem made his appearance there was a general rush around him.

"What news, Mr. Burkem?"

"Is the master in good humor?"

"Will he take the rint from us?"

These and similar questions were put to Mr. Burkem.

"Begad, I think he is," said Burkem, "for he said
to me, 'Burkem, go tell these poor people to come
in. I hope they have the rent; for, God knows, I
rather they had than be turning them out;' 'I think
they all have it, sir,' says I, 'and it would be a pity
to turn them out when they can pay their way;'
'that's true for you, Burkem,' says he."

"You know, boys, there is no harm in having the
good word."

"Sorra harm, Mr. Burkem, and may God bless you
for it."

"Thanks be to God!" were the general exclama-
tions of the expecting crowd.

"Now," said Mr. Burkem, "let ye that have the
money plentiest, go in first; come with me, Mr.
Doyle, I know you have the shiners; nothing softens
a man like them, Mr. Doyle."

"How do you do, Mr. Doyle?" said Mr. Ellis, in
a very bland manner.

"Well, thank your honor," said Mr. Doyle, with
a most obsequious bow.

"I suppose you have your rent, Mr. Doyle, £21
14s."

"Yes, your honor, by allowing me half the rates."

"I cannot allow it this time, Mr. Doyle; so I will
give you a docket for the present; will that do?"

"Yes, your honor; but I'd sooner get the resate; Mr. Burkem told us that you'd allow it."

"Mr. Burkem, that's good! how did Burkem know; ay, Mr. Burkem?"

"Shure I only thought so, your honor."

"Well, you needn't be telling what you think, Mr. Burkem; however, it makes no difference; I could not give a receipt until I see his lordship about these notices. You know I am only a servant, Mr. Doyle; must carry out his lordship's wishes,—write a docket for Mr. Doyle, Hugh, £21 on account."

"Well, Mrs. Cormack, have you the rent, ma'am?"

"Yes, your honor."

"Fifteen pounds, ten shillings, ma'am."

"Here is fifteen pounds, your honor; and may God bless them that gave it to me."

"Pray, who gave it to you, ma'am," said Mr. Ellis; drawing the money towards him.

"Young Mr. O'Donnell; God spare him, he is the tender-hearted young man; he comes in to me and asked me had I the rent. I told him ——"

"See, that will do, ma'am; I'm sure he is a good young man; but," said he, in a mutter too low for Mrs. Cormack's hearing—"A fool and his money soon parts."

"Ten shillings more, ma'am, if you plaise," said Hugh.

"Ten shillings! arrah, hav'nt you it all there except the poor rates."

"We cannot allow any poor rates now," said Mr.

Ellis; "the next time though, the next time; it makes no difference; give her a docket, Hugh."

" What about the notice, your honor ?"

" I'll see his lordship about it; I'm sure when he I ears you all paid he will withdraw it; you know I am only a servant to his lordship, and must consult him."

" Well, good woman, have you the rent ?"

This was addressed to a miserable-looking poor ereature, whose patched garments were scarcely sufficient to cover her shivering form.

" All but a thrifle, your honor."

" Well, I cannot take it without the full."

"God help us! shure your honor knows that a great deal of the praties war black, and four pounds is too much entirely for a cabin and haggard."

" Come, good woman, don't be taking up my time; I'm sure it wasn't I made the potatoes black; as for the rent, why did you engage to pay it ? it's only what you are paying always."

"Call some other one, Burkem; this woman goes out. Mark her down to be ejected, Hugh."

Burkem whispered something to Mr. Ellis.

"Have compassion on the poor woman, your honor; she has some geese—maybe she'd sell them to you."

" God bless you, Mr. Burkem—I have, your honor; but I thought to sell them to buy a stitch of clothes for myself and the orphans; have compassion on us, your honor, and God will have marcy on you."

"To be turned out, Hugh; we can't lose any more time."

"Take them, your honor," said the poor woman, with a sigh; and she wiped the tears from her eyes with her tattered apron.

"There are ten in it, but leave me the old ones, and here is three pounds; God knows it's by pinch-ing and starving myself and children I made it up."

"That will do, ma'am; Burkem, get the docket, and when this woman gives you the ten geese--ten is little enough for a pound—give it to her."

"Yes, your honor."

"God help myself and my poor orphans!" groaned the wretched woman.

It is unnecessary that we should follow the worthy Mr. Ellis seriatim through all the tenants; it is enough to say that the geese, the cows, and some slips of pigs, were all disposed of in like manner.

There was one poor fellow, and it was most affect-ing to see him take his leave of his cow. Magpie was enjoying the luxury of a sop of hay when he returned to her, after her fate being sealed inside.

"Poor Magpie, poor baste, what will we do afther you; come here, poor Magpie."

Magpie left the hay, and placed her head between his hands, as if to sympathize with him.

"Poor baste," said he, kissing her; and then he wiped the big tears from his eyes—"poor Magpie, your corner will be lonely to-night, and the childers will miss you, and cry for you; och, mavrone, it's the bitter news I have for them; but God's will be done," and he wiped his eyes again; and as he left the yard, he looked back, and Magpie looked after him, and followed him.

"No, I can't stand it," said he, and he blubbered out as he went away.

On the whole, the tenants were well pleased with their day.

"He was hard enuff on the poor," said Mr. Doyle; "but anything is better than to be turned out of the house."

"Thruc for you, Mr. Doyle; what fear is there of us? hav'nt we the cabins over us, and our health, the Lord be praised!"

"Well, it is not a bad day's haul," said Mr. Ellis, as he closed the books. "Poor fools, if they but knew the mercy they are to get. Is it on account you have given all the receipts, Hugh?"

"Ya'as, sir."

"Give that woman's docket to Burkem, and let him go for the geese; and mind, let him say it was to buy them I did."

"Ya'as, sir."

"Take it down to him yourself, and leave me alone."

"Ya'as, sir."

Mr. Ellis lay back in his chair, and thus soliloquized to himself:

"So far so good; things are going on smoothly;

we must keep these Ballybruff tenants on hands until after the elections, for his lordship has assured
me that an election will take place in spring, and
Sir W. Crasly will represent the conservative interest.   We must get all these to vote for him; I know
these d——d priests will oppose us; no matter—let
them refuse, if they dare. Well, if we gain our
point, I know I will be made a J. P.; ay, faith, a J.
P.   Hugh Ellis, Esq., J. P., sounds nicely; doesn't
it, though! ha, ha, great change since the day I
came here with a few pounds in my pocket.   In any
case, after the election, we will evict the Ballybruff
tenants.   Here are two letters"—and he pulled
them from his pocket, and read them over, and then
put them into a private drawer.   "One is from John
M. Nale, offering me five hundred pounds if I'd get
him about two hundred acres at a fair rent and a
long lease; another from his uncle, offering me the
same for about three hundred acres; three and two
are five, just what's in the Ballybruff property.   I
know his lordship will want a few thousands shortly
about that building of his, and that will leave me
able to give it.   Capital, that building of his—how
I got him on with that, for fear he wasn't running
down hill fast enough.   Well, who knows for whom
he is building it.   Heigh ho! what would the world
say if I were living there yet—heigh ho! eight and
two are ten thousand; no joke of a mortgage, heigh
ho!" and he leant back in his chair, evidently well
pleased with the state and prospect of his affairs.

When Hugh Pembert went into the kitchen in search of Mr. Burkem, he found that worthy regaling himself on some cold meat and crisped potatoes.

"Taking care of yourself, maun, I see," said Hugh.

"Ay, faith, Mr. Pembert; a man wants something after such a dry day's work."

"Will you please slip into my room when done?"

"Certainly, sir, with pleasure."

When Burkem went into Mr. Pembert's room he found him with a case of pistols on the table before him.

"Weel, Mr. Burkem, take a seat."

"These are purty pistols, Mr. Hugh."

"Weel, weel, there's nae fear of them, maun."

"Ye gang for them geese, Mr. Burkem, ye war spacking about; here is the docket."

Mr. Burkem took the paper.

"Hang them for geese; its a shabby thing for a man to be going after geese, at least," said Burkem.

"Weel, weel, maun, Mr. Ellis sends a chiel on many a poor mission."

"True for you, sir; it's well if he don't get sky-lights made through some of us some of those fine days, if he goes on as he is."

"He dinna no such thing, Mr. Burkem; we maun do our duty; I'm sure ye weel be well paid."

"Sorra a bit too well at all for the risk I run, Mr. Hugh; if ten shillings a week and my chances is good pay for a man risking his life every day, I don't know what to say."

"It's sma'; it's no the thing, no doubt; but then I dinna mind adding a mickle to it. Here maun, drink my health," and he handed him a pound-note.

"Ye maun like one of these braw things," and he handed him a double-barrelled pistol.

"Thank you, Mr. Hugh," said the other, "I will not forget your kindness."

"Ye maun see that, when I'll be master here by-and-bye, Mr. Burkem, I will na forget those that serve me."

"You may rely upon me, Mr. Hugh; you may be sure I will serve you faithfully."

"Weel, I dinna doubt it, so good bye now."

"Good bye, sir, and God bless you."

"I dinna ken, can I depend on that fellow? Weel, I think, I maun; he'll do anything for the baubee," said Mr. Pembert to himself, when alone.

"What the devil is he up to now; he must have something in view, when he gave me a pound, for he's as close as the old shaver. No matter, I'll play my card between them; and I am thinking I won't lose either. I will go over to Mr. O'Donnell's to see that little baggage, Mary Cahill; upon my soukens I am afeard that young Cormack is cutting my cabbage fast; if he be, let him look to himself. That I may never die in sin—but no matter—it would be as well for him not to crass me," and he whistled song, as if to keep off the bad thoughts that were working within him.

When Mrs. Cormack returned to her home, her two sons and daughter were sitting around the fire, eagerly expecting her.

James, the eldest, was a fine specimen of the peasant class. He was above the middle height, with fair features and sandy hair. There was an impulsive, honest expression in his open countenance; his eye was dark and sparkling. He was evidently one that could love deeply; but could impulsively revenge a wrong. His dress was that of the peasant class—a corduroy trousers, heavy shoes, or brogues, with an overcoat or jacket of flannel.

John Cormack was a few years younger than his brother. The razor had not yet touched the down of manhood that covered his chin. Mrs. Cormack was proud of her two fine boys—and well she might; for a mother never reared more loving nor more dutiful sons. She was also proud of her gay, sprightly daughter; and it must be confessed, there was not a lighter foot in the village dance, nor a gayer smile, nor a sprightlier laugh than Nelly Cormack's.

"Nelly, alanna! will you go out and see is mother coming. My heart is heavy, somehow, until I hear the news. If I knew which road she'd take, I'd go meet her," said James.

Nelly went out, but returned immediately.

Here she is, up the road," said Nelly; " and she

in shanachus with some old cosherer. I hope, James,
it's not going to bring in a step-father over us she
is. If so, some pretty girl I know would have a
poor chance." Here she looked most roguishly at
James, as much as to say, "you see I know all about
ye."

"Bad scran to you, Nelly, can you ever sthop, or
hould your tongue," said James, blushing.

"Och, indeed, what color is red now, James.
Shure it's no blame to you, avick machree. Faith,
if I were a lump of a boy myself, I'd be in love wid
her—and a nice boy I'd make;" and she looked
complacently at herself. "It's I'd have the girls
crazy."

"Whist! you scatter-brain, you; and throw out
the praties, and put down an egg for mother; she
must be hungry. Here she's in, and the Rover too."

"Welcome, mother—and blur-an-ages is this you.
It's a week of Sundays since we saw you—cead
mille failthe! Nelly, help mother to take off her
cloak."

"Thank you, James," said the Rover.

"That'll do, Nelly," said Mrs. Cormack.

They looked at their mother, to read the news of
the day in her face. It is strange that when there
is some event of importance at stake we do not like
asking about it—we wish to keep from our minds
the bitterness of disappointment as long as possible.

"Sit down, mother—you must be tired; and, Nelly, roll out the praties."

Mrs. Cormack sat down; and then looked about the house, and then at her children.

"Thank God, we have the house over us, another sthart, anyway," said Mrs. Cormack.

"That's good news. anyway, mother," said James.

"It is, achorra, the Lord be praised, he was in the good humor; oh! it's pleasant to go near a man when he has the smile and kind word for you."

"That's thrue, mother; the Lord bless him for that same to you, bad as he is."

They had now collected around the table of potatoes and noggins of milk, to enjoy their frugal meal.

"Nelly," said Mrs. Cormack, "bring down that miscawn of butther in the room; shure it's not every day the Rover comes to us."

"Nor every day we do have the good news, mother," said John Cormack."

"Thrue enuff, avick mastore."

"Och, and faix I will, wid a heart and a-half," said Nelly.

"There's a good dale of these black, Mrs. Cormack," said the Rover, as he shoved the potatoes aside.

"There is, the Lord be praised; but then it's nothin' I hope; what would the poor do, if they ran black on them?"

"Sorra a one of me knows, ma'am, they wouldn't live at all; shure it's hard enuff for them to manage now."

" God is good!" said James, sententiously.

"He is, achorra; praise be to His holy name!"
said Mrs. Cormack, piously raising her hands in
prayer, and a tear of gratitude glistened in the
widow's eye.

" Did he say anything about the notices, mother ?"

" Yes, John, achorra; he gave us dockets, and
said that the notices were to frighten the tenants
and nothing more; he should see his lordship about
them."

"'I never like to trust the old bodagh," said the
Rover; "there is no time he's so dangerous as when
he has the palaver; he has a bad set about him too;
as for the nephew, he's as hard and as dark as himself; and as for Burkem——"

"He put in the good word, to-day, anyway, for
us; I heard them sayin' he spoke up to his honor,
and told him it would be a shame without taking
the money from us."

" Well, achorra, praise the fool as you find him."

"I will go down to Mr. O'Donnell's; I am sure
Master Frank will be glad to hear the good
news."

" Do, James, asthore; God bless him, but for him
shure I could not make up the rent."

" Take care, James, that you do not see some
other one," said Nelly, with a smile.

" Bad scran to the other one I want to see," said
James, stooping down to tie his shoes.

James pulled very hard at that tie, for he broke it, and when he raised his head, his cheeks were very red; no doubt from the hard pulling.

When James went into Mr. O'Donnell's kitchen, Mary Cahill was alone at the fire, baking bread.

" God save you, Mary," said James, with something like a stammer in his voice.

" God save you kindly, and you're welcome: sit down."

" That I will, alanna," said he, placing his seat near her.

" You might keep out from a body, though, James, and not be going with your cumhethers," and she pushed her seat over from him.

" Och, musha! how contrary the people is getting," said James, pushing after her, and taking a stocking she was knitting in his hand.

" How the deuce do ye knit, Mary; I could never larn it."

" Shure you ought," said she with a laugh; " and make a sheelah of yourself."

" Ye do have as many twists and turns and ins and outs in it as there do be in a woman's heart."

" And as many crooked ones as there do be in mens', take that, James."

" I dunna, faix, what turns does be in mens' hearts, at all; for when a purty colleen, like you, Mary, puts the soft sawder on one of them, sarra bit they know what they do."

" Faix, James, ye do be chicken-hearted entirely;

och, botherashun to ye and yer blarney," and Mary
looked at him with a most provoking, roguish look.

"Deuce the blarney then, Mary. Shure, darlin',
your funny eyes and pouting lips would burn a holo
in any man's heart."

James moved his chair nearer to her, and placed
h.s hand around her waist.

"Arrah, will you sthop, James; look at the bread
the way its burning," and she hurried away from him.

"Faix, I know somebody's heart that's burning
worse, Mary."

James placed his hand most pathetically over his
to show where the volcano lay.

"Bad cess to 'em, can't they throw water enuff
upon it," said Mary, taking her seat again. "Now,
James, if you don't sthop I won't sit her another
minit."

"Mary, will you ——— ?"

"Arrah, whist, James."

"Will you?"—and he took her little hand in his;
"will you tell me ——"

"Now, can't you have patience, James."

"I want to know iv you ——"

"Oh, James, don't be in such a hurry," and Mary
blushed and held down her head.

"Shure, Mary, it's time," and he squeezed her
hand closer; "shure it's time that ——"

"Oh, don't James; give me time to think; don't
be in such a hurry."

"About what, Mary?"

" About asking me."

" Ha, ha, Mary, alanna, I was only asking you to tell Masther Frank to come down to me."

Mary withdrew her hand.

" Bad scran from you, James; shure I thought it was going to ask me to marry you you were."

" Faith an' may be I'll be axin' you to do that same, some of those fine mornins, achree, as soon as I have things settled."

" Choke your impudence; I knew you hadn't the courage, sorra a bit."

" Maybe I havn't, Mary, my darlin' !" and he pressed her to him, and imprinted a kiss upon her pouting lips. " Mary my love, will you be——"

Here his declaration, whatever it was—and there are few of my bachelor readers but could give a good guess as to what it was to be, at least,—was interrupted by the opening of the kitchen door, and our friend, Ned Burkem, walked in with a most in-nocent look, and a " God save all here."

Mary and James' confused manner was enough to betray them, if Mr. Burkem had not witnessed any of the interesting love drama—but he did; for, hearing the voices inside, he looked through the key-hole. A scowl of revenge, dark as that worn by Satan, when he saw Adam and Eve in the garden of Paradise, crossed Mr. Burkem's features. The demon of revenge had entered his heart, but the smile of Judas was on his face, as he opened the door.

"God save you, kindly, Ned!" said James Cormack, as soon as he recovered his composure. "Sit down, Ned. This is a fine evenin'!"

"It is, the Lord be praised; and it was a fine day altogether. The tenants got on well to-day, James."

"So my mother told me; and you wor no bad friend to them either, Ned, I can hear. Give mo* the hand for that."

"Shure it's only nathural I would do anything I could for my neighbors. God help me, I often do things I'd rather not; but thin if I didn't another would, and maybe he wouldn't keep the light hand, as I does."

"Thrue for you, Ned; shure the tenants all feel that. Tara-an-ages, but it would be the bad day if you should take it into your head to give up."

"Sorra a bit of me likes the business at all. It's only for their sakes I'm sticking to it."

The servants were now home from their work, so the conversation turned on general topics.

CHAPTER XIV.

CHRISTMAS AT HOME.

"Hark! where it rolls!—It thrills their souls! arise and bend
the knee;
He comes, who blessed the wedding feast In Cana of Galilee."

WHEN the poor wandering minstrel that wrote
"Home, sweet home" rambled about the streets of
London, without a roof to cover him, and heard
the sad voices of wretched ballad-singers chanting
"Home, sweet home!" how his desolation must have
crushed his mind. The world was before him, but
no home for him that sang of a happy home. Verily,
the tender sensibilities of fine minds are often tried
with a vengeance. He who felt most keenly the
charms of home and domestic bliss could never call
them his own.

"Home, sweet home!" How little do we think
of home when intoxicated with the gaieties of fashionable life; yet home is the haven of rest, where
the weary spirit seeks repose, where the affections
bloom and blossom. If assailed with bodily or men-
tal trouble, where can we turn for pure sympathy
but to home. You may have wealth, and wealth
without sympathy, but not without admiration and
envy. Admiration will not make us happy without
love and sympathy; and where will these be found

in all their depth and purity, but at home. Home is the union of all these social ties that bind brothers and sisters, parents and children, in one holy bond —a holy bond of mutual love and brotherhood.

A man of a loving heart, with good moral resolution, and the genius of moral discipline, can make home a paradise indeed. Home is woman's province the sphere of her love and duty ; it is her kingdom; and how grandly does a wise woman rule her little empire.   Her words are words of peace and love. She rules her household with a moral influence that delights the heart of her husband.

Young men are too apt to be taken with the allurements of society; still these charms possess nothing so endearing as the sweets of domestic affection.   These expand the heart with the truest sensations.   What artificial enjoyments can compare to the greeting smile of a fond wife or the prattling of pretty babes.   There is no charm of society so dear as that arising from the confidence and mutual thoughts and plans fostered and designed by man and wife.

He who is worthy of love, and can appreciate all its fervor and purity, will find them in the endearments of his wife and children.   Man seldom appreciates the gushing warmth of woman's affections. There is a purity in her devotion that our rougher natures cannot well appreciate ; we seldom comprehend the depth of her love, the purity of her intense affections.

Such a home as I have attempted to describe was

Mr. O'Donnell's. It never witnessed these little domestic scenes, these family broils, that generally alienate the affections and deprive home of its truest blessings. Mr. O'Donnell was a kind, affectionate father, but not a too indulgent one. As for Mrs. O'Donnell, home, indeed, was her little kingdom, which she ruled with all the moral government of a well-ordered state.

Her family sat around their little table, quiet, cheerful, and friendly; without an unkind word; without a frown to mar their happiness.

In such a home as this how happy must our friend, Willy Shea, find himself, even if there were not the sacred tie of love to bind him to it.

Alice Maher, too, had come over to spend the Christmas at Glen Cottage.

Kate was visiting at her uncle's, and when returning home got leave for Alice to accompany her.

It was Christmas-day—that day of high festival—and there were merry hearts in cabin and hall. The village bells were pealing forth in merry tones, and seemed to say: "Christmas comes but once a year, and when it comes it brings good cheer." The bells were pealing, and happy faces crowded along the village way. Men and women and children throng the way, for the merry bells seemed to grow joyous, and clang out—"It's Christmas-day, Christmas-day." And they chimed and they chimed, until merry hearts took up the burden of their song, and wished each other a happy Christmas.

"A merry Christmas," greeted our friends as they proceeded to the village Mass.

" Ay, a merry Christmas, and a great many, too," —for Mr. O'Donnell and his family were beloved by the poor.

How often did he get some friend, for form sake, to secure a poor man in *his* bank, for his rent, to keep the house over him.   For form sake, I say, for well did that friend know, that if the poor man failed, he would not be called on to pay.   How often did his son, Frank, give from his scanty means to make up the widow's rent, and his wife and daughter pay visits of charity and mercy to the sick and needy.   It is no wonder, therefore, that they were greeted from every side with, "a merry Christmas, and a great many, too."

Why was the sublime feeling of adoration purer, warmer, and more ardent to-day than any other? To-day, for it was Christmas-day ; it took its inspiration from that pious and mystic ecstacy created by the solemn and awe-inspiring belief, that we are commemorating the birth of a God that died to save sinful man from eternal perdition.

The sleet was pattering on the windows, and the wind was moaning dismally around the houses, but few heeded it, for it was Christmas night, and there were bright fires and brighter hearts within.

A bright fire, and smiling faces and merry voices, are a cheering picture of domestic bliss.

There were light hearts and merry voices around

Mr. O'Donnell's hearth that Christmas night. He sat, as usual, in his easy chair, and around him were seated his wife and family, and their two welcome guests.

Bright lights streamed from the table, and bright sparks glowed from the yule-log that burned in the grate, for they loved and cherished the good old customs yet. A Christmas tree, with its glittering fruit, and card, and ribbon, and gold and silver ornaments, stood in all its effulgent grandeur, upon the centre table. Holly and ivy and berries were entwined around the frames and cornices ; even the very kitchen was a perfect wilderness of them. The mistletoe hung from the centre, and many a laugh, and joke, and kiss, were interchanged beneath it that Christmas night. The kitchen rang with the song, and tale, and jest; for they were merry with good drink and cheer, and kept Christmas night a jubilee.

"Here is a health to the good old year, that's fast dying out ; and may we live to enjoy its offspring," said one.

"Amen! Amen!" shouted the others, and emptied their glasses.

"Here is that the holly, the ivy, and the shamrock, may grow green for ever," said the Rover.

"Hip, hip, hurra!" and the kitchen rang with merry shouts.

"Here is that we may have good hunting next year ; tallyho! tallyho! in the mornin'," shouted Shemus-a-Clough.

"Here is a health to the brave; and may the laurel wreathe their brows, and beauty's smile cheer their hearts," said Uncle Corny.

"That's it, Sergeant; that's a purty toast," said the Rover.

"Here is the thrush in the bush, and the bush in full bloom; my love in my arms, and that very soon," said James Cormack; who had come over to spend Christmas night at Mr. O'Donnell's.

James, to carry out his toast, jumped up and caught Mary Cahill. Mary, of course, struggled and cried out, "won't you'sthop you schemer; bad scran to me if I don't call them out to you." Despite all this, however, she got over, somehow, very easy under the mistletoe, where James caught her two hands to prevent her from clasping them on her mouth; and then impressed a warm kiss on her pouting lips.

"Bad scran to you; did anyone ever see the likes of you; look at the way my hair is all tossed wid you," and Mary gave him a harmless slap on the cheek.

"Take that now, you schemer; maybe you won't do it agen."

"Och! musha, Mary, but you have blinded my eye," said James, putting up his hand; "you must marry me now."

"Arrah! the deuce take your impudence."

"Well, here, if you don't, take back your kiss," and James returned it with interest amid the shouts and laughter of the company, and the slight struggles of Mary.

There were light and loving hearts in that old kitchen, on that Christmas night. We need not wish them a merry Christmas, for their own hearts joyously rang out—"A merry Christmas."

The French have a saying, that peace is first-cousin to *ennui;* but it was not so with our happy party in Mr. O'Donnell's parlor; for the yule-log blazed and sparkled; the candles shone forth, and the Christmas tree glittered and glistened as if some fairy had touched it with her wand. The tea table lay spread near; the shining tray looked temptingly; its rich butter, its yellow cream, and its hot cakes cut in fantastic shapes—all Miss Kate's making. Our party near the fire were on easy terms with one another; for they laughed, and sang, and joked, and gave and solved riddles and conundrums.

They now took their tea, and then a glass of wine; and Mr. O'Donnell took an additional glass of punch, and rubbed his hands, and looked at the young folks so happy, and rubbed his hands again, and laughed, and felt superbly glad and contented.

After playing at 'Acrostic Charades,' 'I love my love with an A——,' and such like, they had a game of forfeits. Nor did Mr. O'Donnell chide, but laughed heartily at the fond kisses beneath the mistletoe. Then,

> "The game of forfeits done, the girls all kissed
> Beneath the sacred bush——"

Our party assembled around the fire, and sang and chatted away.

They then drew their prizes from the Christmas tree.

The hail and snow pattered on the windows without.

"Let it dash away," said Mr. O'Donnell, looking at the blazing fire, the cheerful room, and more cheerful faces. "Let it dash away. It won't reach us."

"But, papa," said Bessy, and she left her hands upon his knees, and looked into his face; "papa, how many a poor person without a home to-night, without a fire to warm them, or good cheer and fond hearts to make them happy!"

"That's true, darling," said Mr. O'Donnell; and he kissed that frail-looking child. "That's true, darling. There is misery in the world, no doubt; but then, if we allow these feelings to overcome us, we will only make ourselves miserable, without making others happy."

"But, papa, shouldn't every one try to make as many as they could happy?"

"Yes, darling. If they did this, there would be no real misery in the world. This is the true spirit of charity."

"And why don't they do it, papa?"

"Really, I cannot say, my pet. You see our Saviour was neglected in a manger, and forgotten by those He came to save."

"Oh! wern't they cruel, papa?"

"Yes, indeed, child, but I fear we are not a bit better. Our Divine Master says, as often as we relieve the poor we relieve himself; and now tell me puss, what have you done for the poor this blessed Christmas?"

"I will tell you, papa; in the first place, mamma made up a basket of meat and bread, and tea and sugar for us, and then Kate and I went up to poor Mrs. Sullivan's, and——"

"Hu," said Kate, "little tell-tale; you know the Scripture says, let not your left hand see what your right hand giveth."

"True," said Mr. O'Donnell. "And now, Bessy darling, go sit near your mamma."

Bessy did sit near her mamma, and nestled her head upon her bosom, and prattled with her in low tones.

While this conversation was going on, Willy Shea was in a deep reverie. His elbows rested on his knees, and his face upon his open palms. Of what was he thinking?

Ah! he thought of the good old home where he spent many a Christmas night such as this; where father, mother, brothers, and sisters all joined to make it a merry Christmas. Where the yule log burned, and the Christmas tree glistened, and where light hearts, and merry faces, and jocund laughter made a merry Christmas indeed. Where were all these now?

On such a Christmas night as this did his kind gentle mother—the last of her race—sleep for the first time in her cold grave. As he returned to his bleak home, the sleet and rain pattered without, but there was no yule log, nor Christmas tree, nor fond hearts to greet him within.

"Ah! my good tender mother, where are you?" he exclaimed, half audibly, as the tears trickled between his fingers.

"Willy, what ails you?" said Kate, leaning her hand upon his.

"Nothing, nothing dear!" and he brushed away the tears, and tried to look cheerful.

"Come," said Alice Maher, "Willy, get your flute and come to the kitchen, we will set up a dance there."

"Agreed, agreed!"

And the kitchen became merrier, and resounded with the song and dance of light and loving hearts, until the old clock in the hall chimed twelve, and then that merry Christmas had passed away.

When Willy rose in the morning, he went to the window to look out. The ground was covered with a slight sprinkling of snow. He looked towards the farm-yard. A long range of ricks of hay and stacks of corn crowded behind the house. The noise of the flail resounded from the barn.

In the yard was Kate O'Donnell and Mary Cahill, with a whole troop of gabbling turkeys and geese, cackling hens, and ducks around them. Over and about these fluttered a lot of busy pigeons. Kate, in a plain dress, with her sleeves tucked up, was feeding them with oats from a sieve, which Mary held.

A pigeon was cooing from her shoulder jealously at another that was busily pecking on the sieve.

"This is happiness, indeed," said Willy ; "and with such a noble, loving girl I would gladly live and die amidst such scenes."

When he came down to the parlor, Alice Maher and Frank were enjoying a pleasant *tête-à-tête* on the settee near the fire.

They seemed very happy, and evidently on very good terms with one another.

Mr. and Mrs. O'Donnell shortly joined them. Kate and Bessy soon came in with two plates of hot butter cakes, which they were after baking in the kitchen.

After breakfast, as the day was too unpleasant to go out, our party amused themselves playing drafts, backgammon, and other games. Then they sang and played on the flute and concertina, and read amusing books alternately.

About noon, their recreation was enlivened with the most discordant attempts at music imaginable, proceeding from the little lawn in front.

"Come here," said Alice, looking out of the window ; "come here," and she laughed heartily. "Such a motley group I have never witnessed ; what the deuce are they ? "

They all ran to the window.

It was no wonder that Alice laughed, for a more picturesque group of rags and patches you could not see.

"The wren boys, the wren boys," exclaimed the party.

The wren boys, or, as they called themselves, the wran boys, now came up to the window, and commenced to puff and blow their spasmodic instruments.

One fellow had an old flute which would elicit for him, despite all his puffing and blowing, only a few shrill whistles. Another was scratching at a fiddle, whilst another was trying to force the wind out of an old asthmatic bagpipes; but all these were completely thrown in the shade by an old drum.

Their appearance was not less ludicrous than their music.

Some had petticoats and gowns, mounted with ribbons, drawn over them; others had shawls for sashes and hatbands.

The fool or harlequin was the most laughable of all. He had a mask made of an old hat, with holes for his eyes, nose, and mouth cut in it.

The front was painted red, with plenty of hair stuck to it with pitch.

Some stumps of quills protruded from the mouth for teeth, and his dress—this was the crowning point of all. He had an old red gown buttoned over his body It was split in the middle and the

lower part sewed over his legs to answer a trowsers
—something in the Turkish fashion.

His bare feet were painted red.

This fellow cut many antics and capers, and
showed his teeth in a manner to please the servants,
who had now collected from all parts to see them;
and I must say also that he amused our friends in
the window.

Mary Cahill went near him, when he ran to take
a kiss of her; this, of course, set Mary screaming,
and all the others laughing.

Another held the wren dressed out most gaudily
in a bush, and sang under the window:—

> "The wran, the wran, the king of all birds,
> St. Stephens' day he was caught in the furze;
> Altho' he is little, his honor is grate,
> So git up, madam, and give us a thralt."

"Why is he called the king of all birds?" said
Frank.

"Shure I'll tell your honor," said the other.
"You know, your honor, there was a great compe-
tishen intirely betune all the birds to know who'd
be king; well, they couldn't agree at all, so they settled that whatever bird could fly the highest he was
to be king. Begor, sur, the eagle was mighty proud
intirely, for he was shure of winnin'. 'Let ye's
all meet on such a day, and we'll set off together,'
says he. Well becomes them, they all assembled.
'Where are you goin'?' says he to the wran. 'Begor, to see the fun, your honor,' says the wran.

So they all laughed at the poor little wran. While they were gettin' ready, well becomes the wran he stuck himself in the fethers under the eagle's wing. 'Away now,' says the eagle. Shure after a time they all felt tired but the eagle, and he flew on until he got tired. 'I'm king now,' says he; 'I may go home; I am not able to go another peg.' 'Not yet,' said the wran, flying from under his wing as fresh as a daisy. Begor, the eagle was fit to be tied, he was so mad; but divil a use in it. That's the way he became king, you see. Throw something to the boys, your honor."

"Thank ye; long life to ye, and that ye may be all married this day twelvemonth. Begor, if we met every house as good as this, naboclish."

Mary and all the servants gave their mite to the wren-boys, who went off well pleased.

CHAPTER XV.

ALL the world knows that St. Patrick's day falls on the 17th of March, and that Irishmen revere the saint's memory with all due honors.

Mrs. Butler took care to have an additional supply of potteen, and a few barrels of beer in for the occasion.

A big red-nosed horseman swung over her door, with a pint of creamy ale in his hand, and announcing, "Entertainment for man and horse;" and a fiddler scraped away inside, to let people know that Mrs. Butler's establishment was alive and stirring.

Mrs. Butler came frequently to the door, and looked very anxiously about, and wondered people were not coming to pay their respects to the saint.

"The Lord be praised, what's become of the people, at all, at all; maybe it's haythens they will shortly become;" and Mrs. Butler looked askance at the two barrels of beer, and sighed at the growing depravity of the times. She then commenced practising a little sum in arithmetic on her fingers' ends.

"Fiveteen and fiveteen is thirty—thirty shillings ;

I want to know where it's to come from, though, if
they don't come to drink it; that's the thing; but
whist, here is somebody; och, shure it's only the
Rover." And Mrs. Butler sighed in a manner that
implied that the Rover was not likely to add much
to the required sum.

It so happened, too, that the Rover was after
making a resolution, that he would pass Mrs. Butler's house without going in to drink.

"Now," thought he to himself, "if she sees me,
she'll be out with me, and she's not a bad sort of
woman; and, faix, there she's at the door. O, murther, what will she think of me, at all, and there's
the music, too; bad cess to me, what a time I made
you."

"Good evenin', Mr. Delany," said Mrs. Butler, in
her blandest of tones.

"Good evenin', kindly, ma'am; how are you?"

"Well, thank you. Won't you come in?"

"I'm in a hurry, ma'am, I thank you."

"Well, I dunna what's the world coming to; look
at that fellow, that I often thrated to a shaugh and
a glass, too, and he wouldn't come in; well, well,"
and Mrs. Butler looked horribly shocked.

"What will I do?" said the Rover. "I have it;
shure I only promised to pass the house, I didn't
say anything about turning back,—well done, resolution, I will have a glass on the head of you;" and
he slapped his thigh, and returned to Mrs. Butler's
warm corner.

"Arrah, faith, I thought you warn't goin' to come in, Shawn," said Mrs. Butler.

"Faix, I thought so, too, myself, ma'am; shure I made a resolution not to come in, but I tricked it, though."

"Mr. Delany!" said Mrs. Butler, looking very dignified and highly offended—"Mr. Delany, would you have the condesenshun to tell me what I did to you, or what's to be laid at my dacent door, that you should make a resolution not to enter it; ay, Mr. Delany, would you tell me that? O, holy Mother! maybe it's resolutions them all made, oh, oh!"

It is strange how very polite people become when they wish to be otherwise; now, Mrs. Butler seldom addressed Mr. Delany otherwise than as Shawn; however, she emphatically addressed him now, Mr. Delany, and nodded her head at him with each word, and then raised a soiled red calico handkerchief to her eye.

"See, now, Mrs. Butler, sorra a one of me——"

"Oh, oh," sobbed Mrs. Butler, "any shlur to be thrown upon me dacent house and karakter. O, you ought to be ashamed of yourself, Mr. Delany."

"Arrah, hould your tongue, woman, and listen to rason; divil a shlur anyone could cast upon your house nor karakter either. Shure it is only the last seshins his lordship said to me, 'She keeps the dacentest house from this to Cashel.'"

"Did he say so, Shawn."

"Ay, faix I never sees anyone drunk nor shout

ing there; and shure if she sells a dhrop itself, she's a poor, lone widow, that must be let live," says he.

"Faix, his lordship is the right sort; not like other spalpeen magisthrates, that would be tryin' to hunt a poor, lone widow out o' the house," replied Mrs. Butler.

"True for you, ma'am. This fish makes a body very dry," and Shawn spat out a couple of times.

"Faix, it does, though; maybe you'd have a drink of beer, Shawn?"

"Wid pleasure, ma'am, if pleasing. Here is your health, ma'am, and that you may shortly have some one to mind the house for you."

"Git out, Shawn; shure it's not a woman of my age, after rearin' her family, you'd have thinkin' of the like."

"Why not, Mrs. Butler? there is Nell Croak, that got married the other day; I'd take the Bible, she is not a day under fifty; now, I'd swear you are not forty."

"Just forty-one next Lady-day, Shawn. I was married at eighteen, and my poor man is dead six years, God be good to him; he was the good man, Shawn;" here Mrs. Butler indulged in some lachry-mose reflections. "Ah, he was the kind husband, Shawn; shure, isn't it surprising, the impudence of some people, to think of Nelly Croak gettin' married; oh, oh, she's every day of fifty years, Shawn. Shure I recollect when she was a child I was a slip of thackeen myself; oh, oh, at her time of life; what's the world coming to ?"

Shawn was all this time taking an inventory of the stock of the concern, and just considering to himself, " wouldn't it be a great deal pleasanter to sit in his own corner, drinking Mrs. Butler's—Mrs. Delany's, though—porter, than be trudging from place to place ;" he appeared to have come to a very satisfactory conclusion, for he rubbed his hands and smiled.

"She's over sixty, though, as sure as she's a day ; what harm ? sure it's not I'll be picking her bones ; she has a snug house and place," said he to himself.

" Who could blame the poor woman after all," said Shawn, taking Mrs. Butler's hand affectionately in his ; " sure its pleasant to have one's own house."

" True for you, Shawn "—and Mrs. Butler looked about with an air of great satisfaction.

" To have some one to talk to—to keep us comfortable—to console us when sick, to——"

" Ah, Shawn, Shawn, you spake the truth," and the widow sighed at her own desolate condition.

" To have some one to cheer and console us in time of afflictions"—Shawn squeezed the widow's hand, and she looked gratefully to him—" to have," he continued, " to have some one to love, to "—— here his pathetic discourse was interrupted by shouts and laughter from the outside.

" They are coming, the Lord be praised," said Mrs. Butler, jumping up.

" Dhoul take them," muttered Shawn.

" Musha! ye'r welcome, boys; how is every mother's soul of ye," said Mrs. Butler to her new arrivals; "and the colleens, too, God bless them."

" What the dickens use wid we be widout the crathurs; throth they are the life and sowl of us, Mrs. Butler," said James Cormack, leading in Mary Cahill, smiling and blushing.

"Where's the musishiner? Oh, here he is stretched ashleep; get up, man alive, and give us a bhlast to warm our toes," and he shook the fiddler to waken him.

"Aye, what will ye have? Pathrick's day in the mornin', I suppose."

" That will do; up wid it; anything at all man, to knock the cobwebs from our hearts." Then four couples took the floor, and danced until they began to get wearied, when they were replaced by others.

" That's it, Mary, lie into it; deuce a bit but you'll tire him out."

' Success, Jem; don't be too hard upon the colleen."

" Musha then, that for his best!" says Mary, snapping her fingers playfully in his face.

" By my sowl, Mary, but I'll sober you before we lave the flure for all that."

" Faiks, avourneen, you may do your best; you never seen the day that you could beat a Cahill on the flure," and Mary strengthened her boast by a fresh display of agility.

"Arrah! Mary, alanna, is that it; sure you know the Cormack blood never gave in," and James, too, would improve his speed in heel and toe, and snap his fingers, as if in defiance.

"Success, Mary! he's flagging *a ban choir!* Lay to it James; bravo! whist!"

"I'll hould a gallon on Mary."

"Done! said another; a gallon out of James."

"No, boys, no," said James Cormack; "I think the colleen has enough of it; as for myself, *avourneen machree!* I have too much, so let us stop," and he took Mary by the hand.

"Ha, ha!" said Mary, with an arch smile, "I knew that my feet were too light for you, James."

"Sthrike up the fox-hunter's jig," said Shemus-a-Clough.

Shemus commenced dancing it by himself, keeping time to the music with his feet and club.

"Success, Shemus. Dhoul a better. Arrah! that's the music; you'd think it is the bow, bow, wow of the hounds you'd hear," said Shemus, all the time keeping his huge feet moving.

"Musha! isn't it pleasant; faith it would nearly make me jump through the windy: there it is again, bow, bow, wow, tallyho harkaway; here Dido, ho Juno, tallyho, tallyho, in the mornin'!" and Shemus finished his capers amid roars of laughter.

Reader, have you ever seen an Irish dance? It is none of your stately drawing-room affairs, where you lead your partner with slow and measured step through the mazes of a full set; no such thing. There they are, four, or perhaps eight couples, twisting, turning, capering, snapping their fingers, hitting their hams with their heels, in the full buoyancy of spirits.

"Musha! I think ye have enuff of it now for a sthart; arn't ye betther sit down and have a dhrink," said Mrs. Butler.

"I think so too, ma'am," said the Rover.

So they all sat down around a large table with their girls by their sides, and Mrs. Butler's flowing cans of ale and porter before them, to each and all of which they did ample justice.

After a time a voluable flow of soft nonsense, snatches of songs, and sundry hip, hip, hurras! gave forcible proofs of the strength of Mrs. Butler's drink, and also to the very decent manner in which the saint was treated. Shemus - a - Clough's voice rose like a little tempest above the rest, as he mingled snatches of his favorite hunting songs with others in honor of the saint—

> "Harkaway, harkaway, tallyho, my boys!
> I hear the cry of the fox and hounds."

> "The seventeenth of March is Pathrick's day,
> And he was the great saint of our isle,
> Shure never a wor.' to us does he say,
> While we are drinkin' and sportin' the while."

> "Say your prayers, the huntsman said,
> Before the hounds will tear you;
> I have no prayers, poor Reynard said,
> For I was bred a Quaker.
> Harkaway, tallyho, harkaway!

"O, you wor the saint, acushla macbree;
To handle an alpeen, shure you wor able;
You hunted our varmint, and allowed us a sphree.
Here's your health, while there's a dhrop on the table,
Cead mille falthe, a cushla machree
　　Whooroo, tallyho, harkaway,
　　　　Sweet Tipperary and the skhy over it!"

"That's a purty song, Shemus," said one.

"It is, the Lord be praised; but it is so hard to sing the two together; you see the hounds, bad scran to thim, do be running in on the saint."

"Never mind, Shemus, he'll keep out of their way."

"Faith he ought, for Dido would not respect him one bit. Shure one day she caught myself in the kennel, and she ought to know me betther than the saint."

"Will you go to the election, Shemus," said another.

"Faiks an' that I will; didn't Father Phil say to-day that every one ought to go and not allow themselves to be walked over, and driven like so many pigs by shooneen landlords and agents."

"It's hard for the people to know what to do, boys," said James Cormack; "there is Mr. Ellis after sending word to all the tenants to vote for Sir W. Crasly, and there is the priest after advising the people to vote against him. Now, if the people vote against the landlord, they are shure of being turned out, and if they vote for him, or his man, rather, they are shure to be ballaraged by the priest."

11

"It is unpleasant business, no doubt," said Ned Burkem; "I'm thinking of giving up my situation; I never felt anything so much as to have to go and tell the tenants to vote against themselves and their priest."

"It is hard enuff on you, Ned," said another; "but shure you can't help it; and if you left, they would get some one else; so you might as well keep your place."

"Sorra a one of me would keep it twenty-four hours, only that I can do some little good for the tenants, now and then."

"Good luck to you, Ned, there is nothing like the kind word."

"Are all the tenants to meet at Mr. Ellis's, Ned?" said another.

"They are to be there on Tuesday morning, at eight o'clock; that is the word he sent, and to have them not disappoint at their peril; if they do, they know what will happen them."

"It is a drole country," said the Rover; "the landlord ought to tell the tenant that he must get his vote as well as his rent. If he made these conditions when lettin' the land the thing would not be so bad afterwards. I know if I had a vote, I'd see him to the dhoul before I'd give it to him. Ay, indeed, vote for a man to tyrannize over yourself and your religion!"

"Thrue for you, Shawn; thrue for you!" was the exclamation of the whole party.

"We are low-lived fellows to put up wid it," said a little fellow with a lame leg.

"What can we do?" said another.

"Not to let the voters go wid thim," said the Rover.

"All balderdash," said another; "how soft you sphake."

"Faith, maybe it's no balderdash at all!" said a young fellow, who, with his hands leaning on the table, was silently listening all through; but who now raised his head, and there was a flashing kind of anger in his eye, "maybe it's no balderdash at all!" and he slapped the table with his clenched hand.

"Pooh! what could you do, Lawlor?" said another.

"We could rescue them; shure, I know that the poor wretches of tenants must go against their grain."

"Bravo, Bill," said Burkem; "give me the hand! I wished I could join ye; but ye see I must be on the other side; but, faith, if it comes to a fight, I know who I will help," and he gave a nod, as much as to say, depend upon me boys.

"Come, boys, we have eьuff about it, let us have a song or a story. Did I ever tell ye how I made a teetotler of the greatest drunkard in the whole country."

"No, no, Shawn; out wid it."

"Hem! ha! I'll drink yer health, boys, first, and

then the story—mighty good drink it is, the Lord
be praised." Shawn hem'd and ha'd, and wiped his
mouth with his sleeve, and then commenced :—

"'Tis, let me see, about twenty years gone, since
I was working at the Mardyke colliery. One day a
man was passin' by, in a car, and he blind dhrunk.
The mule stood grazin' about the banks of the pit.
I went over, but not a stir was in him. So as I was
always fond of a joke, I got some of the boys to take
him down into the pit with me. When we reached
the bottom, we took him about two hundred yards
farther, and then tied chains to his hands and feet.
He slept very soundly for about two hours ; when
he came to himself he thought he was in the mule's
car. 'Prooh ! prooh !' said he. He then felt the
chains. So he rubbed his eyes, tried to look about,
rattled his chains, but could make nothing of it ; he
was perfectly bewildered. 'Where am I?' said he
to himself ; then he felt himself, to make sure of his
identity, and felt the place about him to see could
he make out where he was, but he was still in the
dark. He reflected. Could it be that he had died
in his drink and that he was in hell. 'Oh, wurra,
wurra,' said he, 'what will become of my poor wife
and childers ; oh, wurra, wurra ; Lord, have mercy .
upon me, a poor sinner ; O, the darlins, what will
they do after me,—and to die in my drink ; heaven
have. mercy upon me ! O, Kitty, alanna, will you
forgive me all I ever drank upon you and the poor
childer. O the darlins, what will they do after me ?

O, holy Mother, intercede for me: oh, oh,' and he
commenced a regular course of tears, prayers, and
lamentations. After having prayed and cried himself just sick, he began to think. 'It's a curious
place, anyway; I wonder is there anyone here but
myself; well, I might as well see.' In attempting
to stand up, he knocked his head against the roof,
with such force, that he fell back again. 'Oh,
wurra, wurra, I am kilt now or never. Oh, murther, murther; my head is smashed. O, holy Saint
Joseph, protect me; where am I, at all; it's as dark
as pitch, and if I sthir, maybe it is into some hole
I'd rowl. O, Lord, O, Lord, have mercy upon me!
oh, what will I do, at all, at all; O, Kitty, alanna; if
I had you here to console me, asthore!' and he sat
down sobbing and lamenting. I stuck some candles
in my old hat, and tied chains to my body, and
crept on all fours towards him. My face and body
all covered with culm, the candles' glimmering light,
and the rattling chains, made him take me for the
devil. As I approached, he threw himself upon his
knees before me exclaiming, 'My lord, spare me,
and tell me where I am, or what brought me here?'
'Don't you see you are in hell?' said I, making my
voice as strong as possible. 'O, Lord, have mercy
upon me! am I to remain here always?' 'You are
to remain here until your body is buried; you are
then to be removed to a place filled with never-
quenching fire.' 'Oh, Mr. Devil,' says he, 'och,
darlin'! what will become of my poor wife and chil-

ders?' 'How do I know?' says I; 'I am only the porter here; however, I can tell you that your wife will shortly be married again, and that your children will have to look sharp.' 'O, God help them.' 'Now, don't be mentionin' the name of God, if you plaze,' says I, very angrily. 'No, your honor, if you wish it; but you said that my body was to be buried, but here I am, body and all.' 'You are not well dead yet, man; but when your body is buried upon earth, you will depart from it here and go to hell, for ever and ever.' He burst into tears, and bewailed all his past crimes and sins; he beat his breast and tore his hair; he appeared in the greatest anguish and terror. 'O, my wife and childers, I have been a bad husband and father to you; I have spent your means in drink and folly. O, Lo——, ah yes, what can I do? oh, oh; if I could see ye again, oh, how changed I'd be.' So great was his paroxysm of grief, that I took compassion upon him.

'Have you any money?' said I to him. 'I had five shillings when I died; I can't say I have it now.' 'Search your pockets.' 'Begad, here it is, your honor.' 'Well, give me that; perhaps I could do something to get you out of this, for the devils scarcely know you are here at all; so if you promise to mend your life, I might get you off.' He threw himself upon his knees, exclaiming, 'May God Almighty bless you; 'tis I will make the good, kind husband and father; and divil,—oh, I beg pardon—

sorra a dhrop of whiskey I will ever touch agin'.'
' Well, take care,' says I, ' and keep this in token of
your promise,' and I gave him a purse with an old
coin in it. I then went and brought the worth of
the five shillings of whiskey for the boys ; I brought
down some that I mixed with tincture of opium, and
gave it to him to drink. After drinking some, he
remarked, 'Isn't this very like the whiskey we had
on earth. Och, but I'd nearly swear they are the
same ; no matter, shure I had better dhrink, anyway ; your health, your honor,' and he finished his
pint. He shortly began to sing and shake hands
with me ; calling me a good kind of a poor divil ;
then, when it began to work, he fell asleep. We
then quietly hauled him up, and placed him in the
car, and turned the mule homewards, for some of
the men knew him.

" When he went home, they took him out of the
car, and put him to bed; he shortly awoke, and
casting his eyes fearfully around, he asked where he
was. 'Shure, you are at home, in your own warm
bed, achorra,' says his wife. He rubbed his eyes.
I can scarcely believe it ; am I alive at all, or who   !
are you, woman ?' 'Oh, avourneen, I am your poor
wife ; don't you know me ?' Well, well, I don't
know what to say,' and he felt for the purse ; 'there
you are, shure enough ; all I can say, if I am alive,
I am afther comin' out of hell, thanks be to God.
The wife, hearing this, and seeing his wild looks,
called in the neighbors. .They all collected, and

hearing him rave, as they thought, about the horrors of hell, and the like, nodded at one another and tapped their foreheads, as much as to say, 'he's not right here, poor fellow.' At length he gave such good accounts of the place, and exhibited the purse, as corroborative evidence, some began to think that perhaps he was taken there for a start in punishment for his sins; anyway, from that forward, he became a changed man, and led a pious, sober, good life. He is firmly resolved that the devil shan't catch him again. He often tells the story about his journey to hell; and if any one doubts him, he shows the purse he got from the devil, in confirmation of it. Who can doubt such evidence, particularly, as it was all black; but some malicious people said it was with culm. No matter, his wife and childers bless the day that I took him to hell."

"Faiks, you were better than Father Matthew to him, Shawn," said one.

"Strange things happen," said Mr. Freany; a little withered specimen of a fairy doctor, that had come to the neighborhood to practice his healing art upon some cows.

"Ah, it's you knows that, Mr. Freany," said Mrs. Butler, with great deference; "shure they say you see the good people walkin' about."

"Indeed I do, ma'am," said Mr. Freany; "they are about the room here this blessed minute; there is one little dawny fellow drinking out of your tumbler, Mrs. Butler."

"Lord protect us," exclaimed Mrs. Butler, drawing back, and making the sign of the cross upon her forehead.

"Don't be afear'd, ma'am, he'll do you no harm; he is an innocent fellow; but there is a schemer trying to take a kiss from Miss Cahill." Mary bounced aside, and somehow into James Cormack's arms, who, I must say, took the start of the amorous fairy.

Mr. Freany was distinguished in his way: he could cure the fairy-stricken; he could bring back butter, milk, or any other property unlawfully abstracted by these thieving little gentlemen. He certainly managed his business iu a manner to impose upon the poor credulous peasantry. He lived near Killough Hill, a hill, he asserted, that grew all the "harbs" that were required in fairy medicine. His cabin contained two rooms; the inner one was separated, by a thin boarding, from the outer. When any person came for Mr. Freany he was sure to be from home. His mother, in the meantime, drew a full history of the disease from the visitor. Mr. Freany was all the time listening with his ear quite near the speaker; he then passed into an out-house, by a private door from the room, and went into the fields. The mother went out and ran in again. "Thank God, you're in luck; he's coming. You might as well go out and meet him." Our dupe goes out and finds Mr. Freany on the side of the hill picking herbs, and laughing to himself. "Stay

back, honest man, I know what you want." And
then he would relate all the particulars of the disease, whether of person or beast, with an accuracy
to astonish the other, and make him look up to him
as infallible. When he went home he told how he
knew the disease, the times the fits seized the patient, and the like unto his friends ; so Mr. Freany
became famous, and lived well upon the credulity of
his dupes.

Mr. Freany's class is now fast disappearing. However harmless they were in themselves, they were
mischievous to society at large.

"Faiks, Mr. Freany, it is not pleasant to have
them so near a body," said Mrs. Butler.

"Sorra a haporth they'll do to you, ma'am ; they
are the quiet, tricksy creatures unless they are vexed,
then, nabocklish !"

"Faiks, I believe they are dangerous, then, Mr.
Freany," said a wag who had little faith in their
boasted powers.

"Dangerous, you may well say that. I recollect
I was sent for to cure a man, not far from this,
either. He was one night walkin' out, when he heard
the tramp of people comin' towards him ; he waited
until they came up, and there they were, a dacent
funeral. 'God save ye, neighbors,' says he, goin'
over and puttin' his shoulder under the bearer.
With that they all gave a shout, and left him, coffin
and all. When he opened the coffin there was a
stump of a stick in it. He took to the bed. I

couldn't do anything for him ; he was too far gone when they sent for me. Another man came to me. His cows used be always milked by a white hare. I told him to go home, and when the cows would be milking to put the coulter in the fire, and then have some fast dogs and hunt the hare. They did so, and the dogs come up to her and tore a piece out of her leg ; however, she escaped and ran into a house ; they followed her, and instead of the hare there was an old woman stretched on the bed all covered with blood. The cows were not milked any more."

" Here, Mrs. Butler, this talking is dry work ; bring us more drink," said James Cormack.

Mrs. Butler went to the kegs and found them empty. Mrs. Butler was not sorry for this, for she found that their money was all spent, and the only payment she got for the last two gallons were some strokes of chalk upon the back of a board. Mrs. Butler returned empty.

" Sorra another dhrop in it, James," said she.

" No matter ; bring us a drop of the hard stuff."

" O, holy mother! do you hear this. Going to drink sthrong spirits after two half barrels of beer."

" Come, come, ma'am ; let us have it."

" Sorra a drop, James, sorra a drop ; I wouldn't have it for a sin on my sowl. So go home now, like dacent boys. Shure ye wouldn't be keepin' the colleens out any longer."

All remonstrances were useless with Mrs. Butler ; for she knew that she had emptied their pockets.

But her chief defence was "the colleens. Shure it was time for dacent girls of karakter to go home."

The dacent girls supported Mrs. Butler; so the lords of creation were forced to yield to such influence.

"Oh, milla murther!" said the Rover, as he ploppsed into a lough, on his way home. "Och, holy Saint Pathrick! look at all I am suffering on your account."

He then staggered across the road into another.

"Och, blessed saint! look at that agin. Shure I am earnin' you well!"

And as the Rover took a dive into almost every hole on the way home, he certainly brought the saint under a very heavy obligation; which I am sure he will honorably acknowledge when he meets our friend above.

CHAPTER XVI

HOW WE MANAGE ELECTIONS IN IRELAND—LORD CLEAR-
ALL'S OPINION OF PRIESTS AND PEOPLE—HOW TEN-
ANTS' CONSCIENCES SHOULD BE MANAGED.

CLEAR CASTLE, as Lord Clearall's princely residence was called, was beautifully and romantically
situated. It was built upon a rising ground; and
commanded a wide view of a fertile and picturesque
extent of country. The extensive lawn was inter-
sected with roads and avenues, and adorned with
stately oaks and sycamores.

A pleasant little river babbled on its way by the
castle and pleasure grounds, now shaded by the
overhanging trees on its banks, and then prattling
through some rocky glen. I might apply to it the
words of the poet :—

> " Sweet are thy paths, oh passing sweet!
> By ———— fair streams that run
> O'er airy steep, through copsewoods deep,
> Impervious to the sun."

As we have nothing to say to the river, and little
to say to Lord Clearall, but what we can learn of
him through his worthy agent, we will not take up
the time of our readers with one or the other.
However, we must introduce our readers into his

lordship's study ; where himself, his agent, and Sir
W. Crasly are making arrangements for the coming
campaign.   The library was a fine, spacious room,
well furnished with richly-bound books, easy chairs,
lounges, and the like, as if the muses were to be
wooed and won in ease and luxury.

His lordship was seated in an easy chair, at the
head of the table.   Near him sat Mr. Ellis, looking
over some accounts; whilst Sir W. Crasly reclined
on a lounge near the window, apparently watching
some orange and lemon trees, that were peeping
out of the conservatory into the library window.
There were several busts, on marble pedestals, of
his lordship's noble ancestors around the room ;
these, too, seemed to occupy much of the honorable
gentleman's attention.   Perhaps, he was thinking
how distinguished he would look in effigy, one of
those fine days—for he had little doubt that, as
soon as he got into parliament (of which he had no
doubt at all) he would so astonish the conglom-
erated wisdom of England, that he would be honored with a niche among the penates of his lordly
friends.   It is no wonder that he should think so
well of himself, for he had spent four years in Ox-
ford, and got a medal in oratory, after reading a
speech that a poor plebeian, with more brains than
cash, composed for a consideration.   He should
have graduated, also, if he got his merit ; and, to do
him justice, there was not a better player at tennis,
or fives, or a more expert intriguer in the college.

He had now come to start his oratorical wares
among the "hignorant Hirish." Sir W. Crasly was
something of a Cockney in his way. He was a
young man of some note in London ; a great favorite with the ladies, as he had considerable property
in possession and more in expectation. He was, indeed, a very eligible match, and as his heart was
rather soft and sentimental, many a penniless beauty
had laid her snares to entrap him. He had never
been in Ireland before, though he had considerable
possessions in it : but he left the uncontrolled management of his estates to his agent, who liberally
fleeced the poor tenants to feather his own nest. It
is true, he had a great dread of the Irish ; for, from
all he had read about their cold-blooded murderous
crimes and assassinations, all of which were en-
dorsed by his agent, who did not wish him to come
over, perhaps to frustrate his own comfortable system of managing his property, he concluded that
they were a very "hignorant, barbarous set." He
thought that he conferred a great favor on them by
coming to misrepresent them, and wondered with
what apathy they were receiving him.

"Well, are they ready, Mr. Ellis?" said his lordship, looking up impatiently from a book he was
reading.

"Yes, my lord. Shall I trouble you to look over
it?"

"Certainly ; though, no—let me see what's the
gross amount? I hate poring over accounts—twenty

thousand three hundred and twenty-one! Why Mr. Ellis, at my father's death the rental was nearly two thousand more. Now, after ejecting the old tenants, we have spent about ten thousand on building houses and improving the land, and what have we got in return from your cannie Scotch friends?"

"You must consider, my lord, the improved state of the land, with its elegant farm-houses and fences, when compared with the barren, impoverished state it was in when we got it up."

"Certainly, there is an improvement that way; but then a reduction of nearly two thousand, beside the outlay and interest of nearly ten more, is a great drawback. Shure, these fellows, the old tenants, I mean, said they would build houses and drain the land if we but gave them leases."

"You couldn't believe a word they say, my lord. They promise you everything, but perform very little. They are a thriftless, idle race."

"I think, Clearall," said Sir W. Crassly, with a yawn, "you are better not interfere with them. That is just what my agent says to me; and he knows them better than we do. Your Scotch tenants will have a beneficial effect upon the Hirish. I declare, I never saw prettier farmer's places than you have about here."

"Yes, your honor; his lordship knows what kind of a wild place this was twenty years since. Now, look at it; is it not an honor to his lordship?" said Mr. Ellis.

"Yes, indeed; and you have a devilish pretty little place, too, Mr.—Mr.—what I call you?"

"Ellis," suggested his lordship.

"Ay, Mr. Ellis."

Mr. Ellis winced a little at this, but composedly answered: "Yes, your honor; thanks to his lordship's kind patronage and encouragement, and to my own industry."

"What are we to do with these Ballybruff tenants, Mr. Ellis?" said his lordship. "I think you were telling me something about serving them with notices to quit, or the like."

"Yes, my lord; there is a year's rent due on the whole property. You know it is sub-divided into small farms—even adjoining the demesne."

"But have they not paid you some rent lately. I see their names here on the rent roll," and he pointed to the sheet before him.

"Yes, my lord, near a year's rent; but there is another due, and they havn't the means of meeting it. Why, it was cows and geese they offered me to make up the last year's; besides, my lord, it interferes with the appearance of the property very much. I was, the other day, travelling with a gentleman from Scotland, 'Who owns this estate?' said he, pointing to some cabins; 'isn't it a sin to see such fine land going waste?' I declare, my lord, I was ashamed to own it was yours."

Lord Clearall took great pride in the embellishment of his house and grounds; and as Mr. Ellis knew this to be his weak point, he took advantage of it.

"Why not knock them down, and build good slate houses?" said our would-be legislator.

"Well, well; do as you please, Mr. Ellis," said his lordship.

"I think, Clearall, we shouldn't interfere in those things at all," said Sir W. Crasly.

"Well, perhaps you are right, Crasly," said his lordship, in a dubious tone, as if there was something wrong somewhere.

"Have you noticed all the tenants about the election, Mr. Ellis?"

"Yes, my lord."

"Well?"

"A good many promised; others said that it would be hard for them to go against the priest and their conscience."

"Priests and conscience the devil!" exclaimed his lordship, with great warmth. "I don't see why these popish priests should be poking their noses into everything; as for conscience, what conscience have they but the priest's? I tell you, Ellis—and tell them so—we will level the houses over every mother soul of them if they don't vote for us; and then let their priests give them a living."

"I think, Clearall," said Sir W. Crasly, "that there should be a law passed to make priests stick to their psalms. I know I will introduce one, and also one to abolish Maynooth, that hotbed of priestcraft."

"They are a meddling set, Crasly," said his lordship. "Just think you, one of them has written a whole lot of letters about me for turning out some lazy tenants; as if a man couldn't do what he likes with his own. Why, they would fain manage our properties for us."

"Ay, and pocket the proceeds to say masses to send us to heaven," said the honorable gentleman, with a laugh at his witticism, in which laugh his lordship and Mr. Ellis joined.

"I tell you what, Ellis," said his lordship, "send them word again that you will have cars ready for them at your place on Tuesday morning, and mark the men that refuse. Curse them, to refuse voting as I bid them, and I giving them a living; well, let them try it, though!"

"I would make examples of them for others. I had some fellows on my property that refused voting as I bade them; my agent cleared them off at once, except a few that had leases. I think, Clearall, a man shouldn't give leases at all, it makes these fellows so independent; I like to keep the lash hand over them, you see," said the honorable gentleman. His lordship was all this time walking up and down the library in a great fume, to think that his slaves dared gainsay his will—that they dare vote but as he willed and wished; so his lordship said nothing for a considerable time but "Hang them! hang them, priests and all! the ungrateful lot! but let them try it though. I tell you what,

Ellis, go to them, and say that I sent them word to
vote for my friend, and if not, let them be ready to
march ; do your business, Mr. Ellis, and my friend
here and I will recommend you to his Excellency to
be appointed a J. P."

"Certainly, Mr. ——. Oh, yes, Ellis, his Excellency is a particular friend of mine ; will feel
devilish happy to do that for me," drawled Sir W.
Crasly.

Mr. Ellis took his leave ; he was in a fix ; he was
ambitious of the honor of gaining the bench, yet he
wished that the tenants should not support Lord
Clearall's friends, as this would show his lordship
what an ungrateful set they were, and set aside any
qualms he might entertain as to the propriety of
getting rid of them ; however, ambition triumphed.

It is needless to recapitulate the fine promises
made by the rival candidates and their friends—the
very handsome and polite compliments they paid
one another. Sir W. Crasly came forward on true
conservative principles. He was for reform, for free
trade, for running canals through the country to
drain the land, and make every inland town a mari-
time one. He liked religious equality ; it was a
good thing ; everyone should be allowed to use
their own religion ; but then, he hoped, in his heart,
he wouldn't meet any troublesome papists in heaven.
He was for supporting the viceroyalty, for he expected to honor Ireland by becoming Lord Lieutenant some fine day. On the other hand, his hon-

orable opponent cajoled his dupes with far more
liberal promises. To' the speculating and selfish,
he held out, in a private way, the bait of colonial
and custom-house appointments ; to the patriotio
and no-compromise class, ay, he was the man for
them. " He would not sleep quietly on his bed ; he
would not look upon himself as a freeman possessing a nationality until he wrung from an alien parliament, Repeal of the Union ;" loud cheers, and
cries of bravo, you're the man for us. "Dublin
must become in every sense the capital of Ireland,
ay, of Europe. Our absentees must return to enrich
it by spending their money there—money they have
dragged out of the hard industry of the toiling
peasant ; trade and commerce must be restored ;
the people must be secured from tyranizing landlords, of which,. unfortunately, we have too many.
Our towns will flourish again ; industry and capital
will combine to enrich ; in fact we must enjoy the
millennium of Irish prosperity ; and how is all this
to be achieved? only the one way my friends, by
repeal of the Union ; then let your motto be, repeal
and no surrender! hurra for repeal!"

If cheers and shouts be any criterion of the
good effects of a speech, Sir William Placeman must
be highly gratified at the stunning effects of his
oration.

"Repeal, my friends," he continued, "is the grand
panacea of all our evils ; it will make of us a free
people, inhabiting a free nation—

Great, glorious and free,
First flower of the earth
And first gem of the sea.'

And this is to be gained by returning men true to
the cause and country; men who will spurn place
and pension to serve their country.   Let ye have no
placemen ; hunt them from the hustings ; cry them
down.   Make every man, who would have the honor
of representing you, pledge himself to independent
opposition, *as I do now, so help me God!*   Independent opposition means opposition to every government that will not grant tenant right and repeal of
the Union.   There is an old adage, 'tell me your
company, and I'll tell you what you are.'   Now, who
are Sir W. Crasly's companions, why, my Lord
Clearall, that has made eviction a plaything; that
has cleared his estates of most of the Catholic tenantry to make room for Scotch settlers; but the
honorable gentleman has a happy knack of clearing
his estates himself, and need not get any lesson from
his lordship, on the rights of property, which means
the clearance system.   In sober seriousness, I do not
for a moment think that there is a man among ye
that would vote for one who is the sworn enemy of
your race, your religion, and your country.   You
tell me you will be forced to do so—forced! nonsense ; stand together as men should do, and if
violence should be used, have you not strong arms
to resist force by force."   If he didn't get an ovation
of cheers, it is a queer thing; and then the people

went home to prepare their sticks and rusty pieces, to repel, according to his precepts, force by force. If I were to give you all the cajoling speeches made by both parties and their friends, and all the rival puffs by rival editors, for which they were well paid, no doubt, both in cash and with the handsome perspective of a snug berth, somewhere ; if I were to give you all these, I should give a chapter to themselves, or rather one to each candidate and his friends.

An Irish election, and I believe an English one, too, produces much rowing, drinking, and ill-will in the country. Irish elections, though, are losing a great deal of their boisterous spirit now, for the people are becoming quite indifferent as to who is returned. They find one class of candidates radically opposed to their interest, and the other but waits for a good market to sell them to the best advantage.

On the election morning, Mr. Ellis had a large number of jaunting cars, and vehicles of every description, ready to convey the voters to be polled.

There was a breakfast of cold meat, and plenty of bread and beer, ready for all. There was a motley group of Scotchmen, Protestant dependents, and a fair sprinkling of Catholics ; the former laughed and ate with great gusto, the latter held down their heads, and slunk into corners. At length the procession formed into marching order. A huge four-horse car led the van ; Mr. Baker, Mr. Ellis, Hugh

Pembert, and several others, all well armed, occupied this.   They had neither banners nor music, as they wished to get off as noiselessly as possible ; for, notwithstanding all their preparations, they did not feel too safe.   They knew that they had boasted for weeks before that they would go in spite of the people—ay, and drive the tenants with them, too When our party came near the village of Straggle-town, their way was blocked up by a large pile or barricade of stones, placed across the road.   A number of people, armed with pitchforks, picks, and old guns, were crowded behind these, who raised a shout of defiance, and whirled their rude weapons about.

"What do ye want ?" said Mr. Ellis, standing up on the car.

"What do we want, indeed !   We want to have ye go home, with the few honest men ye forced wid ye."

"We're not forcing any one," said Mr. Ellis ; "any one that likes may go home."

"Ay, but dare they," shouted the crowd. "Shure if they did, they wouldn't have a roof to cover them shortly."

"Come, come !   Remove these obstructions; if not, we will force our way.   We are well armed."

"So are we, honey.   Take your ease, Mr. Ellis ; it's not a house you are going to level now, avick machree."

"Get down, boys," said Mr. Ellis to some of his

men, "and remove these; we are well armed; this is the queen's highway, so we will pass in spite of them. So get your arms ready."

A wild, derisive shout from the crowd followed this announcement.

"Oh! stop, stop, for God's sake!" said Mr. Baker; "let us turn back, or let me stick myself somewhere. Oh! oh! I knew it would come to this. Oh! the d——d papists will murder every mother soul of us. Oh! boys, honey, don't do anything rash!"

"Ha! ha! ha! poor Jack Baker," shouted the crowd. "Where are all you ever killed now of the d——d papists? We will pay you back now."

"Oh! sorra a one I ever killed; I wouldn't hurt a hair of your heads," shouted Mr. Baker.

"Mr. Baker, you may return, if you choose," said Mr. Ellis, "or hide in the well of the car there; it is spacious enough. As for me, I am resolved to go on, in spite of these dogs, too; so, boys, get ready, and the first man that prevents the obstructions being removed, I'll pop him."

"Hurrah! hip, hurrah! for Mr. Ellis," derisively shouted the crowd. "Arrah, he is the man to knock the house over the poor, God bless him. Shure it is the great change since he came here with the bag on his back, now to be at the head of a lot of blues, driving poor Catholic tenants to vote for their enemies. Arrah! we'll teach you a lesson now, Sawney."

"Clear away these stones, boys," shouted Mr.

12

Ellis to his men, who had all collected about him
" and let us see who will prevent ye."

"Faith, Mr. Ellis, avourneen, maybe it's the day-
light will be shining through your ugly carcass, if
you attempt firin'," shouted the mob.

"We'll give up the Catholics; sure we don't want
to take the decent men against their will," said Mr.
Baker.

"Hold your tongue, if you please, Mr. Baker.
We will give up nothing, but force our way through
them," said Mr. Ellis, very resolutely.

A large crowd had now collected at both sides of
the barricade ; women and children joined in a regular chorus of screams ; with the shouts of the men
at one side, whilst the party at the other was making
the best possible display of their guns to intimi-
date the others.   Some now began to tear away the
stones and blocks, and a regular hand to hand melee
ensued.   Clods, dirt, and stones, were flung at the
voters. Mr. Ellis took mark at a man that appeared
a leader, and fired ; the man fell.   A shout of execration and fury ran through the crowd.

"Lawlor is shot; let us have revenge; hurrah!
down with the Orangemen," was the wild cry of the
people, and they made a dash with stones and other
missiles at their enemies. Those near the barricade
dashed over it and grappled the guns of the others.
Shots were fired by both parties, and a desperate
conflict ensued. Mr. Ellis got a blow of a stone,
and was knocked off the car. His servants dragged

him to the rear. Mr. Baker availed himself of Mr. Ellis's advice, and stuffed himself into the well of the car, taking care to draw the lid after him. It now became a scene of fearful strife and confusion. The struggling and curses of the men were enlivened by shots and raps of stones, joined with the screams of women and children. Horses, too, in their fright, dragged their cars against each other ; some were rolled into the dykes, whilst others turned back and fled. The people began to collect in multitudes from the neighboring country, and Mr. Ellis's party, seeing that they were getting the worst of it, and that reinforcements were arriving, began to retreat. Some ran into houses, some unharnessed horses, and jumped on their backs ; others trusted to their feet. Mr. Ellis's servants secured a car for himself and his friends, and, having collected a body-guard of cavaliers, mounted on horses with their harness dashing around them, they effected a beautiful retreat.

A party of policemen came up in time to cause a diversion in favor of the flying enemy ; otherwise, they would not have been so successful.

The people now hurrahed and cheered in the wild frenzy of victory. They dashed the cars about —they dragged them into the village and piled them together, and then threw a few loads of turf among them, and set fire to all.

"Sthop!" said Shemus-a-Clough ; "I must break up this ould divil of a car," and Shemus mounted it, and began to strike at it vigorously.

Shemus struck one blow upon the well, which shattered it in pieces. A deep groan resounded from the inside. Shemus staggered back with affright.

"Lord have mercy on me! Sure I didn't do anything, at all, at all!" said the voice from the well.

"Who is it?" "Drag him out!" "Set fire to him!" shouted the mob.

"It's I," said the voice. "For the love of God, spare me. I didn't do anything. Sure I am here all the time.

"Who are you, man alive? Come out, and let us see your purty face."

"O! don't ye know me? I am your friend, Mr. Baker; that never harmed anybody."

"Ha, ha, ha! You that killed so many of us, to call yourself our friend. Faith, that's a good joke, anyway."

"Throw in the fire on top of the ould sinner." "Roast him alive." "Let us put it under him, though, and give him time to repent. That's more than he did to the poor men he shot."

"O! good people, spare me, for the love of God. Let me out! I never shot a man in all my life. No; I wouldn't. Sure it is only a way of talking I had. O! holy Joseph, will ye roast me alive!"

Now, in justice to the mob, they had not the least notion of injuring Mr. Baker, for they knew his cowardly, harmless disposition too well; however, they were resolved to enjoy his misery for a time.

Mr. Baker, all this time, lay on his back in the

well; his face was turned up, so that he could see the brands of fire moving to and fro, and believing every minute that they would be hurled in on him. He prayed, and cursed, and thick perspiration ran down his body.

"Can't you come out until we see you?"

"Gog, gog! I can't; for the love of heaven pull me out!"

"Put plenty of fire under him, and smoke him out," said a man with an old musket in his hand, and he winked at the others.

"He is fine and fat; it's no harm to take a little of the sap out of him," said a little thin man, leaning on a crutch.

"Och, murther, murther! the savages. O gog, isn't there any one to save me! Gog, gog! but I'll hang every mother soul of the d——d pa——; no, I won't, though. Oh! will ye roast me alive?"

"Since you'd hang us, we are better, Mr. Baker."

"Oh! devil take me tongue; sure, I didn't know what I was saying. I swear by the holy Bible, that I won't hang one of you. Give me the Bible, and I'll take my oath on it."

"Here are the police, here are the police!" shouted the women.

"Deuce take them, they should come to spoil our fun; but if they don't go back quicker than they come, nabocklish."

The police, having heard of Mr. Baker's situation, resolved to make an attempt to rescue him.

"We only want to get Mr. Baker," said the sergeant.

"Oh, we will thrate him dacently, if ye let us along," said the mob.

"Let him come with us, then," said the sergeant.

"Divil a step, unless we like it ourselves; we have the upper hand now, and will keep it; hurrah, hurrah! down with the bloody police."

"Halloo, gog, don't leave me here, the bloody papists. Oh, they will burn me,—I mean, if ye leave me here; I am burning, as it is," shouted Mr. Baker, with all his might.

"Do ye hear what he calls us? d——d papists," said an old woman with a goggle eye, and a few teeth in the front of her mouth.

"Arrah, honey, as you're burning, I'll cool you," said another, dashing the contents of a chamber vessel in his face.

"Och, murther, murther; I am smothered;" and Mr. Baker began to cough and curse, alternately. "Ugh, ugh, ugh; oh, I'm smothered. Gog, but they'll burn me, the savages. Oh, the damned pa——, ugh, ugh; for the love of God, will ye let me out of this, ye raps?"

"Oh, holy Mother! do ye hear what he calls us? 'raps,' enagh; I want to know who was the rap, but his own thief of a mother? Oh, but burnin' is too good for him."

"Oh, no, I didn't mean it; ye are the decent

women, every mother's soul of ye; let me out and I'll give ye all I have."

While Mr. Baker was keeping up this parley with the women, a regular fight was going on between the police and the men. The mob rushed on them with stones, shafts of cars, burning brands, and the like; and before they had time to fire a shot, the guns were dashed out of their hands, and themselves hunted into the barrack, which was soon demolished about their ears.

During the conflict, Mr. Baker was in a terrible suspense. If he encouraged the police, and if that they were beaten, he feared the people would revenge it upon him; again, if he encouraged the people, it would look like treason, so he compromised the matter, by calling out—

"Och, murther, do you hear that rapping? oh, these women will burn me. Gog, they will kill one another. That's it, stick the bloody pa——, ahem. Oh, boys, honey, don't ye kill one another. Shure, they will let me out of this. Why don't ye fire, ye cowards — that's, I mean — don't, don't kill the bloody pa——, ahem—that's, gog, what on earth am I saying?"

Now, a bright thought struck him, so he appealed to the women.

"Och, honeys, darling! will ye let me out; all this fighting is on my account; shure, I'll make peace."

Some of the women, whose friends were engaged,

tore open the well, and dragged him, half dead, from it.

"Run, now, Mr. Baker, for the love of God, and make peace."

Mr. Baker did run, as well as he was able, but it was into a house, where he ensconced himself under a bed, from which he did not stir until the appearance of a troop of dragoons in the village. This fight was a great epoch in Mr. Baker's life, and often did he relate the marvellous feats he performed.

With wild cheers and yells the mob returned to the burning carriages. The dragoons even had to return without the voters ; they only succeeded in rescuing the police and Mr. Baker.*

The people gained a great victory ; some were killed, no doubt, but what of that, more were killed of the other party ; and Sir William Placeman was returned victoriously,—Sir William—the advocate of free trade, reform, Repeal of the Union, and I don't know what not. Sir William praised the people, their devotion to the sacred cause of nation-

* I have not drawn on my imagination for this election shindy. Such occurrences are rather frequent in Ireland, witness Six-mile Bridge, Limerick, &c. The people are seldom so fortunate as in my little row ; but any one that has witnessed the fight between the electors and the mob near the village of Newbirmingham, in 1842, will confess, that I have not done justice to that precious skirmish, in which there was more blood shed than the rival candidates were worth. As to Sir William Placeman, no one will be at a loss in mistaking him for his prototype, Billy Keogh.

ality ; what a sacrifice they made in returning him, the humble advocate of a holy cause, a cause dearer to him than life.

Sir William shortly sold them, himself, and the cause for a snug berth ; who could blame him, shouldn't he turn his useful talents to account? besides, he was a penniless barrister.

There were some of his clamorous supporters ridiculous enough to grumble at Sir William's change ; but then, he silenced their absurd objections, by getting places for themselves or their friends.

CHAPTER XVII.

WE must now draw the curtain over two years. It is not that these two years were barren in stirring or exciting events. Never were two years laden with more misery to an unhappy people. The partial failure of the potato crop, which threatened the peasantry in the early stages of our tale, had now become general and fatal. The potato was the staple food of the peasant ; it fed his pig to meet the landlord's claims ; it supported himself and family in health and robustness ; it left him his little garden of oats or wheat, to supply himself with clothes, and other little luxuries. So, in these days the Irish peasant had no fear of hunger or want ; for the potato seemed to spring up abundantly every place. The peasant had enough, and some to spare, with a cead mille failte, for the wandering boccagh and the houseless poor. These times had passed, and misery and starvation, such as never afflicted a wretched people before, now reigned in the country.

We have passed over two years, two years of starvation ; but we come to the time when the country was lying prostrate with fever and famine, and when the energies of good men were aroused to stay or alleviate their dreadful ravages, and of bad men, to stimulate them, in order to exterminate a helpless and now cumbersome tenantry.

The famine was doing its work, and had already sent thousands to premature graves, and thousands to die in foreign lands, and thousands more to feed the fishes of the Atlantic.

You may ask me what was the Government doing all this time? Was it not passing remedial measures to give employment to the poor? England derives an immense revenue from Ireland ; surely she could not let her starve. My friends, how was the Union carried, but by coercion and bribery ; and now, what better levers could be found to upset an in-cipient rebellion — the yearnings of a people for nationality—than famine and starvation. Ah! they were a God-send more effective than thirty thousand British bayonets!"

This potato blight and consequent famine were powerful engines of state to uproot millions of the peasantry, to preserve law and order, and to clear off surplus population, and to maintain the integrity of the British empire.

But, then, there were measures passed. England wished to show her humanity to the world. There were about ten millions voted for the relief of Ire-land. How this was administered we mean to show. What could be expected from a government whose leading organ—when a wailing cry of starvation arose from Ireland, when such as could, fled, fright·

oned at the dreadful ruin at home; when the grave closed over a million of starved peasants—called out in a jubilee of delight: "The Celts are gone—gone with a vengeance. The Lord be praised!" Hear ye that: "The Lord be praised!!" For what? Because about a million and a-half of fellow-creatures had died of starvation; because about as many more had fled beyond the Atlantic, to nestle beneath the sheltering wing of the glorious stripes and stars, or to sleep in its welcome bosom.

Ah! this was a grand and Christian consummation to sing a "*Te Deum*" over! But, then, they were mere Irish. Whilst the Irish were struggling to outlive a famine, such as never devastated a wretched country before, about six millions of the rental of Ireland were spent annually by absentee landlords in England. Irish produce, to the amount of about seventeen millions sterling, was annually exported to England, and yet the Irish were starving at home. It is strange that they should export beef and butter and corn to such a vast amount while struggling against a fearful famine. In no other country in the world but Ireland would this strange anomaly be allowed; for it was calculated that during the worst years the produce of the country was capable of supporting double its population. But the farmer had to sell his crops to pay the landlord, who was as exacting as in the best of times, and even more so, for the spirit of eviction had gone forth, and now was the landlord's opportunity.

After parting with the produce of his farm to meet the landlord, the poor farmer was left as destitute as the laborer. He had not the potato ; he had to try and till his farm to support his family and servants, and to meet poor rates and county taxes, and various other calls.* Indeed, the only thriving

* It is impossible to give in the pages of a novel, without detracting from its merits as a novel, a correct account of how the money, voted and given to relieve the famine, was squandered and wasted.

It is calculated that England draws from Ireland, yearly, the vast tribute of near six millions through absentee landlords, and about eighteen millions of imports, besides a vast revenue. When we consider this, and that one of the terms of the Union was, that each country was to pay the annual charge upon her own debt. Ireland then owed but twenty-one millions, a part of which was for bribing members to sell their country to England! England owed the nice sum of 448 millions. What did she do? Like a dear sister, that she is, she joined her national debt to ours, or, to use a proper phrase, "Consolidated them." Well, this was affectionate—wasn't it. Considering that we owed but 21, and she 448 millions! But this was but a small item of the benefits arising from the Union. Considering all this, one would not be surprised if England came forward liberally and opened the exchequer to save us from the horrors of so dreadful a calamity.

In 1846 the landlords, not to be taken short, seized on the cattle and crops to secure their rents. The poor rate man, the county cess collector, and all other claimants followed in his track, leaving the poor farmer reduced to beggary, soon to become a pauper himself.

In January there was a grant of £50,000 for public works, as much more for drainage of estates. These grants were placed at the disposal of the Commissioners of Public Works, and, I might safely say, that £10,000 of the whole never went into the pockets of the poor, which £10,000 would be but as a drop of water in the ocean. Irish members had the spirit to claim money, not as alms, but as their right ; but the idea was laughed at, to think, indeed, that Ireland should have any claim on the exchequer. It is no wonder that English Journals bantered us. To keep us from grumbling, we got coercion bills and arms acts, *ad infinitum.* The next famous engine of destruction was "the Labor-rate Act." This was an Act to enable the treasury to advance money, to be repaid by rate-payers, to carry on public works sanctioned by the *Government.* This impost impoverished the rich without classes now in Ireland were deputy sheriffs, bailiffs, and rate collectors. These had plenty of employment in levelling houses, distraining for rent and taxes, and the like pastime. These were very profitable transactions then, for the sheriff had constant employment and was well paid. The others, too, were not idle; and as the poor farmers were not able to buy up the stock, the considerate drivers bought them for about half their value themselves; add to this, large deductions by way of fees, and you may form some notion of the amount placed to the wretched owner's account.

It is true, we got in return for all our export, Coercion Bills, Arms Acts, and the like. We also got an additional force of about twenty thousand men to keep us from grumbling. So, you see, the

benefiting the poor, for it was wasted on unproductive works. It discouraged private enterprise, and dragged landlords, farmers, and laborers to one common ruin. Next came the out-door relief system, with its quarter-acre clause; so that any poor wretch holding a quarter of an acre was disqualified from relief unless he gave up his little farm.

Had these various sums of money been spent in some useful, reproductive employment, they might have effected a vast amount of good. Had they been employed in tilling and seeding the poor man's farm, they would indeed do a great deal towards benefiting the country; but, no, they were spent in testing political economy and practical philosophy; in building soup-houses and erecting boilers; in levelling hills; and in extending government patronage by employing commissioners, inspectors, clerks, overseers, and the like, of whom there were no less than 10,000 salaried out of money given as loans and grants for the poor. This is the way the money went, and the poor were left to starve!! Landlords, too, through a selfish and narrow spirit of self interest, oppressed the farmers, and thus hurried their properties into the Incumbered Estates Courts. They acted like the members of the body when they rose in war against the stomach—they did not see that their well-doing was mutual.—AUTHOR.

Irish had no reason to complain, unless they were too hard to be pleased. We also got a loan of about ten millions, half of which had to be repaid by instalments; add to this some private grants, and we ought to be grateful indeed. When we consider that the same England gave about twenty millions to turn negroes wild from whom she never received the least benefit, we are not to be surprised at the noble generosity that urged her to give us, who send her about twenty-three millions of our produce and money annually, a loan of ten millions to keep us from starving, or rather to protract our wretched fate.

All this time the British Parliament was voting millions to enlarge English dockyards, to strengthen English fortifications, to beautify English parks and museums, and to make faster her iron gripe upon her "dear sister island." When we complained of the apathy of the English government about an Irish famine, we got an Arms Bill. When we complained of the ruined state of our trade, war ships were sent into our ports with arms and ammunition. When we said we were starving, give us employment, powder mills and fortifications were set to work.

In 1827, after the defeat of the Catholic question, five millions of bullets were ordered to Ireland to quieten her; some one then wrote—

> " I have found out a gift for my Erin,
> A gift that will surely content her,
> Sweet pledge of a love so endearing !
> Five millions of bullets I've sent her."

England seems to have great confidence in this, her favorite panacea, for all our ills even yet; so she is very fond of repeating the dose.

Local committees were appointed throughout the country for the management and distribution of public money—grants, rates, and the like. Useless public works were fast setting in. Of course Lord Clearall was the manager of one of these committees. Mr. Ellis had a grist-mill near the village. There was a small private house adjoining; in this the committee held their deliberations. Lord Clearall was in the chair. Several of the neighboring gentry and respectable ratepayers were also present.

"I have," said his lordship, "got about a thousand pounds, which we are to spend on some public work, such as levelling a hill, or filling up a hollow, or the like; now, this will give a great deal of employment, and I hope it's only the forerunner of more. We have now to select what work we will commence at—our selections, of course, to be approved of by the Board of Works; but this is a mere matter of form, as one of the commissioners is my particular friend."

"I think, my lord, there is no work more necessary than to level Knockcorrig hill; it is almost impassable it is so steep, and it is a regular thoroughfare to the village."

"I think so, too, Mr. Ellis," said his lordship; "but, then, we must take the opinions of these gentlemen—what do you say, gentlemen?"

Now, as all the gentlemen present were more or less dependent on his lordship for favors, patronage, and the like, it was not reasonable to expect that they would oppose him, though they well knew that the levelling of Knockcorrig was of no earthly benefit to any one save to his lordship and Mr. Ellis, for it was on the road to his lordship's residence and to Mr. Ellis's mills, so they all bowed their assent.

"Will ye agree to that, gentlemen?"

"Yes, my lord."

"Now, we have to nominate a pay-master, overseer, and clerk; as there must be a great deal of money intrusted to the pay-master, he must be a person well secured; I think Mr. Ellis would be a very fit person; I will be his security."

They all, of course, nodded assent.

"What's the salary, my lord?" asked a broken-down gentleman, that expected it for himself.

"Why, I can't exactly say; perhaps ten pounds a week."

"Oh! my lord," groaned the other.

"I think we should also nominate Mr. Pembert and Mr. Burkem as overseer and clerk; their wages are low; one has but thirty shillings a week, the other a pound."

There was a nod of assent, followed by a stifled groan of disappointment from the members.

"There will be several other clerks and gaugers wanted, I shall be happy to get appointed any

worthy person you should recommend, gentlemen."

There was a general vote of thanks to his lordship.

" Now we have to see about a house for our meetings, and for giving out-door relief ; I think this a
very suitable one, indeed," and his lordship looked
about the comfortable room, with its blazing fire."

The others thought so too.

" Now, Mr. Ellis, what might be the rent of
this ?"

" Oh ! whatever your lordship choose."

" No ! no ! I haven't the selection ; name your
rent, for these gentlemen to consider ?"

" Would ten shillings a week be too much, my
lord ?" said Mr. Ellis, with the air of one making a
groat sacrifice for the cause of humanity.

" Really I think not, considering its appearance
and usefulness," said his lordship.

" Would not a cheaper house do ?" timidly suggested one of the committee. " I merely ask it for
information's sake, my lord," said he, correcting
himself.

" Well, perhaps so," said his lordship ; " but then,
where is the great saving in a few shillings a week ;
besides, look at the comfort of this house, and the
safety of having it so near the mills, within a call
of the police ; you know such houses have been attacked already."

" We agree with you, my lord," said the others.

A vast crowd of half-starved, half-naked wretches were collected outside the door, waiting the issue of the meeting. Some were living skeletons, tottering with disease and weakness. Some looked like scarecrows, dressed up in rags, and moved by some inward machinery.

"Arrah! shure it would be dacenter for ye to kill us intirely," said a wretched-looking woman, crouched beside a wall, with a child at her breast.

"Thrue for you, Peg," said another; "sorra a morsel I ate these two days but turnip-tops and cabbage, and there is Jack dying with me at home."

"Lord help us," said another; "they are the terrible times intirely."

"I haven't a bit nor a sup, nor a spark to warm myself, and my four children," said another poor wretch.

"Will we bear to be stharved this way?" said the men; "shure it's better for us to be kilt at wanst, boys, and our poor wives, and the childers."

"Let us throw down the house over them; there's male inside," shouted another.

"Arrah! don't ye," said another, with a scornful laugh; "ye'll get a great deal from Lord Clearall, that hunted us out of the houses himself, and his skinflint divil of an agent; shure tell him ye are stharving and that will do."

"Success, Jim, you're right," shouted the crowd.

"Give us something to eat, or we'll pull down the house over ye," shouted the mob.

"Let us brake in the door!"

Some heavy stones were flung against the door, and wild yells rang from the men, and a wail of hunger and despair from the women and children.

"We are going to commence work on Knockcorrig on Monday next," said his lordship from the window.

"What will feed us until then?"

"Pull in your head, you tyrant you, that threw my poor ould father out of the house, and he dying, and wouldn't lave him the house over him to gasp in."

"Och! shure that's his thrade; 'tis he knows how to quinch the poor man's fire; but he'll get into a warm corner for it some fine day himself."

"Bad luck to the tyrant; let us drag him out, himself and his d——d bastard of an agent!"

"Break in the house. Give us male! Ye have it inside there, ye old cadgers."

"It is better to divide what meal is in the house, Mr. Ellis," said his lordship, turning very pale; "you'll be paid for it."

"I think so, too," said Mr. Ellis, who feared that it would be taken without his leave.

"If you keep quiet," said his lordship, addressing the crowd, "what meal is in the mill will be divided upon you, and you will all get work at the hill on Monday next."

A wild cheer echoed from the crowd. Lord Clearall and Mr. Ellis slipped away backwards.

Mr. Ellis returned home satisfied that he had made good use of the day. He had set his house to advantage; he had also got a handsome salary for himself for doing nothing. He had been lately appointed a justice of the peace, so that he could now sit on the bench equal in magisterial power with his lordship. His lordship was the sheriff for the ensuing year, and he was to be his deputy. He had cleared off the Ballybrack tenants, and had pocketed a thousand pounds by the event; so, all things considered, Mr. Ellis ought to be a happy man. Yet, he did not feel too happy. He knew there was a wild spirit of revenge abroad ; he knew that he was a marked man. Only a few months ago an assassin fired at him, but missed.

He now began to cling to life ; he would wish to enjoy the sweets of hard-earned wealth and honors ; so, in his soul, he resolved, if he had but a few more estates cleared, to change his life, and become a different man altogether.

Though a bold man, Mr. Ellis was wavering in his resolutions. He felt that life was sweet, and that it was possible to lose it by the hand of an assassin. Besides, it was terrible to be hurled before his God, without a moment's preparation, for Mr. Ellis felt that he was no saint; in fact, he had the reputation of being as gallant a widower as he was a bachelor.

He began now to act from policy, and because his nephew and Burkem were eternally dinning into his ears that the Cormacks were resolved to shoot him, he gave them a nice lodge on his property, and constant employment, at remunerative wages; he also took Nelly Cormack into his employ as housemaid. Mr. Pembert and Burkem never expected this, so they were disappointed in their plans; but they laid with greater success, new and more fatal plots for their victims.

Mr. Ellis had received a new guest into his family, the Rev. Robert Sly, or, as he was familiarly called, Bob Sly. The Rev. Mr. Sly was a smart, rather well-looking young man, of about thirty. He was a very sanctimonious man, this Rev. Mr. Sly. His very dress was quite clerical, all black, except a most immaculate white neck-tie. He was so very spruce and neat in his dress, and so demure and pious-looking in his very appearance, that you at once set him down as a man of great sanctity. It is no wonder, then, that he became a great favorite with Mr. Ellis, and also with his daughter Lizzie. Lizzie Ellis was a gentle creature of impulse and sentiment. Her father could spare her little of his company; so her heart longed for some one to commune with. There is a deep feeling of love in the human heart, which must be directed in some channel. If we receive a good moral training in early life, this love may be the source of our happiness. If directed right, it will be the sunshine of our existence; if not, it will be a cloud of darkness in our path. Lizzie Ellis was left alone without society, to ramble about the splendid rooms of her father's house. Her flowers, her pictures, her little pets were now become too familiar to her mind; so her heart craved for some one to respond to that mysterious something that throbbed within it. She loved her father dearly; yet he was a cold, business man, that little understood or appreciated her gentle, clinging disposition. Not that he was a bad father —by no means. He surrounded her with all the luxuries that wealth could supply. She wanted nothing material, so he thought that she ought to be very happy. Wealth and position were his criterions of happiness; he little knew that there is a something in the heart, particularly of youth, that wealth cannot supply. A cheerful smile, a kind pressure of the hand, a deep sympathy of joy or sorrow, awake a warmer feeling in the heart than the most costly attributes of wealth. Thus thrown upon her own resources for happiness, Lizzie Ellis clung with deep affection to anything or person that gained her favor. She had also met with some novels, which fanned this latent fire within her bosom. She had not strength of mind enough to look upon them as mere fictions, created to paint and please society. She often wept at the imaginary struggles and sorrows of some hero and heroine. She then rejoiced in the successful career of her hero, and "wished that heaven had made her such a man."

It is no wonder, then, that one so young and untutored in the ways of life, with such little knowledge of the workings and promptings of her own heart, should feel flattered by the attentions of so pious, so keen, and so worthy a man as the Rev. Mr. Sly. It is surprising though that so shrewd and calculating a man as Mr. Ellis did not see the danger of leaving a creature so young and so susceptible exposed to the seductions of the Rev. Mr. Sly's blandishments ; but then Mr. Ellis looked upon clergymen as noble, pure, and generous, above the passions and sordidness of life ; he did not calculate on a wolf in sheep's clothing getting into the fold.

It must be on this account that the Rev. Mr. Sly was in a manner as great a favorite with the father as with the daughter. It is only right to state how he became introduced to Mr. Ellis at first. There is a body called the Exeter Hall Tract Society. This society has been established for the laudable purpose of raising funds and sending out missioners to propagate the Gospel to heathen nations. Now, the directors of this society, deeming the Irish a most heathenish and benighted people, and compassionating their wretched, starving condition, came to the Christian resolution of sending over a regular brigade of missionaries to enlighten them in the true faith, and console them with Bibles and tracts.

They got up a number of schools, and as they wished to save both soul and body, they got up soup kitchens and meal depôts in connection with several of them. On this account they were called "souper schools," and their ministers "soupers." Whether it were the Bibles and tracts, or the meal and soup that influenced them, several turned over; but I must say that as soon as they were able to get a living again, they abandoned the new doctrines for their old religion. Some of these missionaries were zealous, sincere men of education, who acted from conscientious motives; but others, particularly the Scripture-readers, were illiterate men, who made a traffic of the word of God. Though the Rev. Mr. Sly took the title of Rev., still it is to be doubted very much if any college or bishop conferred this dignity upon him; however, as he has it, by courtesy we will style him such.

He was a Scotchman, and had some acquaintance with Mr. Ellis's friends, from one of whom he got a letter of introduction; this secured him a welcome to Mr. Ellis's house, and his own plausible, insinuating manners, a continuance of it there. The Rev. Mr. Sly was attended by a servant. He bore a very brotherly resemblance to him; his name was Adam Steen. Adam Steen was as zealous and pious as his master, and could wear as sanctimonious a look too.

Adam wore threadbare, seedy - looking black clothes, with a white neck-tie, in imitation of his master. They, for aught I know, might be cast-offs of his master, for, as I said, both men were wonderfully alike both in size and appearance.

The Rev. Mr. Sly was sitting on a settee near a

18

fine cheerful fire, in Mr. Ellis's parlor; beside him sat Lizzie Ellis, and she looked into his face with a confiding, childish scrutiny, as if to catch the words that fell from his lips, or to read the thoughts that flitted through his fertile brain. The table was laid, and glasses and decanters sparkled in array, for dinner was waiting Mr. Ellis's arrival.

"Your papa is late to-day, Lizzie: he is generally in at dinner-hour; I hope that nothing of importance has delayed him?" and Mr. Sly looked at the dinner-table and sighed.

"Oh, he'll be in shortly," said Lizzie; "he is seldom later than dinner-hour."

"Do you ever have any fear for his safety, Lizzie; you know he is not popular?"

"Why so, Mr. Sly; I thought that my father has done nothing to make people dislike him?"

"Not exactly; but you see, people will not reason between cause and effect; now, your papa, in the discharge of a painful duty, no doubt, had to eject several families; these are unreasonable enough to charge him with being the sole cause of their ruin; so we often hear of an agent being shot, when the landlord, the cause of all, escapes."

Lizzie raised her eyes, swimming in tears at the thought of such an affliction.

"My poor papa! what would become of me?"

"Now, Miss Ellis, I am really sorry that I should distress you, by alluding to such a possibility; one, I hope, that will never occur; don't fret yourself!"

The Rev. Mr. Sly passed his hand around Lizzie's waist to console her.

"Oh, Mr. Sly, I never thought of the like before; what would become of me?"

"Why, darling, friends would care one with such flattering prospects; ay, they would fawn upon you."

"Oh, but I have no friends, no one to love me, no one to care for me, but him and ——"

Lizzie looked into his face and blushed amidst her tears.

"Say the words, Lizzie, love, say it, and make a heart, that has been left as desolate and uncared for as your own happy. Oh, Lizzie, there are others, there is one, at least, besides your papa, who could care you, who could love you, who could die, but to make you happy; allow him but the privilege of stating how his affections are wound up in you, and he shall be happy, though you should scorn him then."

Lizzie hung her head upon his shoulder and sighed; her little heart throbbed violently against her side. The Rev. Mr. Sly smiled upon her; his heart was cold, there was not one responsive throb in it; he gloried in her weakness, and felt sure of his victory. Lizzie sighed, and exclaimed—

"Oh, Robert!"

What a sweet sensation throbs a man's heart as he hears his name for the first time from the lips of the woman he loves; it tells him that all cold barriers are separated, and that a sacred tie has sprung up between them. The Rev. Mr. Sly's heart experienced no such feeling; for he did not love that frail, confiding creature ; he loved her large fortune, her brilliant worldly prospects. He felt that he was betraying the confidence of his host, in thus stealing, or rather tampering with, the affections of an innocent, loving, girl ; but then, the bait was large, indeed, and worthy of any sacrifice. Since he came into the house, under pretence of instructing her innocent mind, he was implanting a baneful passion, which he found too ready to take root.

"Lizzie, say you love me, darling." He held down his head, and pressed her to his bosom.

" Robert ! "

" Well, love ? "

" I love you," she whispered, in a tone scarcely audible.

" Darling ! heavens bless you ;" and he pressed a lingering kiss upon her lips.

It is true, he would not be mortal, if some feeling of love did not dart through his heart then ; but if there did, it was but for a moment, for he looked about the room, and thought upon that fine house, the stock and lands that she was to inherit, and he sighed with excessive happiness, when he reflected that all these might be his.

There was a loud knock at the door.

" Here is my papa," and Lizzie sat up and arranged her hair.

The Rev. Mr. Sly sat over on an easy chair, and began to read his Bible.

CHAPTER XVIII.

FAMINE TREATMENT, CONTINUED — THE REV. MR. SLY'S CHARITY—NELLY CORMACK TEMPTED—HER DELIVERER —MR. SLY MEETS HIS MATCH AT SCRIPTURE.

THE Rev. Mr. Sly was quite composed, but Lizzie looked somewhat confused as her father came into the room.

"I fear I have kept dinner waiting?" said Mr. Ellis, as he looked at the table, and then noticing Lizzie's agitated appearance, he asked:

"What ails you, Lizzie, love?"

"She was getting rather alarmed at your delay. I was telling her that it was all on account of business; sure, a man having so much on his hands as you, sir, cannot count his time his own. Whatever made her think otherwise, she was alarmed, lest some accident befel you."

"Oh! is that it? Why, child, if you let every trifle that way annoy you, I fear you'll have an unpleasant life of it. No, pet, there is no one going to hurt your poor father yet I hope; now, cheer up."

Lizzie smiled, and they sat to dinner.

"Why, Lizzie," said Mr. Ellis, sleeking her head

with his hand, as she sat near him, " you must have
some presentiment of things.   Really, a lot of hungry scoundrels attacked his lordship and myself—
we had to get out backwards."

"Why don't you give them something to eat,
papa ?   I see poor creatures about the house ; some
of them frightened me in the kitchen the other day;
they had not a stitch upon them, and one would
think that it was out of the grave they came, they
looked so poor, their clothes in rags, and their
beards all grown."

"There are so many in want now, child, that a
man can do but little among them all.   It looks like
a judgment upon the people.   What do you think,
Mr. Sly ?"

"I agree with you, sir ; the people have become
so wicked and idolatrous, and so much addicted to
priestcraft and all such things, that I should not
wonder if this blight, like the plagues of Egypt, has
come to afflict them for their sins."

"If it be an affliction from God, as you say, which
I am sure it is, it would be only running counter to
Providence to relieve them."

"I wish we could make that relief answer two
purposes ; if we could point out to them the error
of their ways, it would be right to support the elect ;
if we could get up a soup-house in connection with
the schools, it would show the people that we have
their interest at heart."

"Ha, ha ! Mr. Sly, you see I look after your business. His lordship and I have agreed to get up one in the out-office near the school. We can keep a supply of meal and the like in the mill—ye will want vegetables, which I will send down at a fair price, you know."

"Certainly, sir."

"Well your man, Adam, can preside over it; he can give them lessons in Scripture whilst taking their soup. I have ordered Burkem to notice all the tenants to send their children there at their peril; they will be both instructed and fed; you see what a blessing that is for them."

"This is all very kind and thoughtful of you, Mr. Ellis; like the good Samaritan, you are sowing the seed of righteousness unknown to us all."

"Not at all, man, not at all; you would fain have all the good to yourself, as if others have not souls to save as well as you, Mr. Sly?"

"Perfectly true, sir; we should work in the vineyard of the Lord, for He will reward every one according to his good works," said the Rev. Mr. Sly.

"Well, Lizzie, child, will you help us?"

"I shall, papa; Mr. Sly is instructing me, so that I think I could make a brave little missionery myself."

"That's it, darling; I am sure Mr. Sly will not instruct you in anything contrary to his sacred calling."

Lizzie blushed, and looked at Mr. Sly.

Mr. Sly replied: "Indeed, sir, I fear her education in some things has been much neglected; I shall endeavor to enlighten her as much as possible."

"Yes, yes! that is what I expect, my reverend friend. I know that her education, in many respects, has been much neglected; you see I was so busy with the world, making a fortune for her, I hadn't time to look after her; then I couldn't spare her to go to school, I'd miss her too much, for I am fond of her; why shouldn't I too. Her poor mother educated her; but, then, when we lost her, I couldn't spare my Lizzie, her presence is sunshine about the house; so, Mr. Sly, instruct her in her religion and all that sort of thing; I intrust her to your honor. I never minded religion much myself. No, I hadn't time; but, then, I did my duty, I hope, and I have faith in the saving blood of our Saviour."

"My good sir, it couldn't be expected that one so much engaged with the cares of the world as you could spend too much time about religious matters; as you say, you have done your duty, and this is all God requires of us; let us have faith and charity and do our duty, and God will place us with the good and faithful servants. As to Miss Ellis here," and he turned with a smile to Lizzie, " her soul is fertile with the good seed; it shall be my care to bring it forth and to ripen it with the sunshine of grace."

"That will do; take care of her. She's a good child! I will now leave her to your instructions, as I want to go to my office," and Mr. Ellis rang the bell.

Our old friend, Nelly Cormack, who, as I have said, was now in Mr. Ellis's employment, or rather in Miss Ellis's, answered.

"Nelly," said Mr. Ellis, "bring a light up to my office ; I want to go there."

"Yes, sir," said Nelly.

Mr. Ellis left for his office. The Rev. Mr. Sly sat beside Lizzie, and placed his hand around her waist to commence his instructions.

Mr. Ellis lay back in his chair as he entered his office, and sighed.

Nelly Cormack placed the candle upon the table.

"Do you want anything else, sir?" said Nelly, with a smile on her pouting lips.

"Not exactly, Nelly, let me see—oh yes," and he looked at Nelly, who all the time stood waiting his commands. She, no doubt, looked to advantage ; the rose of health was on her cheeks, and a gay good humor twinkled in her eye.

Mr. Ellis looked at Nelly again and sighed.

"Nelly," said he.

"Well, sir ! "

"Sit down, Nelly, and let us chat awhile."

"It's not to the likes of me you'd like to be chatting, sir ! "

"Why not, Nelly, arn't you as good as I am, but that I am richer? I don't feel happy at all of late, Nelly."

"Shure you ought to be happy, sir," said she

" wid these fine houses and lands ; shure there is no end to your riches."

" True, Nelly, true enough, but then riches never make us happy ; some one to love us, to smile on us, to gladden our hearts, can make us a hundred times happier than riches ; what use are they after all ; sure we can eat and drink but enough—well, what use is any more ? I'll tell you what, Nelly, I'd rather some pretty little girl like you to love me than half my wealth."

Nelly blushed and held down her head ; yet, she did not seem displeased, for she was a coquette, and it was something to be noticed by the wealthy Mr. Ellis.

" I'll go, sir," said Nelly ; " you are only making game of a poor penniless girl like me."

" Stay now, Nelly ; what do I care about fortune ? I only want some one to love me."

" Haven't you Miss Lizzie, and can't you get a wife wid a fortune ? You are young enough," and she archly glanced at him.

" Oh! as for Lizzie, she'll shortly get to love some one besides me, I'm sure. Then, as I said, I don't want a fortune ; and if I looked for a high connection they'd reflect upon me. So, Nelly, don't be bantering me ; I wish I could win yourself, my pretty little love ! "

Nelly was conscious of her rustic beauty. She observed Mr. Ellis admiring her very much lately. He was old, to be sure, but what of that ? He was

immensely rich ; what a fine thing it would be to be
dashing about in her coach as the admired Mrs.
Ellis ?   Ah, Nelly, Nelly, beware !   Ambition was the
ruin of angels, and you're but mortal !

Lizzie Ellis became most zealous in aiding the
Rev. Mr. Sly in his missionary labors ; they visited
the neighboring cottages of the poor together. They
distributed meal and soup, and tracts to the right-
eous, and advised the obstinate to forsake their worship of idols, and to embrace the purity of Protestantism. Owing to the pressure of the time some were
unable to resist the temptation, but they were few
indeed.   It is a fearful trial, no doubt, to see one's
wife and children for days without eating a morsel
of food, except cresses and turnip-tops, and the like,
and then to be offered food and raiment, but to put
on the semblance of apostacy ; yet thousands preferred death.

These men must be actuated by a Christian spirit,
who could hold bread to the lips of the starving poor,
and then snatch it away, because they would not forsake their religion ; this is the charity of loving your
neighbor as yourself.   There is many a heartless
Dives in this world, whose idea of " who's my neighbor ? " is—" every rich and respectable person, whose
religion and politics are in accordance with my
own." As to the poor wandering outcasts, the houseless poor, these little ones of our *Great Master*, he
knows them not.   Ah ! Dives, when you look upon
your splendid house, your fertile fields, and ample

stores, think on the parable of the rich glutton and the poor man, and consider that yon naked, trembling wretch, is, perhaps, dearer to the Lord, than you, who are clad in "purple and fine linen." Think that the great Law-giver has said : "As often as you give to these little ones, you give unto me." His followers were both Jews and Gentiles, for He came to save all that obey his laws.

The works on Knockcorrig had commenced, and liberal wages were given. The old and young, men, women and children, sought work there. Children were employed there so young, that they had to be brought on their parents' backs, and old persons had to be carried by asses.

This was in the middle of a severe winter ; the ground was covered with snow ; sleet and snow and rain drenched the wretched creatures. The old and young were put to breaking stones. There they sat, from morning until night, their bodies half naked, and the rain and snow and sleet pouring upon them. It is no wonder, then, that fever and dysentery were prevalent, and that each morning several were crossed off the books without the least comment or remark—they were dead, that's all.

The Rev. Mr. Sly frequently drove about from house to house. Lord Clearall's tenants had to receive him with seeming courtesy at least ; they knew the consequences too well if they acted otherwise. Even now a fresh screw was placed upon such as refused sending their children to the "souper school."

Not only were they threatened to be evicted, but they were also refused employment on the public works. This was easily managed, as Lord Clearall's deputies had the sole management of them. So, it was easy to find some pretence for refusing the obstinate.

Mr. Sly had the seat of his gig crammed with Bibles and tracts ; he also had a quantity of bread and broken meat. Lizzie Ellis sat beside him.

" What way shall we go to-day, Lizzie ? " said Mr. Sly, as they were going out of the avenue.

" I don't well know. What would you say if we called on that Mrs. Sullivan ? She was with me this morning ; her son was on the works, but was sent home, as she wouldn't send the other children to the school ; she wanted me to get him back."

" Do you think has the Lord moved her ; is she penitent, Lizzie ? "

" She looks to be very poor. I'm sure she is ; for I told her there was no use in interfering unless she let the others go to school. She said nothing, but sighed."

" What a stiff-necked people they are, love ; but God hardens those He will destroy."

Nelly Sullivan was sitting at the table with her poor children ; before them was a dish of turnip-tops and cabbage leaves, sprinkled with salt. The children eat ravenously of this coarse fare.

" Mammy, won't you ate any ? " said one.

" No, alanna, no ; ate away ; shure there's not enuff for yerselfs."

"But, mammy, you were walking all the mornin';
shure you're hungry, and you didn't ate anything
these two days."

The mother looked at the coarse food, unfit for
pigs, and her eyes glistened; she then looked at
her wretched children, and she turned away as the
tears trickled down her withered cheeks.

"No," said she to herself; "bad as it is, they
haven't enuff. God help them! My God, I'm dying;" and she squeezed her hands upon her sides,
and sat upon an old stool.

"Oh! mammy, mammy! it is so tough I can't
ate it; it's choking me," said one little thing.

"And me too," said another.

"Oh! if we had a bit of bread or a sup of milk,
or a pratie," said another.

"Here, pet," said Johnny, a little boy about twelve
years; "here," and he picked the softest bits for the
youngest. He then got some and took it to his
mother. "Here, mother, ate this," said he, and he
placed the coarse food in her hand.

She groaned. He rubbed her face—it was covered
with a cold sweat.

"Mammy, mammy, what ails you?" shouted the
boy. "Oh, mammy is dying!" he exclaimed.

The others ran to her, clasping their little hands,
and calling their mammy.

"Johnny," said she faintly, "bring me a drink."

He brought her a vessel of water, from which she
drank; she then ate some of the leaves.

"What ails you, mammy?" said a little thing, nestling at her knees, and placing her tiny hands in hers.

"Nothing, pet; nothing. I am well now," and the poor woman stroked the little flaxen head.

"Oh, mammy, here's a lady and jintleman!" said another, as he saw Mr. Sly drive to the door.

"Thank God!" said she, clasping her hands and looking up. "I hope they have come to save us."

"Good-day, ma'am!" said Mr. Sly. "This is a miserable place, ma'am;" and he looked about the wretched cabin in a most commiserating manner.

"Indeed it is, sir," said Mrs. Sullivan, with a curtsy. "It is a poor place for a lady and jintleman to come to; but then, if people can keep from starving now, it's enuff. I am sorry I haven't a sate for the lady," and she bowed to Miss Ellis.

"Don't mind, ma'am," said Mr. Sly; "we can stand. Would you let this little chap hold my horse for a moment?"

"Yes, sir. Run, Johnny, and hould the jintleman's horse."

Miss Ellis was all this time taking a view of the cabin. The roof was broken in several parts, and the rain had formed into little pools on the clay floor. In a corner a bed of straw lay on the cold ground. A vessel was placed in the bed to receive the dropping rain. There was an inner room, but it was deserted, as being unfit to be occupied, for the roof had nearly fallen in. A few embers burned on the

hearth, and the emaciated, half-clad looking children
crowded around it.

Miss Ellis knew little of the poor; caged in her
father's splendid house, surrounded by every luxury,
she wondered why the people should be poor at all,
or have such wretched hovels to live in.   It is only
lately she began to comprehend the causes that
made them so.   As she accompanied Mr. Sly, her
young and sensitive heart was touched at the tales
and scenes of misery she had heard and witnessed,
She might have become a ministering angel; but
her artful guide smothered these aspirations of gentle
pity in her breast, by telling her that all their sufferings were sent by the Lord to afflict them for
their sins, and to lead them to righteousness.

"How do you live here at all, ma'am?" said Lizzie,
as she glanced at all the signs of wretchedness that
surrounded her.

"Really, I don't know, miss; we haven't had a bit
these two days but some cabbage and turnip leaves.
I didn't ate a bit myself to-day.   God knows I am
starving!"

"Run, Robert," said Lizzie to the Rev. Mr. Sly,
"and bring them some bread.   You see we have
some with us, ma'am, for urgent cases."

"God bless you, miss!" said Mrs. Sullivan.

"Go, Robert, if you please?" said Lizzie, turning to the rev. gentleman, who all the time stood
still.

"Yes, darling, yes; but first let us see, has this

poor woman seen the error of her ways, and is she moved to grace? I am sure——"

Here his speech was interrupted by a regular scramble at the door, and cries of "Give me a bit!" "Tom has it all!" "Bring it into mammy."

"Bless me!" said Mr. Sly, "but these brats have taken all the bread;" and he ran to the door.

Johnny got into the gig, and seeing a loaf of bread, and hearing the lady telling Mr. Sly to bring it in, he seized it, and was bringing it when the others assailed him at the door.

"The brats!" exclaimed Mr. Sly, as he seized the bread.

"Here, mamma," whispered Tommy, as he slipped a part of the loaf, unseen, under her apron, "ate this."

She was hungry. Perhaps that crust of bread might save her life. Who could blame her if she paused. She then drew forth the bread ——

"No, child, no. It's not ours; it would be sinful; give it to the jintleman."

"Here, sir," said Tommy, handing him the bread.

Mr. Sly took and placed it in the car.

"Leave it to him," said Lizzie.

"No; it would be encouraging robbery, Lizzie. Well, my good woman," said Mr. Sly, "your son was turned off the works?"

"Yis, your honor."

"Your reverence, ma'am, if you please," said Mr. Sly, with a bow. "I think, ma'am, he must have deserved it; you see he's a dishonest boy; how soon he stole the bread."

"I never knew him to act dishonestly, your ho—— riverence I mane. I'm shure he wouldn't take the bread but he heard the lady telling you to bring it in."

"Indeed I wouldn't, mammy," said Johnny; "and shure I was bringing it in to the jintleman when they stuck in me."

"Likely story, that; no matter, I will see about getting him reinstated."

"God Almighty bless your riverence!" said the poor woman.

"But, ma'am, you must send these other children to my school, where they will be well treated. They will be educated and fed for you for nothing, so you ought to be grateful, ma'am."

Mrs. Sullivan did not look grateful, but held down her head and wept.

"Well, ma'am?" said the Rev. Mr. Sly.

"I can't do it, sir; I'll starve first, and God knows I am near enuff to it already. Oh! give us some bread, sir, and get work for my boy, and may God reward you. Oh! Miss Ellis, will you aid the poor widow, and her blessing fall upon your head.

"Do, Robert, do," said Lizzie.

"Well, ma'am, do you repent?" said Mr. Sly.

"I can't—I can't sell my sowl. Shure the priests told us not; that ye are trying to make soupers of us all."

"The priests, ma'am, are a great humbug; teaching you to adore idols, and worship saints, and living people like ourselves."

"No, sir—your riverence I mean—the priests are our only comfort; they visit us when sick and afflicted; and if they had the means we wouldn't want."

"So you refuse sending them to hear the word of God!"

"I refuse sending them to *your* school, sir."

"Then the consequence be upon yourself. You are refusing warm clothing, plenty to eat, and a snug house. Recollect, sinful woman, 'I called and you refused.'—'Evil-doers shall be cut off.' I will now leave you to yourself and your priests. Mind, you will not only be refused employment, but this very house shall be levelled over you. This is Lord Clearall's orders." *

"God's will be done!" said Mrs. Sullivan, clasping her hands together and looking towards heaven.

---

* Lest my English readers should think that such coercion exists only in the writer's imagination, I had better give them a few extracts regarding Lord Bishop P——t's interference with the consciences of his tenants. One man swore :—" The Rev. Mr. P——r and Miss P——t called upon me to send my children to their school. As I had a large and helpless family I did, but God knows the bit I eat didn't do me any good from that out." Another witness swore "that she refused to send her children, as she was sure that they would be perverted. Next day the bailiff called upon her for possession, and served her with notice to quit." Several other witnesses swore to the same effect. Such is the liberty of conscience in Ireland!

"Come, Lizzie," said Mr. Sly; "let us leave this house of iniquity. Here, however, is food for your soul," and he handed her some tracts.

Lizzie was following him when Mrs. Sullivan threw herself on her knees, and seized her dress, exclaiming:—

"Oh, Miss Ellis! for the love of God, don't let them ruin the poor widow and her orphans. I am dyin' with hunger; oh! get us work or something to ate—do, and may God reward and bless you, and mark you to grace. As for that bad man, may— —."

"Don't curse, ma'am," said Lizzie, slipping a shilling into her hand, "and I'll do my best for you."

"God bless you, my sweet young lady!"

"Come, come, Miss Ellis, it's time to go," said Mr. Sly.

Lizzie got into the gig, and was quite reserved. Mr. Sly noticed this, and said: "Cover yourself well, love, the day is very cold; allow me to put this rug about you. I declare it went to my heart to refuse that poor family; but, then, we have a duty to perform; if we allow them to set us at defiance this way we could do nothing. I'll bet you she will come to terms; now, when hunger will press on her to-night, she'll send them to school to-morrow; see what a victory that'll be; if not, I'll do something for them, since you wish it, love?"

"Do, Robert, do; perhaps you're right, but, then, they are so poor."

"They are poor, no doubt; so is almost every one you meet."

"Somehow, Robert, I feel an interest in that poor woman, no matter how obstinate she is: 'The Most High is a patient rewarder,' and shall judge us according to our good deeds."

"My little love, you'll shortly be able to preach Scripture as well as myself; you'll make a brave little missionary."

"I hope so," said Lizzie, recovering her good humor.

Mr. Sly had not gone far, when another visitor entered Mrs. Sullivan's cabin. She had a basket under her arm.

"Good-evening, ma'am," said she, in a soft voice.

"Good-evening kindly, and you're welcome, Miss O'Donnell," said Mrs. O'Sullivan.

Kate O'Donnell took the basket from under her cloak, and brought forth plenty of bread and meat.

"Here, Mrs. Sullivan," said she, "perhaps you are in want, for who is otherwise now? and on account of family troubles of my own, I was not able to visit you some days back."

"We all have our troubles, Miss Kate. I didn't ate a morsel these two days."

"God help us!" said Kate; "here, eat some now," and she placed the food before her.

After eating a few bits, Mrs. Sullivan fell back in a faint. Kate sprinkled her with water, and she soon recovered and partook of the food. She then told her all about the Rev. Mr. Sly's visit.

"God help us!" said Kate, "it is a wretched country, where men, calling themselves ministers of God, can trade on the misery of the poor."

"Shure it's too bad, Miss Kate, to try to make us sell our souls, to keep our bodies alive."

"It is, Nelly—it is so monstrous that even honest Protestants and true ministers blush with shame."

"Why, isn't Mr. Sly a minister, Miss Kate?"

"Indeed, from all I have heard of him, I should think not; if he were, I would expect him to be a gentleman, but I suspect he's only some low Scripture-reader."

"Very likely, Miss Kate; he's not a jintleman nor a Christian anyway."

"Well, Nelly, what do you mean to do?"

"I don't know, Miss Kate; I fear I must go into the poor-house. I know they won't give me employment."

"I fear so, Nelly; and only that times are changed with us, you should never go there; however, I fear it is your only course now. I can do very little for you; our stock is seized, and, perhaps, we will be shortly without a house, like yourself."

"God forbid, Miss Kate; ye were good and charitable, and God will not forsake ye."

"I hope not, Nelly, I hope not; though I always took little pride in riches, I long for them now when I see so many dying around me. It is only yesterday, Frank went into a cabin in the bog, where he was fowling; there he found a poor woman dead, and two children sucking her breast."

"Thanks be to God! that's frightful," and Nelly cast a look at her own poor children.

"Nelly, as my father is a guardian, if you wish to go into the house—and I fear you must—I'll get him to put you in."

"Thank you, Miss Kate, I'll think of it."

The Rev. Mr. Sly passed by Knockcorrig, on his way to the school; seeing so many ragged, wretched creatures together, he could not lose the opportunity of giving them a lecture on the evil of their ways. He drew up his gig in the midst of them. A suppressed murmur ran through the crowd. He alighted, and Adam Steen held his bridle.

"Here is the souper parson."

"The devil take him, and shure he will some fine day."

"I wish we could give him his due," was muttered by the crowd.

"Brethren," drawled the Rev. Mr. Sly, and took and opened a Bible. Hammers rapped, stones, and spades, and shovels were set to work with such vigor as to drown his voice.

"Mr. Pembert, I think you ought to order these men to stop work while the word of God is preaching to them."

"Lay down your tools and listen," said Mr. Pembert. The men sulkily obeyed.

"I thought these men were here to do government work, and not to be preached to," said a Catholic steward.

"What's his name, Mr. Pembert?" said Mr. Sly.

"William Fogarty; he's a steward."

Mr. Sly took out a pencil, and wrote down, "William Fogarty, steward."

"Had Lord Clearall anything to do with his appointment?"

"Yes, sir."

Mr. Sly wrote down again, and then said,—

"Young man, I'm sent here by his lordship and his excellent agent; I shall let them know of your conduct."

The young man thought for a moment; he had an aged father and mother and two young sisters dependent upon his hire; if he were to act as a man what would become of them? A blush of shame and indignation mantled upon his cheeks, and the tears rose to his eyes, as he muttered,—

"I didn't mean to offend you, sir; I hope you'll overlook any hasty word I said."

"Well, well, I'm glad to see you repent; I'll consider it."

The young man turned and muttered—

"Oh, my God, how we are scourged!"

"Brethren, the Scripture tells us that, 'if the blind lead the blind, both will fall into the ditch;' now, ye are in the blindness of sin, and quacks, that are as blind as yourself, pretend to lead ye. 'They are glad when they have done evil," sayeth the proverb; so with your priests, they sow the seed of iniquity in men's hearts, that they might empty their pockets, but the Scripture says, 'evil doers shall be cut off.' Our Saviour called each servant to account for the talents entrusted to his care. Now, what could your priests say, they are living in idleness."

" Oh, oh!" murmured the people.

" Hould your tongue, you schamin villain," shouted some man from behind.

" Shut your thrap."

"Go, preach to Miss Ellis, behind the ould chap's back," said another.

" Faith, he's practising betther than he's preach ing, there," said another.

"Who could blame the stharved divil," said a little thin fellow, almost without a rag upon him.

Mr. Sly looked horrified.

Miss Ellis wondered what it all meant, and asked Mr. Sly to come into the gig, and drive away.

" No, Miss Ellis; I have a duty to perform, and I will," said he, heroically.

" I tell every one of ye," said Mr. Pembert, "if I hear another word from ye, I'll stop the work and send ye home, so take your choice."

" Shure he's abusing the phriests, that always sthuck to us."

" Take your choice now,—go on, Mr. Sly."

"Ye all know that your priests will not do any thing without payment. It is with them as if I were travelling, and lost my way, and fell into a deep pit; I chance to catch some branches on the edge, and cling to them; a man is passing; I call to him, for the love of God to pull me up; he asks me, 'Have you a half-crown?' 'No.' 'Oh, well go down, I can't help you.' So your priests will let you go where you like, if you haven't the money. Again, they tell ye that no one will get to heaven but Catholics, as if Christ did not shed his saving blood for all Christians. Now, let us take a parable, when, say Mr. Ellis dies, he will go to the gates of heaven; Saint Peter will ask, 'Who are you?' 'I am Mr. Ellis, sir.' 'What kind of life did you lead?' 'A good, charitable life; gave every man his due, and wronged no man.'"

Here there was a general titter at the picture he drew of Mr. Ellis's life.

"Faith," muttered one, "I think he'll scarcely see the gates at all."

"Nabocklish," said another, "if he do, Saint Peter will be ashleep."

"Well, the Saint will say, 'all very good, but now, what was your religion?' 'I was a Protestant, sir. 'Oh, ha, if so, you must leave this,' and he shoves him down to hell."

"Faith, in troth, true enuff for you, it's there he'll go."

"Aye, and into the warmest corner, too."

"Shure, he'll have company ; they say the best of quality are there."

These and similar expressions were muttered.

"Well, take the other side ; some ruffian dies, whose hands are red with the blood of his fellow-creature. Saint Peter asks him, 'How did you live?' 'Only middling, thank your reverence.' 'I want to know, what kind of a life did you lead?' 'No great things of one, for, the devil take me, if——' 'Don't be cursing.' 'If I was not a raking, drunken fellow.' 'Bad enough, but what's your religion?' 'Arrah, faith, in troth shure I'm a Catholic, and every mother's soul that ever came before and after me ; and, more betoken, my——' 'Hush, hush, that will do, come in, the joys of heaven await you.' You see the bigotry and narrow-mindedness of your priests ; they would consign the good Christian to hell, because he differed with them in religion, whilst they would send the murderer to heaven. Again, they will not allow you to read the Bible, lest your eyes would be opened ; the Scripture says,—'Be not deceived, God is not mocked.' We will give you the Bible, the word of God, and point out to ye the way of life. We are the light."

"Yes, a new light."

"Aye, and a d——n dark one, too."

"A light that will quench in darkness."

"It would be no harm to cut your wick," muttered the crowd.

"Again, your priests tell you to pray to images,

and to worship the saints. You pray to the mother of God, as if she were a God, while she is merely a creature like yourselves. God is all grace, with Him is salvation ; what need, then, is there of praying to a woman ? she has no influence ; she——"

"Sthop," said an intelligent old schoolmaster, who was a ganger on the works, and who prided himself upon his knowledge of the Scriptures ; he had committed them to memory, and was looked upon by the peasantry as a second Father Maguire. "Sthop ; don't we say, 'Hail ! Mary, full of grace ; the Lord is with thee——?' "

"Yes."

"Then the Lord is with her ; we only ask her intercession with the Lord."

"Rank heresy, my man."

"Why was she asked to intercede with him at the wedding of Cana and Gallilee to turn the water into wine ? "

"But he refused her, my man, and said his time was not come."

"Ay, to show that he wouldn't do it for any other one ; didn't he do it, though ? "

"Bravo, Paddy ! that's it," shouted the crowd.

Paddy elbowed his way in, and stood fronting Mr. Sly.

"I ax you, sir, if you wanted a favor of Lord Clearall, wouldn't you go to Mr. Ellis to intercede for you ? "

"Faith he would, Paddy ; that's a poser."

"Ba! he's done up; that sthopped his fine speech."

"Shure ye have no religion," continued Paddy.
"You are divided into so many sects that ye are
changing every day. Socinians and other sects
scarcely believe anything at all, and yet they belong to you. No, the Spirit of God cannot teach
contradictory things, and 'there is but one Lord,
one faith, one baptism ;' and how can all your faiths
then be right?"

"Success, Paddy; sthick it into him; he hasn't a
word."

"Begor, Paddy is the great man entirely," shouted
the women.

"You are wrong, my man ; all Christian sects
believe in the fundamental articles of faith; they
believe in the grand dogmas on which eternal salvation depends."

"Do they, indeed? Is it an article of faith to
deny that our Saviour was God? It will not do to
believe small things. Ye must believe all things.
Hear what our Saviour said to His apostles : ' Go
ye, therefore, teach ye all nations : baptizing them
in the name of the Father, and of the Son, and of
the Holy Ghost; teaching them to observe *all things*,
whatsoever I have commanded you.' Again—'Every
plant which my heavenly Father hath not planted,
shall be rooted up.' Who founded our religion?
Ay, will you tell me that? Luther and Calvin, and
Henry the Eighth, and Queen Bess ; a precious and
chaste lot, no doubt—nice apostles to preach the

word of God! Oh! your religion is a rotten humbug, sir ; got up to favor rapine and plunder, and
every kind of injustice, and the worst of passions.
It is divided into contradictory sects, without union,
without——"

"Stop, sir ; if we haven't the union of sects, we
have the union of faith, and faith——"

"Arrah! hould your tongue, man ; how can ye
have faith when ye believe different doctrines ; and
as to charity, shure ye have it!—Arrah! isn't it the
nice charity to go into the houses of the sick and
stharving, and to try and timpt them with meal and
money, and when they wouldn't sell their sowls, to
lave them to die as you did to-day, and as you're
doing every day.   Look at the priests ; they are
going into fever hospitals, into fever cabins, attend-
ing and consoling the poor.   Shure they haven't a
shilling—they can't dhrive in a gig.   And the poor
are forced to send their children to hear their religion and the Blessed Virgin reviled."

"We are but leading them from darkness.   As to
the mother of God, it is blasphemy, heresy, to pray
to her ; she's a woman, she is——"

"Arrah! now, do you know better than the saints.
Saint Bonaventure says, 'Mary is most powerful
with her Son ;' and Cosmas, of Jerusalem, that 'The
intercession of Mary is omnipotent.'   She is called
'As a fair olive tree in the plains.'   The Archangel
said to her, 'Fear not, Mary, thou hast found
grace.'"

"It is blasphemy, my man; rank blasphemy! to attribute to a creature the power of the Creator. Mary is a woman—she's nothing but——"

"Oh, holy Joseph! do ye hear that? Maybe it's something as bad as himself he's going to call the Blessed Virgin," said an old woman from a heap of stones.

"Bad cess to me; did ever any one hear the likes? Dhoul take every mother's sowl of ye, to let the Blessed Virgin be run down that way. Oh, if I were a man." said another, and she commenced rocking herself to and fro.

"Take that," said a virago, flinging a lot of dirt into the Rev. Mr. Sly's face.

"Oh! ye cursed papists," said Mr. Sly, hitting the woman with the whip.

The men were looking on for some time with a kind of sulky stupidness; they felt themselves annoyed and insulted; but what could they do? Ruin stared them in the face if they said a word; but at this insult they could not bear longer.

"Let us dash the devil into the pond beyond," shouted one.

"Kick him about; to the deuce with the whole dirty set,' said another.

"Hurra! give it to them, the soupers!"

The women flung mud at Mr. Sly, and at Adam Steen, who came to his assistance; even Mr. Pembert did not escape. The then hoisted the two first between them, and were dragging them over to the pond, when Lizzie Ellis ran and threw herself on her knees before them.

"She deserves the same thratement for helping the villains!" shouted some of the women. But others thought better of it, and contented themselves by rolling their victims in the mud.

Mr. Sly and his colleague were very glad to make their escape. Mr. Pembert ordered the works to be stopped, and went to lodge information. The works were thrown idle, and men and children prowled, living skeletons, about the country; some stole potatoes and sheep to keep soul and body together; but their owners were well repaid for these by county taxation.

The Petty Sessions came on in a few days. Lord Clearall was the presiding magistrate. Mr. Ellis and another magistrate were the only ones in attendance. The streets were crowded; for there were several indicted for assault upon the Rev. Mr. Sly and Mr. Adam Steen.

There was the greatest possible excitement among the people. The prisoners were convicted, of course, and sentenced to different periods of imprisonment. Lord Clearall made a very touching speech on the heinousness of their crime in assaulting a minister while preaching the word of God; also in creating a riot, which set hundreds, who were depending on their hire for subsistence—for life—idle; but, then, out of compassion for their wretched state, the works would be resumed to-morrow. He then complimented Mr. Sly on his forbearance and Christian meekness.

The poor wretches were then huddled off to jail, and their families left to starve and die.

Lord Clearall held a meeting of magistrates in the jury-room, and it was agreed to petition the Lord Lieutenant for additional police force, to be paid by the county, also to have the county brought under the new Coercion Act, as it was in a lawless state.

All this, of course, was done ; and the Viceroy not only granted their request, but thanked them for their zeal in behalf of law and order !

CHAPTER XIX.

MR. O'DONNELL was, as I said before, not only a wealthy farmer, but also manager of a local bank.

This gave him much influence. A great many loan-fund banks had been established through the county; Mr. O'Donnell, as manager of one of these, conceived the bold plan of converting it into a discount bank. Having got legal advice as to the safest and best mode of proceeding, he opened his bank. The safe and liberal accommodation given by Mr. O'Donnell enabled him to pay large interest to the shareholders. However, the affair being new, he had to secure many of the depositors. With their shares, and what available money he had himself, he had a working capital of some thousands.

Mr. O'Donnell was the poor man's friend, and as he was wealthy and generous, he often ran heavy risks to enable the poor to meet their rents.

His bank was useful also to the middling class of farmers, and the needy landlord. It is no wonder, therefore, that he was a popular and a rising man.

The country was fast collapsing into a state of ruin; Mr. O'Donnell could not foresee this. No

human foresight could foretell the failure of the
potato crop. It came like the withering simoom
of the desert, spreading death and desolation in its
track.

The shareholders applied to him for their money ;
he paid them as fast as he could get it from the bor-
rowers.

Several of these, though, became bankrupt, and
fled the country ; others had to give up their farms
to get relief or work, in order to keep themselves
alive. In this state of things those who held his
notes sued him for the amount; he offered to forfeit all his own money, and to hand over the bank
to their management. No, they'd have nothing to
do with it ; they held his notes, and should be paid.
He then asked time until he would recover what he
could out of the bank. They would not consent to
this, but took executions against him.

Two years have passed since we introduced our
readers to that happy Christmas party, around Mr.
O'Donnell's pleasant hearth. It is Christmas-eve
again, but there is no yule-log burning on the
hearth, or Christmas-tree sparkling on the table.
Times are changed indeed.

Mr. O'Donnell sits near the fire ; his head is bent
upon his hands ; his hair is quite grey, and he seems
as if twenty years had passed over him in so short a
time. There is nothing of his former strength and
gay good-humor about him.

Mrs. O'Donnell, too, looks very thin and pale ;

care and trouble are wearing her down. Beside her
sat Bessy ; she looked quite sickly ; the thin, blue
veins showed through her hands and face ; black
rims were under her eyes, and she had a short, dry
cough. It was evident that consumption was fast
doing its work.

"How do you feel now, darling ?" said Mrs. O'Donnell, turning to Bessy, after a fit of coughing.

"Better, mamma ; I'll lay my head upon your
lap."

"Do, pet."

Bessy nestled her little head in her mamma's lap.
Mrs. O'Donnell looked at Bessy, then at her once
fine manly husband, and sighed. He raised up his
head and looked at her, then at Bessy, and sighed
also.

"I wonder," said he, after a time ; " what's keeping Frank ; I hope he'll bring good news."

"I hope so too, John ; my dear, you take things
too much to heart. It will not mend matters to fret
this way ; how many, in those times of affliction,
have cause to mourn as well as we ?"

"True, love ; Heaven knows our cup is bitter
enough. There is actual poverty staring us in the
face, and I fear that's not the worst either," and he
gave a mournful look towards Bessy.

"God help us ! John ; it is true, we could bear
poverty, but other afflictions ——" and she wiped
the tears from her eyes.

Bessy slept on, and a hectic flush now and then

mantled her cheeks, and then came that short, dry cough.

" If Mr. Ellis doesn't stand to us, we're ruined ; and it is melancholy to see ourselves and our children reduced, perhaps to want."

" It is, husband ; but God's will be done."

" Blessed be His holy name," said Mr. O'Donnell.

" You couldn't help it, John."

" No, love ; I always thought I was doing the best; no one could foresee the ruin that was coming."

The door opened, and Frank entered ; he sat down wearily upon the chair. Mr. and Mrs. O'Donnell looked at him, to see what news could they read in his countenance.

" How is Bessy, mother ?" said he ; " I see she's asleep."

" She is, Frank ; I think she's something better, thank God !"

" Thank God ! that same is a relief," said Frank.

" What news, Frank ?" said Mr. O'Donnell.

" Nothing good, sir ; I didn't get a pound from either of your friends," said Frank. ·

" My God ! how often did I assist them ; Frank, I even lent them money to take land ; in fact, they owe their riches to me."

" So I told them, sir ; but they said ' they thanked their own industry ; that you were too ambitious; that you ——' "

" That will do, Frank ; stop, my heart will break. What did the attorney say ?"

"That he wouldn't enforce the execution for a few weeks, but couldn't keep it any longer ; I had to give him two pounds as a consideration."

"Frank, our only resource now is Mr. Ellis ; God knows I have no great faith in him ; still we must trust him.   He will be sheriff in a few weeks ; I will get him to seize on the stock, and cant them ; you can buy them up, and, as our lease is out, we must try and get a new one in your name."

"I have no faith in him, father," said Frank.

"Nor I either, Frank ; but I don't see what we can do otherwise ; we must trust him.   We owe no rent, thanks be to God ! he can seize them for the running gale ; you can buy them up, and sure they can't refuse giving a lease to you.   We can then pay these executions by degrees.   It would be pleasant, Frank, to keep the old home of our childhood, that witnessed so many festive scenes, over us," and he looked about the room, and sighed ; for fancy and imagination were busy peopling them with happy faces, long since gone ; with the laughter, and song, and mirth, of many a merry Christmas and happy New-Year in Glen Cottage.

"I don't see what we can do otherwise," said Frank ; "we must run the chance, though it looks like putting your hand into the lion's mouth."

"It does ; but then Lord Clearall must consider old respectable tenants ; besides, I saved the life of his father.   I was going up the hill of Knockcorrig, just the year I was married ; I heard a coach com-

ing down at such a rate that I at once conjectured
the horses were running away. I heard a voice
calling out to stop them for God's sake. I had a
stick, so I stood in the middle of the road; as they
came dashing towards me, I struck the foremost
horse, and then grasped the rein. They plunged
and dragged me under their feet; yet, I held them
and forced them against the wall. His lordship
came out—for it was he that was in it—and ran to
my assistance. It appeared that the coachman
somehow fell off, and that the horses dashed away.
Had they gone a few hundred yards more to the
short turn at the bridge, they would be all dashed
over it. His lordship thanked me most warmly, and
told me to ask any favor I liked. As I looked upon
it as a mere act of charity, that I should do for anybody, I would not accept any favor, but told him, if
I ever needed his interest, I would call upon him.
I had to go home with him to get my wounds dressed,
for I was all bruised and torn; the driver wasn't
hurt, so we proceeded along, I in the coach with his
lordship. If there be a spark of natural affection
in Lord Clearall, he will befriend the man that saved
his father."

"I remember the occurrence well," said Mrs.
O'Donnell.

"I hope his lordship will remember it as well,"
said Frank.

"Well, I trust he will," said his father.

"Where are Kate and Willie?" said Frank.

"They are above stairs in the little parlor," said Mrs. O'Donnell.

"I have a letter for Willie; we had better call him Doctor now, I suppose, since he has got his diploma. I have another from Father William, asking us over to spend to-morrow with him."

"I hope you'll go, Frank," said his mother; "this house is getting too gloomy now for light young spirits; go and try and make yourselves happy for a day at least."

"Yes, my boy, I think ye had better go," said his father.

Kate O'Donnell was sitting upon a low stool embroidering. She now and then looked lovingly into Willie's face, for he sat beside her reading that touching picture of misguided love, "The Sorrows of Werter." The unfortunate Werter breathed forth his passion with all the depth of human feeling. Willie did justice to the subject, for he had a full, deep, pathetic voice.

A tear now and then stole from Kate's eye, and moistened the embroidery.

"Kate, love," said Willie, as he closed the book, "will you sing a song? Somehow I feel so depressed that it requires your sweet voice to dispel this cloud."

"What shall it be, Willie? One of your own. I shall sing 'Lovely young Bessy.'"

"Even so, Kate; any song from you will have a charm for me."

LOVELY YOUNG BESSY.

"Come, sweet maid! it's a mild morn in May,
  The dew's on the grass, so pearly bright,
And the flowers are peeping out so gay,
  And the sun is up with its golden light
Softly streaming o'er hill and dale;
Come, Bessy, to pluck flowers in the vale.
              Come, young Bessy!
              Girl of the raven hair,
              The mild blue eyes,
              And the queenly air

"List to the milkmaid's song upon the hill,
  And the streamlet rippling through the glen,
And the low, humming click of the mill,
  And the warbling little birds—and then,
Harebells and primroses are looking out I ween,
Smiling a welcome to their fair young queen.
              Come, young Bessy!
              Girl of the raven hair,
              The mild blue eyes,
              And the queenly air.

"Come, sit here, love! where the wild blossoms glow,
  Sweetbriar and woodbine have twined us a bower;
The lambkins are sporting in the meadows below,
  And fragrant the perfume of the wild flower.
See our cottage! it gleams in the distance above;
Ah, is it not a sweet morn—a morn for love!
              Come, young Bessy!
              Girl of the raven hair,
              The mild blue eyes,
              And the queenly air.

"I prison'd her snowy soft hand as I said,
  Ah, Bessy, sweet love, my own darling fair!
Be the light of my heart, my peerless maid!
  Look and say is there love for me there.
She raised her mild eyes—oh, rapture divine!
The flower of the valley—young Bessy's mine.
              I love young Bessy!
              Girl of the raven hair,
              The mild blue eyes,
              And the queenly air."

As Kate finished the song, Frank entered the room.

"Here is a letter for you, Willie," said Frank, "and I have another from uncle, asking us to spend to-morrow with him." Willie read his letter and turned pale.

Kate looked at him; he handed her the letter; she read it through, then let it fall and clasped her hands together.

"She's fainting," said Frank. "What have you done to kill her, man?" and he ran to support her.

"Stop, stop! my God. Kate, darling, what ails you?"

"Oh! Frank, water! water!"

Willie held a draught of water to her lips, and then sprinkled her face.

"That'll do, I am better now; Frank support me to my room?"

"No, no," said Willie, taking and placing her on a sofa; he then knelt at her feet.

"Hear me, Kate, my love, hear me! Read that," said he, handing the letter to Frank.

Frank read:—

"Liverpool, Dec. 29, 1847.

"Dear Sir,

"We have appointed you as surgeon to the ship Providence, bound for Melbourne. The terms are £20 and full rations for the out voyage. As she sails on the 7th, you must be on board the 5th Jan.

"Steeber & Co."

"What does this mean?" said Frank; "have you trifled with my sister's affections, now to forsake her?"

"Hear me, Frank, and Kate, love, hear me, and do not wrong me. I have not trifled with her affections; no, Kate, darling! Heaven knows, life would be a blank without your gentle love to smooth my way; but, seeing the altered state of your once prosperous affairs, I knew I couldn't expect any fortune with my Kate from her dear father, and then knowing the difficulties a young doctor has to contend with, particularly in the present state of this wretched country, I came to the resolution of earning some money first; I wrote for an appointment on board an emigrant ship; I did not tell you this, as I did not wish to alarm my own love, and as I couldn't be sure of succeeding."

"Now, Kate, love, here in the presence of your brother, here, before my God, I pledge myself to be yours, to love and cherish you; whether you come with me now, or wait my return, I swear to be yours. Now, sweet girl, do you forgive me?"

"I do, Willie," she whispered.

"And you accept me, Kate, and bind yourself to me?"

"Yes, Willie," she whispered.

"God bless you, darling!" and he sealed their pledge of mutual love with a kiss.

"Frank, have I done right?" said Willie,

"I think you have," said Frank.

"Well," said Willie, "I think we had better ask your parents' consent; I hope they will agree?"

"No fear of that at all," said Frank, "for when they had wealth to give her, you were the man they wished to wed their daughter; now, when they have nothing but their blessing to give her, I'm sure they won't refuse."

"Kate, love, you are dearer to me now than when you had wealth; now you will believe me when I tell you that it is yourself alone I love."

Kate smiled fondly on him.

"I think ye might as well come down," said Frank, "and I will go before and prepare for your reception;" so saying, he left the room.

"Well, my sweet girl, my time is short; hadn't we better prepare and get married after to-morrow."

"No, Willie, no; I couldn't leave my parents now in trouble, and my dear little Bessy, I fear, dying; we are now betrothed; after your return I will consent."

"Bless you, darling, I cannot blame you; your love will cheer me, pray for me."

Mr. and Mrs. O'Donnell received them with open arms.

"I thought, Willie, that I could give you a good start in life with her, but times are changed; however, you have a treasure in herself," said Mr. O'Donnell.

"A treasure which I prize above all the wealth Lord Clearall possesses; oh, father, you now make me happy"

"God bless ye both, my children."

They knelt down, and as their father and mother breathed their blessing over them, they renewed their vows.

"I wished to get married now," said Willie, "but Kate has refused; she says she couldn't leave you, but will consent on my return."

"Ever the good, considerate daughter; I think she's right, Willie."

Though poverty was staring them in the face, there were happy hearts in Glen Cottage that night.

It was settled overnight that they should drive over to Killmore to Mass in the morning, and spend the day with Father O'Donnell

CHAPTER XX.

CHRISTMAS morning was ushered in with a grim,
sleety appearance. There was nothing of that genial
warmth about it that open men's hearts; neither
did you get the smile or the hearty greeting of
Christmas time from your neighbors. Ah, it was a
sorrowful Christmas to many, for, instead of the
feasting, and revelry, and good cheer, that should
welcome Christmas times, and make men's hearts
glad and light; instead of the mistletoe and holly
and ivy, gaunt famine and death were keeping their
dark jubilee in many an Irish home.

Father O'Donnell was robed in the sacristy, going
to celebrate Mass, when our party arrived. The
good old priest looked thin and care-worn, as if the
times were preying upon him.

He welcomed our friends with his usual greeting,
cead mille failthe. Mr. Maher and Alice were there
also to participate in the welcome; they had promised to spend the evening with Father O'Donnell.

Father O'Donnell's chapel, like himself and his
congregation, seemed the worse of the times; the

plastering had fallen off the ceiling over the sanctuary, and the dove had lost another wing, and hung its head despondingly. His motley and ill-clad congregation knelt before him in fervid piety, and though famine had reduced many a once stalworth frame to a living skeleton, there was not a murmur of discontent in that house of God. A feeling of pious resignation, of deep devotion, pervaded all. There is a solemn depth of sanctity, of something beyond man s conception, in the ceremony of the Catholic Church. The senses are first captivated, then the heart is bowed down with a mysterious something, that makes us feel that we are in the presence of our God, and that we are but as dust, as nothing, before his omnipotence. As the priest, in low and solemn tones, pronounced the words, "Sanctus, Sanctus," his congregation bowed down and wept, and prayed the great Lord to have pity upon them. They forgot their poverty, their want; they forgot that many of them had not a dinner to eat, or a home to go to, that blessed Christmas-day; they forgot that, before that day week, the coroner would pronounce over the corpses of many of them, "died from the effects of starvation;" they forgot all but that they had assembled there to honor the Saviour of the world. Poor people, heaven, at least, must be your home; for this world was one of trial and wrong and suffering! After the last gospel he gave them his usual exhortation in the following manner:

" My dear people, this is a sad Christmas to many of ye; I know that there are many of ye that haven't a bit to eat this blessed Christmas-day. God help yo! The potatoes were never so bad as this year; I got a load this week from Mr. Maher—God bless him ; sure but for him and the Rev. Mr. Smith, ay, faith, the Protestant minister, and a few other rich parishioners, I couldn't live at all. Sure I couldn't expect a halfpenny from you, poor crea- tures, and you starving. God relieve ye ! Well, as I was saying, though they were all picked potatoes, there was one-third of them black. I am nearly as poor as yourselves; I'd scarcely have a bit of meat for my dinner to-day, only Mr. Smith sent me a leg of mutton and a ham of bacon, though he's not much better off than myself, for he gives every pound he can spare to the poor. God reward him, and sure He will."

A murmur of applause ran through that mass of human beings, and many a prayer was breathed for the good minister.

" What a contrast, my dear people," continued Father O'Donnell, " to those low, ignorant, ranting, proselytising soupers, that are going through the country with their sanctimonious looks and deceit- ful hearts. They will not give a morsel to poor, starving persons unless they turn, or, what's as bad, go to their schools. Now, I tell ye, don't mind them ; leave them to God, but don't send your children to their schools, as you value their salvation. No, **my** poor people. if you should even die of hunger, God will reward you with heaven, but if you listen to their seductions, hell is your portion for all eternity. Do not ill-use them or abuse them, either, for the law is on their side; but when you meet them, and they offer you tracts, go on your knees, and make the sign of the cross, as you would if you met the evil one."

Father O'Donnell went into the school-room, and he was there surrounded by a host of half-naked, starving creatures.

"For God's sake, give us something to buy a bit to eat this blessed day?"

"Only it's Christmas-day, shure we didn't care."

"God help you, my poor people," and he wiped his eyes, and gave unto each head of a family sixpence or a shilling, the Christmas offerings of his wealthier parishioners.

He then left for home in company with his guests. There was a crowd of poor people about the door of his cottage.

"Well, what do you want?" said he.

"Something to ate, your riverence; we haven't a bit for our dinner."

"Mrs. Hogan!" shouted the priest.

"Coming, sir;" and Mrs. Hogan made her appearance, looking well, considering the times.

"Well, Mrs. Hogan, look at all the company I've brought you."

"Shure they are welcome, your riverence," and

Mrs. Hogan made a low courtesy to those on the car.

"What will we do with these, Mrs. Hogan?" and he pointed at the ragged group.

"Hunt them away, sir; shure if they haunt you as they are, you won't have a bit, nor a sup, nor a stitch to wear, for the matter of that soon. You gave the last shirt you had to that poor man yisterday—would have given your coat, but I stopped you."

"Hush, hush. Mrs. Hogan, like a good woman, bring out the potatoes Mr. Maher sent us and divide them amongst them."

Mrs. Hogan raised her eyes and hands to heaven, and ejaculated : "What will become of us at all, at all ; it's the poorhouse we'll have to go to?"

"It's Christmas-day, Mrs. Hogan," said the priest, persuasively. "How would you like to be without your dinner to-day?"

Mrs. Hogan looked for advice and consolation to those on the car.

"Give them to the poor people ; I'll send you another load to-morrow," said Mr. Maher.

"Thank your honor ; shure I will, your riverence. I was only waiting a sthart," said Mrs. Hogan.

Mrs. Hogan proceeded to divide the potatoes, and our party went into the priest's cottage. The young people sauntered about the lawn, whilst Father O'Donnell, accompanied by Mr. Maher, went to have breakfast.

Alice and Frank walked arm-in-arm along a sheltered walk in the little garden. Willie Shea and Kate had so much to say to each other, so many little affairs to settle, so many promises to make over and over again, that they could attend to nothing else. They sat for the last time together in the old summer house.

"Kate, my love, we have but another week to spend together. Heaven alone knows what may befall us."

"God will watch over us, Willie; my life shall be dark, indeed, until we meet again."

"And will mine be one of roses, Kate, think you."

"I fear not, Willie. Let us love and pray for one another."

"Yes, darling! let us. Kate, remember me in your prayers."

"You need not tell me."

"I know that, my love."

"Should I die far away, or meet any mishap, love, sure you'll never forget me."

"I'll go to the grave; ay, and to an early one, too, should anything befall my first, my only love."

"God bless you, Kate! Here," he continued, "is a locket with a miniature of me; see, there is some of my hair in it also."

Kate placed it around her neck.

"Now, Willie, I have not forgotten you either," and she pulled a gold locket from her breast. "Take this, Willie ; a lock of my hair is in it, entwined with some of yours."

Angels looked down with pity, and sanctified their vows of mutual love.

Alice and Frank walked up and down in silence for some time.

"Alice," said Frank, "I fear fortune is against us."

"I hope not, Frank. At least, we can love one another."

"Yes, it is a sweet dream, Alice. Would that the future were as bright as the past."

"Let us hope for the best, Frank ; a little time might put your affairs right ; I know you are a favorite with my father."

"Do you say so, Alice? But, then, what's the use? I could not ask his child to share a lot of penury ; no, I love you too well for that, Alice."

Alice looked into his face, and her old gay smile played about her pretty mouth.

They were silent for a time ; at length Frank said—

"Alice, if I were poor, could you love me ?"

"As deeply, and more so, than when you were rich ; you know me not, you know not woman's heart, to say so," said the noble girl, as a tear stood in her eye, and again they sparkled with love and reproof.

"Forgive me, Alice ; love and poverty are jealous."

Alice was silent.

"Well, do you forgive me, love ?"

"I do, Frank."

"Alice, I have a little plan."

"Like you, always planning," said she with a smile ; "well, what is it ?"

"This, Alice ; if our affairs do not improve, I'll follow the example of Willie, and win gold in some foreign land, and then return to my own sweet love."

Alice sighed, and wiped away a tear.

Father O'Donnell had finished his breakfast, and was seated in his old arm-chair, enjoying a cosy chat with Mr. Maher.

The wretched state of the country was a prolific subject for gossipers, and politicians, and newspapers ; most likely they had it in hand too.

. At least, Father O'Donnell sighed and shook his head, and spread his thin hands over the fire and finished the discourse with—

"God help them, Mr. Maher ; God help them !"

Our party now entered the parlor.

"You look like the genius of melancholy brooding over that fire, Father William," said Alice, going over and laying her hand playfully on his shoulders. The old priest caught her hands and pressed them.

"Age is always gloomy and exacting, my child," said he ; "but where have you been ?"

"Oh, out in that old garden of yours, looking for heart's-eases and pansies ; but we found nothing but wild roses hedged with thorns," said Alice, with an arch smile at her companions.

"Roses," said the old man; "roses now! why, you surprise me."

'Oh, monthly ones, I suppose," said she again.

"Well, well, Alice, I don't know what to make of you, you are such a madcap! yet I can't scold you; hy, Mr. Maher ?"

"Oh, I'll leave you to settle your little quarrel between you," said Mr. Maher, good-humoredly.

"Sit beside me, Alice!" said Father O'Donnell. "That will do; now, my child, tell me"—and he looked into her face inquiringly—"how often do you act the Sister of Charity now ?"

Alice blushed and said, "Oh, Father William, you know I am, as you say yourself, a madcap, a thoughtless girl; so let my faults lie hid."

"Your faults! A madcap you may be apparently, but I know you, Alice; and you often forestall me in my missions of mercy to the sick-bed."

"Oh! don't, Father William, or I'll leave you;" and she blushed deeper and rose to go.

"No, no, stay, Alice, I'll say no more; yet I could not let your good deeds remain unknown."

Her father took her hand lovingly in his, exclaiming, "God bless you, my child!"

Frank's heart responded, "God bless and protect her!"

"What will the country come to, Mr. Maher ?" said Father O'Donnell to his guest.

"Really, I don't know, sir; it is strange how in-
fatuated landlords are, ejecting poor tenants in hundreds, sending such as do not starve outright to die
in that lazar called the poorhouse, and to multiply
our rates."

"Really, it is strange," said Father O'Donnell;
"there is the land now lying waste on their hands,
and to my own bitter knowledge the poor rate has
been 15s. in the pound for the last year."

"So high!" said Mr. Maher.

"Every penny of it; I know it to my cost," said
Father O'Donnell.

"It was only 5s. with us; but then we have no
evictions; the Earl of K——e is a father to his tenantry; he has ordered his agent to make a reduction of twenty-five per cent. on the rents, and also
to allow the poor-rates in full while the present
hard times continue; besides, he gives a great deal
of employment. I think I might safely say there is
not a tenant in want upon his property."

"God bless and reward him!" said Father O'Donnell, clasping his hands piously together.

"I wish we could say as much for Lord Clearall,"
said Frank.

"I am sorry that you cannot, Frank," said Mr.
Maher; "there are more evictions, and consequently
more misery, upon his property than in all the
county together. He is a bad man, and I fear his
agent is worse."

"It is melancholy, indeed, that such men as he

and his agent should have unlimited power over their poor serfs," said Willie Shea.

" Yet, such are the boasted laws of England," said Frank ; " they give him as much power over his tenants as if they were slaves. It is true, he cannot sell them, but then he can turn them out of their homes ; he can make them beggars ; he can rob them of the fruits of their hard industry. He can force them to sell their souls or starve. The slaves of America are a thousand times better off than the Irish serfs. The master has an interest in his slave ; he is his property, he cares for him, he—"

"But consider," said Mr. Maher, "that parents and children can be separated, and sold to different masters."

" Grant it, sir. I do not defend slavery ; God forbid I should ! for it is a bitter draught ; but then, I say that stern necessity compels Irish families to separate as much as the slaves. In how many a family is the father, the brothers, the sisters, or sons forced to emigrate, perhaps never to return. Are they not separated in the poorhouse, sir ? Oh ! I fear the laws are made to be scorpions in the hands of the rich, and not for the protection of the poor."

" It is true," said Willie Shea. " There is no other people under heaven that would bear so much."

" There is a spirit abroad ; I hope a day of reckoning will soon come," said Frank, and his eyes kindled.

"Frank," said his uncle, "do not feed yourself

with this. We have tried that game too often, and what are we the better of it? No, child, there is too much disunion among ourselves; there is too much power in the hands of our enemies; we are crushed and trampled on, and then taunted. No, Frank, no, we are too weak; they are too strong. We gain nothing by such struggles but widows and orphans, and desolate homes."

"But then we could die at least like men. See what the Americans did with their three millions. Nearly half a million of our people have died already of want—better have them die like men."

"Now," said Mr. Maher, who saw that both Frank and his uncle were getting too warm on the subject, "I think we are too selfish, keeping all the conversation to ourselves. Let us speak on something that the ladies can join us in—eh, Miss O'Donnell?"

"I think you're right, sir," said Kate, who was glad to change the subject.

"Well, I believe so," said Father O'Donnell; and the conversation became general.

After dinner, while the gentlemen were enjoying a glass of punch, Kate and Alice went into the kitchen. Mrs. Hogan was comfortably ensconced in her old corner. Neddy O'Brien, too, lolled in the other corner, in a state of somnolency. Things were going on swimmingly with Neddy, for while the priest's larder had a bit in it, he was sure not to want. He managed his game with consummate tact. He brought Mrs. Hogan and Jack Grace to-

gether. Mrs. Hogan was highly pleased with Jack,
and he with the inexhaustible stores of bed-clothes,
sheets, and a thousand other things she was said to
have stored away somewhere in the priest's house ;
besides, she had fifty pounds, ay, every halfpenny of
it in hard cash, in bank.

Neddy gave a yawn, and stretched out his hands.

"I think, ma'am, I'll go over to Jack's," said
Neddy.

"Do, avick. Shure I didn't see him to-day, I was
in sich a hurry to get the dinner."

"He was axin' me where you were, ma'am."

"Tell him I'll see him on Sunday, Neddy," said
she.

"I will, ma'am. I fear we'll have no sphree to-
day. Shure the times are gone. One can't get a
few boys to take a glass of punch, even on Christmas-day."

"They can't help it, Neddy, they can't help it,
they are so poor. Here, Neddy, is a six-pence for
the night, and stay, I'll slip out a glass of punch for
you."

"Thank you, ma'am. Maybe I won't tell Jack
how good you are, and if we don't have the fun at
your wedding."

"Whist, Neddy ; don't be saying that," and she
gave Neddy a poke in the ribs.

"Faix I will though, ma'am, and that soon too.
Shure Jack says he can't hould out much longer."

"Bad scran to him, the schemer."

" Sorra a óne could blame him, ma'am. Faix, I'd be as bad myself, iv some one thought as much of me," and he looked most coaxingly at Mrs. Hogan.

Mrs. Hogan set up the ghost of a smile.

" Mrs. Hogan, I know something. Shure, I heard it in the garden."

" Whist !"

" Faith, I did, though."

" What was it, Neddy," said Mrs. Hogan, coaxingly.

" Bad scran if I like to tell."

" Do, Neddy, avick."

" Och, faix I don't like to tell, ma'am ; maybe it's not right."

" Do, Neddy, and I'll put two glasses of whiskey in your punch."

" Shure you won't tell any one ?"

" Oh, sorra a one."

" Shure, I was behind the hedge, and I heard the doctor speaking of going away, and axin' Miss Kate to go with him."

" Hould your whist."

' Divil a lie in it. She began to cry, and he caught her this way," and Neddy hugged and rocked Mrs. Hogan as you might a bear, and then tried a kiss.

" That was funny, Neddy."

" Then I looked up ; there was Frank and Alice doing the same."

" Och," said Mrs. Hogan, raising her eyes, perfectly horrified.

"I think they are all disthracted, as the phriest says when he marries the people."

"That's not it, Neddy; it's some other stracted. Shure, we ought to tell on them."

"Och, honor bright, would you like a body to tell on yourself?"

"That's thrue, Neddy; shure it's natural."

"Whist, that's the bell, Neddy; more wather; I'll engage, they won't leave a dhrop of sphirits in the house, and it's scarce enuff."

"Whist, ma'am, here are the ladies."

"Well, Mrs. Hogan, aren't you married yet?" said Alice.

"No, Miss Alice; shure a poor woman like me wouldn't get any one; it's enuff for the likes of you, Miss, to be thinking of that."

"Now, indeed, why, Mrs. Hogan, I'm told there's a boy near here, that has a snug house and three cows, breaking his heart about you."

"Sorra a word of lie in that, Miss," said Neddy, with a grin.

Mrs. Hogan blushed, if the ghost of a blush could find room on her ruddy cheeks.

"You're welcome to your fun, Miss."

"It's the truth, Mrs. Hogan; he's dying about you;" and Alice winked at Kate.

"Maybe there is some one not a mile away dying about yourself, Miss Alice; I know two things, and what happened in the garden, too," said Mrs. Hogan.

It was Alice's turn to blush now.

"The deuce take it, there is the bell again," said Mrs. Hogan ; "I'm coming! Will ye's ever sthop with your ringing? how can my poor feet hould?" and Mrs. Hogan made her exit.

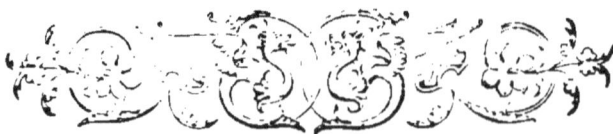

CHAPTER XXI.

NEXT morning, after breakfast, Frank and his
uncle were walking about the little lawn, the good
priest giving a thousand advices to Frank as to the
best manner of settling his affairs. However, they
were so complicated that he contradicted and re-
contradicted himself, until Frank found at the end
of the discourse that he was not a bit wiser than at
the start.

"I tell you what, Frank, I tell you what; I don't
know what to say. I don't like to trust that scoundrel, Ellis; yet, I fear, there's no other course left;
no, I fear not—but who is this?"

A man rode up on a very good-looking horse, and
after respectfully doffing his caubeen, said:—

"Please your riverence, Parson Smith sent me
for you to prepare poor Jack Tobin, that's nearly
dead. He had no other one, so he calls me, and
says, 'Will you go for the phriest to prepare this
poor man, and take my horse and hurry, for I fear
he won't live long,' and wasn't that very good of

him, your riverence ; so off I dashes as hard as I could."

" How will I travel?" said Father O'Donnell, turning to Frank.

" I'll drive my car over with you, sir."

" Yes, that will do, run and get the horse ready. And now, good man, ride back and tell Mr. Smith that I'll be with him directly."

" I will, your riverence."

As Frank and Father O'Donnell were getting upon the car, Father O'Donnell stopped and paused, and then went into the pantry, and shortly returned with a joint of cold meat and some bread. It was funny to see the old priest looking cautiously about him to avoid Mrs. Hogan's observation, or rather her lecture upon his extravagance. He first cautiously shut the door leading from the hall into the kitchen, and then made a dive into the pantry, concealed his booty under his coat, and made for the car.

" Here, Frank, here child, stick these in the well! I know we'll want them ; I did it cleverly, didn't I ? That's it now, drive away ; the old lady would give me such a hearing if she saw me ; I tricked her, though ; how she'll scold by and by, though ; ha, ha, ha!"

" Why don't you let her go, uncle ? I wouldn't be bothered with her that way."

" That's all the harm in her, Frank, that's all, child ; she's with me since I became a parish priest ;

how could I part with her now.   No, I am so used
to her, I turned her away once, and begad I was
sick until she came back.   I'll tell you, Frank, it is
not easy to part those with whom we have lived for
years ; besides, she's not a bad woman after all ;
her tongue is the worst of her ; drive on, Frank.   I
hope we won't be late ; very kind of Mr. Smith, so it
was."

Jack Tobin's cabin was some distance from the
road, so they had to leave their car in a farmer's
yard and proceed along an old boreen on foot.   The
cabin was a miserable hovel, built of sticks against a
high ditch, and these covered with heath and scraws.
The front was built of earth and stones, rudely piled
together.   The rain had puddled the earth around
it.   It was not a bit more comfortable within.   The
water freely dripped through the broken roof, forming pools upon the soft floor.   There was no fire in
the rude grate.   In a corner, upon a damp bed of
straw, lay the wretched man, a death-like paleness
upon his features.   From his emaciated appearance,
it was evident that death was fast approaching.
When Father O'Donnell and Frank entered the cabin,
they found the Rev. Mr. Smith placing some warm
blankets, which his servant had brought with him,
around the sick man.   The patient raised his eyes
as the priest entered, and muttered—

" Thanks be to God ! He has heard my prayer."

" Welcome, Father O'Donnell," said Mr. Smith,
extending his hand to him.   " I'm glad you are

some in time to afford this poor man the consolations of his religion. I have done all I could for him in a worldly way ; so now we had better leave him to you."

The minister and the other inmates retired while Father O'Donnell was administering the rites of his Church to the dying man. His wife and two wretched children crouched outside the door. Frank and the Rev. Mr. Smith stood conversing near them.

"My poor woman," said the minister, turning to the emaciated skeleton at the door, "why didn't you seek work ?"

"So I did, sir ; while we wor able we were on the public works ; then my son took the dysentery from the exposure to cold and hardship ; my husband took it also ; I was sick too ; so when my darlin' boy died, we weren't able to bring him any farther than this," and she tottered over and lay upon a freshly raised mound of earth.

"Good God!" said the Rev. Mr. Smith, "is your son buried there ?"

"He is, your riverence," and the poor woman wept and swayed her body to and fro, over the grave. "He is here, my banchaleen bawn, without a coffin or a shroud to cover him. Oh! my darlin', my darlin' child, I'll soon be with you, and your poor father, too, will soon shleep beside you, my darlin', lovin' boy, that you wor !"

"Don't cry and fret that way, my poor woman," said the Rev. Mr. Smith.

"Oh, sir, oh, sir, if you knew how good and kind he was, you would not blame me. Shure it's a terrible thing to die of hunger, and then be buried like the beasts of the field in unhallowed ground."

"I do not blame you ; it is natural that you should feel the loss of your child deeply."

"Oh, sir, sir, it is terrible ; God knows how we lived ; we have eaten but docks and weeds these four days. We struggled to live some time upon the flesh of an ass, but when this was out we stharved entirely. We worn't able to bury my poor boy ; he was dead three days in the bed, and it is only yisterday that a poor travellin' man helped me to bury him there. And what harm if. he were buried like a Christian in a churchyard. Oh, oh, God help us !"

"Don't cry, poor woman ; I'll have him removed this evening to the next churchyard. I'll send my men with a coffin to bury him decently."

She threw herself on her knees, exclaiming : "God Almighty, bless you and your family. Oh! Lord, hearken to the prayers of the afflicted. Oh, sure," said she, turning to Mr. Smith, "if every minister was like you, this isn't the way we'd be to-day. We were snug and comfortable until Mr. Shly came to the county ; he got us turned out of the lodge, as we would not send our children to his school ; so we had to lave, and then we came here."

"Mr. Sly," said Mr. Smith, musingly. "That man is creating a world of mischief and disaffection in this part. He is no minister; but if he be what I'm told, I will expose him to shame, if he have any."

"If he is not worthy the confidence of Lord Clearall and Mr. Ellis, it is a pity not to have him exposed, for he is creating a great deal of bad feeling between these gentlemen and their tenantry."

"I am aware of that, Mr. O'Donnell. I am told that he is a mere low Scripture-reader; and that himself and that Mr. Steen, who is actually his brother, were hunted out of England on account of their immoral conduct."

"If such be the case, you ought, I think, expose him, sir; for it is currently, and, I believe, truly, reported, that he has gained the affections of Miss Ellis, who is a good-hearted, sensitive young lady, if not perverted by his machinations."

"I cannot act from hearsay, Mr. O'Donnell; but I will fish out all particulars about him, and then, feel assured, I will expose him fully. I will not allow such a wolf in sheep's clothing to go about disgracing our sacred calling."

Here the conversation was interrupted by Father O'Donnell opening the cabin door.

"Ye may come in," said he; "I fear the poor man is dying."

The wife and two children rushed in, followed by the minister and Frank. The poor man was deadly pale, and his eyes were fixed and glassy.

"Thank God! I die content," muttered he.

"Oh, Jack, aroon! what will we do now at all, at all?" sobbed his wife.

The emaciated children wept and cried. The dying man looked at his wife and children, and then imploringly and confidingly at Father O'Donnell and the Rev. Mr. Smith.

"Make your mind easy about them, my poor man," said the minister; "I will see that they shall not want."

"God bless you!" he muttered, and he took his wife's hand, pressed it, and placed it in the priest's.

"I will see them provided for," said the Rev. Mr. Smith again.

The sick man heaved a sigh and lay back; his eyes opened and closed again.

"He's dying," whispered the minister to the priest.

"Let us read the litany for a soul departing!" said Father O'Donnell.

They all knelt down upon that wet floor beside the dying man's bed; and priest and minister, and all, joined in one fervent supplication of mercy for the departing soul. The sick man muttered a few responses, and then gave a few convulsive sighs. He was dead.

The priest and minister, after making arrangement for the Christian interment of the poor man and his son, and assuring the widow and orphans that they should be provided for, took their departure.

The Rev. Mr. Smith faithfully kept his promise; he got the bodies decently interred, and the widow and her two children removed to a snug cottage, where they were comfortably provided for.

As Frank and his uncle returned home, he could not help contrasting the Christian zeal and spirit of the Rev. Mr. Smith with that of Mr. Sly.

"You don't know Mr. Smith, Frank—you don't know him," said Father O'Donnell; "he is the good minister; he goes about to the poor people's houses, giving them food and raiment; he never interferes with their religion; but if he finds any of them dangerously ill, like this poor man, he sends for me. It is often he slips a five-pound note into my hand, remarking, 'You know the poor better than I do, so take and divide this upon the most needy and deserving.' Do you know what he was talking about that time when he called me over."

"No, sir, I'm sure I don't."

"Well, look at this?" And he showed Frank a three-pound note.

"I see it, sir; what has that to do with it?"

"Everything. 'Father O'Donnell,' said he, slipping this into my hand, 'take this as my offering to your Christmas collection; sure your parishioners are paying tithes to me—the least, then, that I should contribute something to you these hard times.'"

"Would to God," said Frank, "that every minister were like him; then we would have no religious animosities or religious bickerings in the country, as the Rev. Mr. Sly is producing; no, we would have a union of Christian brotherhood."

Frank and his party returned home that evening. They could not remain longer, as Willie Shea had to make arrangements for his departure.

We will not attempt to paint the feelings of Kate O'Donnell, as she took her final leave of her betrothed. Ossian speaks of the joy of grief. Never do we feel this so truly as when we take leave of some dear friend, or loved one, who is going to fight the rough battle of life in order to gain a name and station for us. Amidst our tears of sorrow there is a joy that tells us that that manly young heart will succeed in life's rough struggles, and will win us a happy home. Such were the feelings of Kate O'Donnell, as her Willie strained her to his bosom, and imparted the last farewell kiss upon her lips.

Mr. and Mrs. O'Donnell wept after him, for they loved him as their son.

Little Bessy wept upon his bosom, and his tears moistened her gentle face and golden hair, for well did he know that he would never press that darling child to his breast again.

Kate and Frank accompanied him to the next station. Frank looked upon him as a brother, and felt that one of the ties that bound him to life was severed.

There was many a sad parting at that station-house that morning, but none more sincere than that of our friends.

I have often watched the separation of friends at a railway station. It is sorrowful to see the aged father and mother pressing to their bosoms, in one wild embrace, the son or daughter with whom they are to part forever. Oh! to hear the groans that shake that old frame, and to witness the tears that moisten the whithered checks of age! Look at that phrenzied embrace of that young wife and husband as they part, perhaps forever; and listen to the cries and screams of these women and children; good God! it's pitiful. Can the slave markets of Africa produce anything more harrowing? You may ask me why do they go? Stern necessity compels them : they have no choice—go they must, or starve.

As the engine puffed away upon its rapid journey, Willie leaned his head out of the window, and waved his white handkerchief to Kate. Poor Kate sobbed in silence, and intently watched his receding figure. One wild wave of the handkerchief, as they turned a curve, and he was gone—yes gone, perhaps forever. Who could tell?

As she returned home, a feeling of loneliness and desolation crushed her young heart. A sweet, undying love had possessed her ; it entwined its tender tendrils around her affections, until her bosom throbbed with a strange feeling of delight. He, the noble, gentle youth was now gone, perhaps forever! Who could tell what his fate might be! Perhaps her sweet dream of love was but a vision of happiness. Ah! there is a sensitiveness about gentle hearts that makes them cling for love to some worthy object ; they must love some one, or die ; and if this pure love is disappointed or sullied, a corroding desolation takes its place.

Mr. and Mrs. O'Donnell occupied their accustomed seats near the parlor fire in the evening. Bessy was seated upon the settee, with her head, as usual, resting upon her mother's lap. Her mother was playfully twining her golden hair around her fingers. The little dog and puss were also amusing themselves by leaping and playing about the rug and settee, which gambols Bessy enjoyed.

" Ha, ha, puss, how funny you are ; come here !" and the two jumped upon her lap. Mr. O'Donnell's head gloomily rested upon his hand upon the table. Mrs. O'Donnell looked at him, then at Bessy, and as she heard her merry little laugh, and saw her bright eyes sparkle, a ray of hope lit her features, for a mother's anxious heart can never admit the unwelcome truth, that death is silently stealing her darling child. So Bessy took the cat in her arms, and the little dog went to rest upon the hearth-rug.

" Pusheen cat, my darling, would you be sorry after your poor little Bessy, if she went to heaven ?"

Pusheen cat mewed softly in reply, as Bessy gently stroked her sleek coat.

" You would ! Well, I know you would, pussy."

Bessy stroked her back, and pusheen set up a low purring croonaun, and then closed her eyes.

" Poor thing, I know you would be sorry for me."

Pusheen gave another assenting mew, which was interrupted by the little dog catching pusheen by the tail.

"Lie down there, you little brat, and let pusheen alone," said Bessy, drawing the cat nearer; and pusheen raised her paw to resent the insult herself.

"There now, you are not easy until you have another squabble," said Bessy, as pusheen jumped down and dealt a blow of her paw upon the offender.

Mr. O'Donnell occasionally raised his head and gave a sickly smile.

"Bessy darling," said Mrs. O'Donnell, "don't fatigue yourself."

"No, mamma, but it's so funny to see them playing; I am delighted."

"They are tired now, Bessy, as well as yourself; let them rest, pet."

"Yes, mamma," and she placed them upon the hearth-rug.

"Come, Bessy, lay your head upon my lap; that's it—nestle there, my darling; I hope you will soon be as strong as ever—eh, pet?" and the fond mother imprinted a kiss upon her lips and wreathed her hair upon her fingers.

"I hope so, dear mamma, for your sake and dear papa's; for Kate and Frank's sake, I should like to live; only for that I would wish to go to heaven. Oh! it is so bright and glad a place, filled with gladsome songs of joy and love; how sweet must it be, mamma, to be in heaven with our good and

16

blessed Saviour, who calls little children to Him and says, 'of such is the kingdom of heaven.'"

"It is, indeed, child, a land brilliant beyond our conceptions, glorious beyond all that eye hath seen, or the heart of man conceived."

"I was reading yesterday, mamma, about a good monk that left his convent, lured by the singing of a little bird. Its voice was so melodious, that he spent, as he thought, the most of the day listening to it. When he returned, what was his surprise to find the convent changed, and all the monks strangers to him. After making inquiries, it was found that he had been some hundreds of years listening to the little bird, which was no other than an angel. Oh, how delightful to hear the whole choir of heavenly angels chanting hymns of love and praise!"

"It must, indeed, Bessy."

There was a silence for some minutes.

"Mamma!"

"Well, pet."

"Would you wish me to be in heaven?"

"I would, love."

"Then, mamma, sure you won't fret when I die?"

"What makes you think of death?" asked Mrs. O'Donnell, wiping her eyes.

"I don't know, mamma; yet something tells me that God will take me to Himself. I'm sure it must be my guardian angel that tells me so."

"O Bessy, Bessy, don't break my heart by speaking of death."

"I thought, mamma, you wouldn't grudge me to
be happy in heaven ; sure I would get to be your
guardian angel to watch over you and papa, and
Kate and Frank."

Mrs. O'Donnell gave a few smothered sobs, and
the tears rolled down her cheeks.

"Don't cry, mamma, and I won't say it any more,
and, papa, kiss me," and she went over to her papa
and twined her tiny arms around his neck.

" God bless you, child!" said Mr. O'Donnell, as he
raised his head and pressed her fondly to his ach-
ing breast—"God bless you, darling! and spare
you to us to cheer our misery."

Mr. O'Donnell and Mrs. O'Donnell chatted and
laughed and played with that fond child. They forgot that misery and ruin were on their track ; their
hearts were too full of love and hope, and they forgot the dark frowns of the world. Thus they spent
their time until Frank and Kate returned. Mrs.
O'Donnell had the tastefully-laid tea-table spread
before them, and a cheerful fire sparkled in the grate,
and sad, but still loving hearts welcomed them.

During tea the conversation was chiefly about
Willie ; after tea, Mr. O'Donnell brewed his glass of
punch, and Frank did the same to refresh himself
after his journey.

Frank stirred his punch, and then balanced the
spoon upon the edge of his glass, and then looked at
his father ; but the latter was in one of his usual rev-
eries. Frank hem'd and haw'd. and at length said—

"I suppose you called upon the attorney to-day, sir? Is there any chance of a settlement?"

"None, Frank, none in life; I offered any compromise, but none would be accepted; nothing but pay down in full. This is very cruel, Frank—very cruel, considering all we have lost by that unfortunate bank, and that these people had as much right to meet the losses as I. While there was a gain, they had their share—why not of the losses? But now, as they have the writ out, they are pressing to enforce it before Mr. Ellis becomes sub-sheriff. I asked but two years to pay them all off. I told them that if my effects were scattered they would ruin me, without getting themselves paid."

"What will we do, sir?"

"We have only one course now, Frank—that is, to trust Mr. Ellis; let him seize and sell the stock and effects for rent; you can buy them, and get a lease in your name."

"I believe we must do so," said Frank, musingly.

"Yes, Frank, there is nothing else to be done; we can then pay these harpies without breaking ourselves. Frank, my dear boy, you cannot believe what a desire I have of ending my days in this old house of my fathers," and he looked about the room; "so go to-morrow to Mr. Ellis and tell him all. I hope he will act honorably."

"God grant it!" said Frank, doubtingly.

"Well, there is no help for it; we must trust him," said Mr. O'Donnell.

CHAPTER XXII

NEXT morning, after breakfast, Frank proceeded
to Mr. Ellis's residence. In answer to the bell, Nelly
Cormack came to the hall-door.

"Arrah, Misther Frank, is this you?" said she;
"shure you're welcome; walk in, sir."

"I'd scarcely know you, Nelly," said Frank, as he
shook her hand; "you're getting to be such a fine
girl."

Nelly blushed.

"You needn't blush so, Nelly. I am sure they are
very kind to you here."

"Indeed they are, sir. Won't you come in?"

"Yes, Nelly, I want to see Mr. Ellis. Where is
he?"

"He's in the office; I'll tell him that you are
here."

"Do, Nelly."

Nelly tripped into the office, and shortly returned
with orders for Frank to step in. Mr. Ellis was sitting at a writing-desk; beside him was Hugh Pem-

bert. As soon as Frank entered, Mr. Ellis raised his head, and said:

" Good-morning, Mr. O'Donnell."

" Good-morning, sir," said Frank, respectfully.

" Well, Mr. O'Donnell, what can I do for you?"

Frank stated his case fairly and clearly, and told him how his father sent him to him for protection.

" I understand, Mr. O'Donnell, that you want me to make a seizure upon all your stock and effects, and to sell them for rent."

" Yes, sir; in order to protect us from pressing and, I must say, unjust debtors; though there is only a half-year's rent due, the running gale will enable you to do so."

" Exactly so, Mr. O'Donnell. Well, I'll make the seizure this day, and send over Burkem and a few others as keepers. You know we must do these things openly to deter others from proceeding."

Frank bowed, and left the room.

" The fools," said Mr. Ellis, as he heard the hall-door close after him.

" They have a nice place there, sir," said Mr. Pembert; " it's a pity to have it going to rack as it is."

" It won't be long so, Hugh; I often wished to have them in my power, but now I have them. Hurry with that account; we must drive over there."

As Frank returned home he called to see his old nurse, Mrs. Cormack. She was at her usual occupa-

tion of knitting, and was seated near the door, with
her spectacles jauntingly fixed upon her nose.

"Good-day, ma'am," said Frank, as he entered the
cottage.

"Oh, Misther Frank, is this you, and how are you
and all at home? Shure it's a month of Sundays
since I seen you. How is that little darling, Bessy?
I'm tould she's not well. Shure I've threatened, I
dunna how long, to go see you."

"Why, Mrs. Cormack, you seem to forget us altogether. We are all well at home, except Bessy; she,
I hope, however, is improving. You seem to be
very comfortable here, ma'am," and he cast his eyes
around the comfortable cottage.

"We have no reason to complain, the Lord be
praised; the boys have good wages, and Nelly is a
favorite wid the masther. She's housekeeper there.
She brings me many a present of tay and sugar to
sthir my ould heart."

"I saw her to-day, and I scarcely knew her, she
looked so fine."

"She is, thanks be to God; and then we had a
letter from Ned. He is doing well in Amerikee.
Shure he sent me tin pounds—sorra a lie in it—and
said he'd pay all our passages if we'd go."

"Poor Ned, I recollect him well. He was a hard-
working, industrious boy, just the man for America."

"He was, God bless him! Here is the letther;
maybe you'd read it," and she pulled a crumpled
piece of paper from her pocket.

Seeing Frank hesitate about reading it, she exclaimed—

"Arrah do, Misther Frank; shure it gladdens my ould heart to hear it; it is like as if the poor bov wor speaking to me himself."

Frank unfolded the dirty scroll, and read:

"Phillydelphia, Dec. 20, 1847.

"DEAR MOTHER,—

"I rite these few lines hoping to find you and Nelly, and Jem and John, and all the nabors in good helth, as this laves me at present, thanks be to God for all his marcies——"

"The poor boy, isn't it the beautiful letther?" said Mrs. Cormack.

"Dear mother, I have good employment in a sthore, and I am saving every halfpenny I'm not sphindin' to sind ye, becase I hear that ye have frightful times at home. I——"

"Mostha, faith then he heard the truth."

"I sind you tin pounds, and if ye come out here I'll pay yer passage, for it's a fine country for any one able and willin' to work. I have a dollar and a half a day, and I am able to spare four dollars a week. Rite at once, dear mother, and let me know if ye'd come out. We could all do very well together; besides, we would be so happy. Do you know I does be often thinking of the boys and girls at home. How are they all?

"Faix there's many of them dead wid the hunger.

It's well for the poor boy to be where he is, Masther Frank."

" That's true, ma'am."

" I would wish to see sweet Tipprary agin. I have the blackthorn sthick Ned Casey gave me, and the hazel one too ; they say it kills sarpents. I also have the scraugh I took from the field behind the house, and every time I looks at it I thinks of the poor ould home. I do be lonely sometimes, but there is no use in fretting. I saw several blacks. They are ugly looking things, with big noses and eyes, and they as black as my shoe, and they have woolly heads."

" Och, the brutes ! to have wool like sheep. Couldn't they have hair like dacent Christians ?"

" I suppose they can't help it, ma'am; it grew there."

" I suppose so, Masther Frank. Shure they are not to blame ; they'd be like other dacent people if they could help it."

" Very likely, ma'am."

" Go on, Misther Frank."

" They frightened me very much until I became used to them——"

" No wonder ; I'm sure I'd lose my life if I saw them."

" So, dear mother, when you get this rite at once, tellin' me if ye will come out to me. I will send ye more money as soon as I have it. I will never let you want, dear mother. Give my love to all the nabors, and to all my school-fellows. What pleasant times we used to have, when going to Mr. Quirk, playin', and ramblin', and stealin' crabs, though he often payed us for it. Tell Paddy Nolan that I met his brother. He is doing well. Give my love to——"

"There is a whole lot of names here, ma'am; it is too long to read them."

• "That'll do, don't mind them. He is the good son, God bless him," and Mrs. Cormack wiped the tears of affection from her eyes.

"Will ye go out to him?"

"Not at present, Misther Frank. We are doing very well, and I'm too ould now to crass the say; though I'd go if I thought I'd live to see him."

"I am glad that you have good news, anyway; that's more than I can say. Times have changed very much with us, Mrs. Cormack."

"I am sorry to hear so."

"It's a fact; Mr. Ellis is going to seize upon our stock to-day."

Mrs. Cormack let her stocking drop, and looked horrified.

"Oh, och, mavrone, Misther Frank, is it come to that? I'm blessed iv one of my children works another day under his roof, the dirty spalpeen, to seize yere cows, oh, oh."

"It is for our good Mr. Ellis is doing it, ma'am, to protect us from others. Don't do anything rash, Mrs. Cormack."

"No, alanna. Here, Misther Frank," and she pulled an old purse from her pocket, and after untying about twenty knots, she drew forth the check.

"Here, take this, I don't want it, and it might serve ye. I would give my heart's blood, not to say this rag, to serve your darling mother, and the dear young ladies."

"No, no, ma'am, thank you; your money would be no use to us. It is a great sum for you, so keep it."

"No, Misther Frank, you must take it, just to keep it for me."

"I do not want it now, Mrs. Cormack; if I do, I will call for it."

Frank left the cottage, and Mrs. Cormack felt highly displeased, since he would not take the money. On his return home, he found Mr. Ellis and Hugh Pembert taking a regular inventory of the stock and effects; they then made their seizure, and left Burkem in charge. Ned Burkem, with his usual obsequiousness, did his utmost to make himself agreeable to every one in Mr. O'Donnell's employment, particularly to Mary Cahill. To her, he was all attention; he assisted her in her household duties, stood with the cows while milking, and did several other little offices. Though Mary did not love him, still it was something to be courted by a rising man like Ned Burkem—a man that stood so high in the estimation of both landlord and agent. Mary, like most of her sex, had a good mixture of

pardonable vanity in her composition, though she
did not encourage his addresses, still she did not
wholly reject them. It is true, Burkem loved her,
if one of his low, cunning nature could entertain
such a hallowed feeling as love. There are natures
that cannot understand or appreciate love in its
holiest and purest sense, and yet are governed by a
blind passion that drives them to desperation.

As Mary was returning from town, one evening,
about nightfall, Burkem met her a few fields from
the house. He crossed her path as if he were on
his way to Mr. O'Donnell's, whilst in reality he was
watching for her coming fully two hours.

"And is it now you're coming home, Mary. I
wonder you're not lonesome."

"Not a bit, Ned. I'm sure no one would hurt a
thackeen like me; besides, the neighbors aren't
bad."

"That's thrue, Mary, alanna; shure no one would
hurt a purty colleen like you."

"More of your blarney, Ned."

"Sorra a blarney, Mary. But go easy; I'm as
tired as a dog; we had such dancing at Mrs. Butler's
last night, I'm not able to sthir a foot."

"Now, who were in it?"

"Oh! not many. John and James Cormack were
there, and Hanna Russell. Faix I'm thinking that
James Cormack and Hanna are pulling a cord; I
never saw two greater in my life; they couldn't
sthir from one another at all."

Mary changed colors, for Hanna was a noted rustic belle, and a rival of hers. Though it was dusk, yet he knew from her eager, flurried manner that his words had taken effect, so he continued—

"Mrs. Butler tould me that they have the match all as settled. John Cormack is thinking of going to America to join his brother, so they'll have the house to themselves."

Mary walked on in silence.

"Don't you think it is well for them ?"

"Faix I'm sure I can't say ; I suppose it is ; but then it doesn't concarn·me," said Mary, with a sigh, rather too deep for an unconcerned person.

"No, but then people say that you had a liking for him, and that she got inside you, and people don't like to be jilted in that way."

"It's hard to sthop people's mouths ; but sure we must bear it," she replied.

"The way to silence them would be to take the sthart of them ; that would show people that you had no hankering for him."

"I wish them luck, Ned ; but never a bit if I mean to hurry myself on their account."

"You needn't, Mary, for you can easily get as good and better, any day. To say the least of him, he was a palavering sleeveen to be trying to coax any girl, and he going to be married to another."

"Faix," said she, with a forced laugh, "I don't care that about him," and she snapped her fingers. "That I may never meet a greater loss."

"I know one, Mary, that loves you dearer than his own life, that dreames about you day and night, that would give his heart's blood for you, and that is double as good a match as James Cormack, and that would one day make you a lady if you'd marry him."

"And pray, who is going to make this lady of me?" said she.

He pushed near her, and placed his arm around her waist.

"It's I Mary, I love you Mary; you know I have twenty pounds a-year; I'm promised a farm by the master; I will make you happy. Oh, Mary, say you'll be my wife! do love, and sure we'll be happy as the day's long."

She paused; the supposed faithlessness of her old lover rose up in judgment against him, yet she loved him, and a woman cannot tear the sweet pleasure of love so easily from her bosom, to make room for a new one. It is true, she often heard Burkem spoken of as a cunning, deceitful man; yet, she always found him kind and soft-spoken; besides he told her how he oftentimes interfered for the poor tenants; all this made some impression upon her.

"Well, Mary, what do you say?" said he.

"I don't know, Ned; we'll speak about it another time."

"Why not now? Will you have James Cormack laugh at you, when he marries Hanna Russell; besides, Mary, it is pleasant to have your own house and cows, and to have servants, instead of being one yourself."

"It is, indeed."

"Would you like riches, Mary?"

"Faith I'm sure I would," said she, with a smile; "who is it that don't?"

"True, Mary, they are everything; look at Mr. Ellis; he came here a poor steward; no one knew him—look at him now, what a great man he is, stuck up with my lord in every hand's turn."

"It is a fine thing to be rich, no doubt," said Mary.

"It is, Mary, for I'll tell you, but don't tell anybody."

"Never fear."

"Well, Mr. Ellis intends turning out the tenants, and I'm promised a farm, my choice of them you see; so if you like the ould place where you are, I'm sure we'd get it."

"What," said she, with surprise, "Mr. O'Donnell's place you mean?"

"Yes, wouldn't the people stare at us then; we could keep our car and drive about; sure after a time, we'd be rouling in riches, like Mr. Ellis.

Mary Cahill was silent; she was trying to take in the depth of his villany; believing James Cormack faithless, and knowing Burkem to be, in a worldly sense, a much better match, and seeing how deeply he was devoted to her, we cannot blame her if she hesitated as to what answer she would give to his appeal.

The only objection she had to him was, that he

was the servant of a tyrant; she heard always that
he used his influence for the good of the tenant;
still, after all, with that keen instinctive perception,
natural to women, she could never bring herself to
love him; perhaps, this was because she loved another; but now he had forsaken her, would she be
wise in rejecting the offer of so good a match.

Such were the thoughts that ran through her
mind, until Burkem laid open his scheme for becoming rich. He, with the narrow-minded sordidness
of low cunning natures, thought, as she expressed
such a desire for wealth, to dazzle her with projects
beyond her wildest conception. He did not see any
harm in occupying the O'Donnell's place, provided
they were once ejected; but when Mary understood
him, she turned upon him a look of withering scorn.

"Ned," said she, "do you think I'd live in the
house from which my benefactors were hurled forth
to work or starve? Do you think that I'd live in
the house from which any poor family was driven to
have their curses ringing in my ear; no, no, I'd
starve first. I thought you were a friend to the
family, but now I see what you are, you are as bad
as the rest of them; you only want the power to be
as big a villain; so take your hands ov me."

"Here me, Mary, shure I didn't mean ——"

"Hould your tongue, and take ov me."

"But Mary, if they were ejected some one would
have it; shure we might as well have it as a stranger
but if you wish we could get some other place."

"'Take ov me, I say."

" Mary, Mary, forgive me ; oh, if you knew what it is to love, to feel this burning passion, to feel one's heart, as if it were in a furnace, to feel this torture; no, I cannot leave you ; you must be mine."

"Must!" said she, with emphasis, as she strove to extricate herself from his grasp. "No, man, take ov me, I say. I'll never love you, I'll hate you, if you don't let me go."

" Mary, don't say that, say you'll love me.',

"Never, man, never ; I see your baseness now."

"Then, Mary," he exclaimed, "listen to me. Here is a prayer book, swear that you will be my wife."

"No, no, not now, perhaps some other time."

"Now or never," said he. "Here is prayer book,'' and he placed it in her hand. "Swear, or you'll rue it ; we're alone."

" No, no, I can't perjure myself, God help me !"

"You won't do it, then ?"

"No, never, I call upon a just God to assist me."

" You must swear !" exclaimed he, seizing her by the arm.

"I cannot, and will not !" answered she, much alarmed. "For the love of God, let me go ?"

" You must swear to be mine," returned he ; but at the same moment a blow of a stick resounded upon his head and laid him senseless on the ground.

" Take that, devil that you are," said the well-known voice of James Cormack.

"Oh, James, save me for the love of God."

"I will, Mary, my darling, I will—thank God, I was in time." He raised her up and pressed her to him.

"Sthop, James, sthop—that's not fair; you know you are to be married to Hanna Russell, so let me go, but see me home."

"Mary, who tould you that?"

"That fellow," she whispered, and pointed to Burkem, who was wiping the blood from his brow.

"The lying scoundrel, I didn't spake to her these three months. No, Mary, if you refuse being my wife, I'll never marry; you know I love you. When I went to Mr. O'Donnell's this evening, I heard you were in town, and missing Burkem, I thought it would be no harm to come to meet you, so, thank God, I was in time."

"The devil is in it," muttered Burkem, as he looked on with envy, like the serpent in the garden; "if I don't have sweet revenge for this, my name isn't Burkem."

"What are you saying, you double-distilled villin you; do you want more of this?" said Cormack, going over to him and whirling his stick.

"Don't, James, let us pass him; he could harm us," whispered Mary.

"Deuce take him and all the harm he can do. He's not worth minding, the dirty spalpeen."

"Forgive me, James," said Burkem, reaching his hand. "Shure my love for Mary there blinded me. I desarved what I got. I thought to blacken your

name with her to make her marry me, but shure it
was no use. You know what it is to be in love,
James, so you will forgive me what I did ; and you,
Mary, won't you forgive me?"

"Indeed, I will," said she, after a pause.

"I'm sure I'm not the man to keep in a grudge
for a man that axes my pardon," said James Cormack.

"God bless you and make you happy! but don't
mention a word of what happened to anybody, if
you forgive me."

"No fear, Ned."

As he left them, he felt the hot blood trickling
down his face ; he wiped it off, and gave a kind of
chuckle, and muttered—

"Devil take me if that don't be the dearest blow
you ever struck. My name isn't Ned Burkem, if I
don't bring you to the gallows for that, and make
that proud thing kneel to me for marcy. I must be
his best friend, though ; I must get him into my
power, until I crush him like the serpent. Ha, ha!
whose turn will it be then, I wonder. No matter—
ha, ha, ha! you'll rue it, James Cormack. May
God ——, but no, I won't curse ; I'll leave him until
my time comes. Curse this blood—but I'll have
blood for it," and he muttered and cursed as he
went along.

CHAPTER XXIII.

THE O'Donnells' affairs were every day becoming
more discouraging. Though throwing themselves
for protection upon the agent, still, so little faith
had they in him, that they did not feel secure, and
heartily wished that the day of sale was over.

Mr. O'Donnell moved listlessly about the house
and place, his grey hair streaming about his head,
and his once portly form stooped. Strong minds
yield to adversity sooner than weak ones. When
unable to resist it, they are too proud to bear the
world's frown, and that very moral strength that
gained them wealth and respect in their prosperity
now helps to drag them to ruin.

Little Bessy was becoming weaker every day, and
it was evident to the most unpractised that consumption was fast doing its work. The dry cough,
and the hectic flush that mantled on her velvet
cheek, seemed to number her days.

Mrs. O'Donnell and Kate were continually engaged with their domestic duties and their attendance upon Bessy. Frank was the only one upon

whom devolved the painful duty of trying to make the most of their shattered fortunes. Even Uncle Corny became apathetic, for if he went abroad, nothing but want, and wailing, and death, met his gaze ; so he preferred to remain at home. It is true that Shemus-a-Clough kept him company, for with that instinct of poor, half-witted creatures, he found that he could not live roving about as usual, and as there was always plenty to eat and drink, and a welcome at Mr. O'Donnell's, he now stopped there the most of his time ; besides, he said that something was to happen them, and no one would be there to protect them if he went.

James Cormack spent most of his time at Mr O'Donnell's, for since Burkem became a resident in the house, and since his attack upon Mary Cahill, he thought it prudent to keep an eye upon him. Burkem took care to worm himself into his favor again. He expressed the greatest sorrow for his past conduct, and thereby disarmed Cormack's suspicions.

I should have said that Uncle Corny tended and cared Bessy ; he sang and read for her, and amused her with tales of his campaigns. It was cheering to see the fine old soldier with that delicate, frail child upon his knee eagerly listening to his adventures, and then she would look anxiously into his face and ask him—

"If you were killed, Uncle Corny, what would you do ?"

"Why, I don't know, pet; I suppose they'd bury me somewhere."

" It's not that I mean, Uncle Corny ; but sure you couldn't be prepared to die and you fighting? You know we should work out our salvation with fear and trembling."

"Oh, as to the fear and trembling, my dear little puss, I had enough of it on the battle-field ; but anything about my salvation, I fear, never gave me any trouble."

"Why, wouldn't you like to go to heaven, Uncle Corny ?"

" To be sure I would ; but you know, we hadn't time to think of such things then. Soldiers seem born for fightin' and nothing else. When you'd hear the guns and cannons roaring around you, and see dead men upon every side of you, you'd be thinking how you could fight best, or perhaps how you could escape."

" Oh, it is dreadful," said she, shuddering.

" It is, but it's glorious, after all, to kill your enemies."

" Doesn't our Saviour tell us to love our enemies ? Besides, perhaps, that poor man you'd be after killing might have left a wife and children to lament his loss, or perhaps to starve. Think how I would feel if anything happened dear papa, and sure some one is left to feel after every one that's killed. Oh, it's dreadful for people to be killing one another that way."

"Well, I believe it's wrong, after all," said Uncle Corny.

It is strange what influence a child's simple arguments will often have upon the strongest man ; I have known them to succeed where the most philosophical arguments failed. This is because there is a homely innocence and purity in their remarks that touches the heart.

Frank often visited his uncle, apparently for advice, but in reality to meet Alice. Father O'Donnell felt flattered at being thus treated as the family oracle.

The lovers had to meet furtively of late ; for, though Mr. Maher had not forbidden Frank his house, still there was a coldness in his manner that impressed him with the belief that a change of circumstances had produced a coldness on his part. Besides, he told his daughter that she should not encourage the young man to be neglecting his business.

Mrs. Hogan was Alice's adviser. She sympathized with the young lovers, and warmly entered into all their little plans. Alice loved Frank with all the true devotion of an honest, generous heart. They went to school together, they played together, they plucked flowers, and roamed the fields together in search of birds' nests, and now, when their hearts were united, was fortune to separate them?

After one of these passionate love meetings with Alice, he was returning home. His uncle's car had

come a part of the way with him, and then, with his
gun upon his shoulder, he set out to make a short
way through the country.

Alice had told him, with tears in her eyes, that her
father had ordered her not to meet him again. Their
interview was a sad one.

" Frank, love," said she, after relating all to him,
" what am I to do? I cannot disobey my father,
and yet, Frank, I will miss you so much that I would
rather be dead than not see you."

Frank held his hands to his face and groaned.

" Don't fret, Frank," said she.

"O Alice! Alice! I could bear the loss of wealth
well, for I'm young and strong, and there is a wide
field of enterprise in other lands ; but to lose you,
to lose you is losing all that binds me to life: and
my poor father, and mother, and my darling sisters.
O Alice! Alice! but for you I could smile at the
world ; frown at the loss of fortune. I could scorn
all!"

"Frank! Frank! don't fret so ; let what will come
we will not be separated. No! God never made
too honest, loving hearts to make them unhappy.
Don't fret, Frank ;" and she gently pulled his hands
from his face.

"O Alice," said he, "there are times when I picture the future radiant with sunshine ; you my own
sweet wife ; our home hallowed by love, and all the
domestic virtues. And now, such a fair, bright
dream, to be but a dream. Indeed, oh! it's enough

to drive me mad! mad! I have read of men who, unable to bear the loss of so much happiness, penetrated the dark mysteries of the future, sooner than live a worthless, hated life."

Alice looked up and shuddered.

"Only that I have hope in the future, only that I have your love to sustain me, only that I have domestic ties that bind me to life, I fear I should become one of these."

"O Frank! Frank! don't say so, or my heart will break. Let us part now, Frank, and not meet too soon, unless you have very particular business with me, as I do not wish to disobey my father. When you want to see me, you can send Shemus to Mrs. Moran, or to me."

"Be it so, love; I suppose if your father ordered you to marry some one else you could not disobey?"

"Frank!" said she, "I did not expect this from you, after all my promises of devotion. You know my father has hitherto encouraged our love. Now, when my young heart is yours, if he ordered me to wed another, I would be justified in refusing him. No, Frank, if I'm not yours, I'll never be the wife of another."

"Alice, forgive my unjust doubts; you know the unfortunate are always suspicious."

It was after this interview that we met Frank returning home. His heart was full of a deep love, and yet the uncertainty of the future oppressed him.

17

He did not for a moment doubt Alice's love, yet he knew that if he lost his property he would not get her father's consent. He had little faith in Mr. Ellis ; for, in order to put him upon his guard, Mary Cahill told him what Burkem had said. Though he looked upon this as an idle boast, still he knew so much of Mr. Ellis's unprincipled character that he did not altogether disregard it.

As Frank was passing by Mrs. Butler's he heard the sounds of mirth inside.

Mrs. Butler's establishment had undergone a great change for the worse. The ruddy horseman had fallen from his perch ; the windows were all broken and stuffed with rags ; even Mrs. Butler herself had lost her bloom, and now looked thin and faded. The times were telling upon her, and, to use her own words, "she wasn't herself at all." She managed to keep a few gallons and a drop of beer somewhere for the boys whenever they called, which was seldom indeed.

Frank stood at the door listening to the Rover, who had just commenced a song.

The Rover was something of a poet, and a great politician. He wrote most of the rough political ballads for the boys. He had a strong, sonorous voice, so that he did full justice to his doggerel verses.

"Well done!" said Frank, opening the door and walking in as the Rover finished his song. "Where have you been this time back ?"

"Not far, Mr. Frank. How is every inch of you, sir?"

"Very well, though I can't say times are going on well with us."

"I'm sorry to hear so; for it was you kept the good, plentiful house, full of lashins and lavins; but we'll have a change soon, Mr. Frank. Our day is coming, believe me. That was a great meeting the clubs had in Dublin. It won't go like '98 with them this time, I'm thinking. Shure the ould prophecy is nearly out; shure the hills are levelled and the hollows are filled up, and cars are walking on the roads without horses, and the people are dyin' of hunger in the midst of plinty."

"Begor, that's all thrue enuff," said one.

"It is," said the Rover; "and shure it is said that it is an O'Brien that's to hunt the Saxons, as well as it was one that routed the Danes at Clontarf."

"Who knows but it's Smith O'Brien? The Lord be praised!" said another, rubbing his hands with glee.

"I hope so, I hope so; but, Mr. Frank, sure you ought to be one of us," said the Rover; "it's not for an O'Donnell to remain idle when there is work to be done for his counthry."

"That's true," said Burkem, who was of the party. "It's not in their blood. Shure they were always foremost."

"Ay, and will be now, please God," said the

Rover. "We are going to get up a club, and we'll make a president of you, Mr. Frank. Will you join us?"

"Not now; I've too much to attend to, though my heart is with you, and, if need be, my arm too; but, then, no matter—we'll speak over it another time. Haven't you any story to tell us?" said he to the Rover, to change the conversation; for, from what he heard about Burkem, he had no confidence in him.

"Sorra a one, Mr. Frank, only the counthry is in a blaze."

"Do tell us how you tricked the gauger," said another.

"Well, I will," said to Rover; and after a few preparatory hems and haws, he commenced—

"I was, one evening, taking a small dhrop here with Mrs. Butler, when a strange man came in. 'God save all here!' says he. 'God save you kindly,' says I. 'It's a cowld evenin',' says he. 'Begor it is,' says I; 'would you have a dhrop?' 'Wid pleasure,' says he. After drinkin' he went off; and faith he was no other than the rogue of a gauger in disguise. Myself was summoned. 'Och, mavrone,' says Mrs. Butler, 'you'll ruin me, Shaun, if you swear upon me.' 'What can I do, ma'am?' says I. 'Oh, I don't know; but you'll beggar me from house and home.' 'Well, I won't swear on you.' 'Won't you, Shaun, alanna?' 'No, ma'am.' 'Thanks be to God! I'm safe if you don't, Shaun.

Is it my oath you want? Show me the prayer-book ;' and I took and kissed the book. 'Now, Mrs. Butler, I take my oath upon this that I won't swear upon you.' 'Thanks be to God!' said Mrs. Butler. So, when I was called up, the fellow swore that I'd threated him. 'Well, what have you to say?' says the magistrate to me, when I was swore. I looked at the fellow as if I'd never seen him, and then says, 'Upon my solemn oath, if I swore that I dhrank with this fellow at Mrs. Butler's I'd perjure myself.' 'You must have mistaken your man,' said the magistrate to him ; 'dismiss the case.' So, you see, I kept my oath, and saved her."

"Begad you did ; but won't you come up, Shaun?" said Frank, rising to leave.

"Begor, I believe I might as well, sir."

As they went along, the Rover gave Frank a full account of the organization through the country.

"I did not think it was so extensive," said Frank; "but you ought to be more cautious before that Burkem ; I have reason to know that he's nothing good."

"I always thought so much about him myself; but then, as it is all a public business, we needn't fear him," said the Rover.

We do not mean to take up our reader's time with that ebullition that ended in the partial outbreak of '48. It was an unexpected result to the great things promised by that national party that had with it the feelings of the majority of the people. We do not mean to analyze the past; but this we say, that never was a country riper for revolution, and never were the feelings of an aggrieved people more warm in its behalf, and yet it failed miserably.

The two great parties that gave unanimous expression to a nation's will differed among themselves; they quarreled as to the means of liberating a willing people. Division, that bane of Ireland, entered their ranks; they quarreled and fell, and lost their strength in their own disunion. The people lost hope and confidence, and many who might be useful fell listlessly back into retirement.

While the peasant sees the laws protect the landlord as he despoils him of the fruits of his industry, of his once happy homestead, as he drives him a penniless pauper upon the world, he cannot reverence or respect the laws; nor can he look upon the nation that affords such protection to his oppressors but with abhorrence.

A nation's esteem and love are to be gained by equitable and just laws, and not by oppressive ones, that protect the rich and despoil the poor. A rich man's wealth gives him power, so the laws should protect the poor man from every abuse of that power.

Such is not the case in Ireland, and, therefore, while the laws afford protection to the oppressive landlord, disaffection will exist, and plots and secret societies and revolutions will be the result.

Frank was young, generous, and enthusiastic; he

possessed a good deal of family pride, and loved to dwell upon the days when the O'Donnells were princes in the land. It is no wonder, therefore, that he warmly entered into the Rover's views.

"What's Shemus doin'?" said the Rover, pointing over the ditch.

Shemus was busily engaged pulling something black from a tree.

"What are you doing there, Shemus?"

'Sorra much, Masther Frank. It's only Bully; I let him down to rest himself."

"What was he doing?"

"Why, you know, he's always huntin' me about, so I hung him up by the nick. Begor, it was fine fun, to see him flappin' his wings this way;" and Shemus wound his arms about, in imitation of Bully, which was no other than a fine venerable turkey-cock, so called on account of his bellicose nature. "That's the way he went on, flappin' about. Begor it was fine fun; sorra a doubt but it was he that had the work ov it; faith it was pleasant to see him exercise himself. Now he's rested enuff. It's worth your while to come to see him; you never had sich fun; begor, it's pleasant."

"Not for Bully, I think," said Frank, as he took the bird. "He's dead; you killed him, you villain."

"Never mind him, Masther Frank. Now, maybe he'll let me alone. Killed? arrah, who asked him to do it? Sure it was his own fault, bad cess to him."

CHAPTER XXIV.

HOW AN IRISH AGENT FULFILS HIS PROMISE—RUIN OF
THE O'DONNELLS.—MESSRS. BURKEM AND PEMBERT
PLOT TOGETHER—DEATH OF BESSY O'DONNELL.

THE day of sale arrived. Mr. Ellis and the auction-
eer were early on the ground. There were a good
many police, too, and bailiffs in attendance. These
were too indispensable to an Irish agent in the discharge of his duties to be left behind; though, in
truth, to a keen observer, they boded no good to
the poor O'Donnells.

Mr. O'Donnell, stooped and feeble, and leaning
upon the arm of his son, came out to meet the
agent.

"I'm sorry, Mr. O'Donnell," said the latter blandly,
"to see you reduced to this—to see your stock and
effects going to be sold for rent."

"Welcome be the will of God, sir. We can't help
these things."

"I think, Mr. O'Donnell, I and my men had better
buy the stock; we can sell them back to your son.
With executions hanging over you, it would not be
safe for him to buy them now."

"Sure they couldn't touch them if his; there's
nothing against him."

"Certainly not; but people would look upon it as a sham, and, perhaps, distrain again; where, if I buy them and remove them to my land for a few days, they are my property; no one will dare interfere with them; your son can buy them back again, you understand."

"What will I do, Frank?" said the old man, in doubt.

"Really I don't know, father," said Frank.

"Do as ye please," said Mr. Ellis. "If you doubt me, I will withdraw the execution altogether, if you choose."

"God help us!" muttered Mr. O'Donnell.

"Well, what shall I do?" said Mr. Ellis.

"As you please, sir. I know that you or his lordship, whose father I once saved from death, would not injure me or my poor family."

"As to that, Mr. O'Donnell, I have come here at your own wish. If you choose, I'll go home and leave things as they are; if not, allow me to take the safest course, as I mean to do."

"Do, Mr. Ellis; protect me and my family, and God bless you."

The sale proceeded; as the neighbors understood that it was to protect Mr. O'Donnell, they did not bid; so Mr. Ellis and his men bought up the whole at about one-third of their real value. They then removed them to Mr. Ellis's place.

A few days after the sale, Frank called at Mr. Ellis's; he was shown into the office.

" Well, sir," said Mr. Ellis, " what can I do for
you ?"

" My father sent me, sir, to arrange about the
sale."

" Your father himself must come ; we cannot treat
with you about them," said Mr. Ellis, resuming his
occupation.

" He's very feeble ; couldn't I manage the business?   Besides, my father wishes to give up the
management of the business altogether."

" Can't help it ; he must come. What's the widow
Shea's last payment ?" this was addressed to Hugh
Pembert.

" Twenty pounds, sir ; there is a year's rent due
besides."

" Haven't you got your answer, sir ?" said Mr.
Ellis, with all the arrogance of office, raising his
head from the account to Frank, who stood still all
this time.

Frank clenched his hands and teeth, and bitter
thoughts burned his heart ; but he mastered his
passion, and merely bowed and left.

" The devil is in that fellow's eye," said Mr. Ellis.

" He is dangerous when crossed," said Hugh Pembert ; " and Burkem tells me he has joined these
clubs ; so if he gets ahead, I suppose he'll treat us
to a bonfire in our own houses."

" Bad scran to the lie in it," said Burkem. " Shure
they had a meetin' at Mrs. Butler's, and they made
him captain. He vowed that he'd kill all the Pro-

testants in the country. The Rover was in it too,
and he went off with Masther Frank—you may be
sure for no good."

" It is important to know all this," said Mr. Ellis.
"As a magistrate, I cannot connive at it."

"Certainly not," said Mr. Pembert ; "but then,
you have no witness except Burkem, whom it would
not do to bring forward publicly. It is better let
things go on a little ; Burkem will not be suspected,
and we can watch our own time."

" Well, I believe you're right, Hugh."

" There are others, too, that oughtn't to join them,"
said Burkem.

" Who are they?" said Mr. Ellis.

"Och, it's not worth namin' them. I don't like
to injure any one."

"As a magistrate, I command you to name them,
Burkem," said Mr. Ellis, sitting back with a very
dignified air.

" I don't like, sir," said he, scratching his head
with well-assumed diffidence.

" Name them, sir," said Mr. Ellis, sternly.

"There are many of the tenants, sir ; but the
leader is James Cormack ; he's to be sargeant under
Misther Frank."

"Good God! what an ungrateful set they are,"
said Mr. Ellis. Watch them well, Burkem, and you
shall be well paid. I want to meet his lordship at
one o'clock. I will inform him of the state of things,
and what a character this young O'Donnell is, lest

he should extend any mercy to them; and you, Hugh, have that notice to quit made out, for I know they'll come in the evening; and you, Burkem, serve old O'Donnell with it when they leave the office."

" I'd rather not, sir ; it's betther for me keep on terms with them, the way I can know every thing that's passin'. Couldn't Splane do it, your honor?"

" Well, well, let him," and Mr. Ellis left the office.

As soon as Mr. Ellis was gone, Hugh Pembert threw his pen from him, and fixing his hands under his coat tails, turned his back to the fire.

" I tell you what, Burkem," said he, "we are on the high road to fortune, if we take advantage of it."

" And why the devil shouldn't we," said Burkem.

" Look, Burkem," said he, and he placed his hand upon his shoulder, " my uncle will soon turn Mary Cormack out of the house, for reasons of his own."

" Are you sure of that, sir?" said Burkem.

"As sure as that you and I are standing here," answered Pembert. " I overheard a conversation between them the other morning. If you please, she wanted him to marry her, and cried sorely on the head of it; so she's sure to march. Waal, when she's agone, her hot-headed brothers will be looking for revenge, I ken. Perhaps they'd kill this foolish old uncle of mine. No matter ; whoever does it, it will be left at their door. The government will offer a large reward ; you could get that ; besides, I wad be your friend, for I will fall in for this place ; for this swaddling old chiel will pick Lizzie off our hands some day or other. Do you understand me ?"

" Perfectly, sir."

" I think I can trust you, Burkem. I have always found you a loyal chiel, and you know it wouldn't be safe for you to peach. Here is five pounds as an earnest of favor."

" Before God, I swear to be thrue !" said Burkem, as he buttoned up the note.

" It will be your interest to be. You must keep on the best terms with the Cormacks and this young O'Donnell."

" I'd rather have nothin' to do with O'Donnell, sir. They reared a brother of mine, and sent him to America ; but I hate the Cormacks. I have sworn to see James die on the gallows."

" Very good, very good ! Waal, as you like. We must get the Cormacks out of the work ; hunt Mary home ; supply them with arms, so that we can swear to them afterwards, and if this ould carl should be killed, shure there's no other one to do it."

" That's thrue, sir, that's thrue. I'll have revenge."

" Considering that I'll come in for the property, I wouldn't mind adding one hundred pounds to the reward, to any one that would get me into possession soon."

" I understand you, sir," said Burkem, with a wink.

"I dunna ken what I said," said Hugh Pembert.

"Not much, sir, not much; just iv a certain jin-tleman forgot drawing his breath some night, you would give one hundred pounds to whoever brought you the news first; besides, the government would give a few hundred more, and shure there is no one to do that but certain jintlemen I have sworn to see hanging on the gallows. Isn't that it, sir, isn't it?" said he, with a demoniac look.

"Waal, waal, something that way, but bide your time. Fools only half do their business."

"Ha, ha, ha! I half do it, indeed. No, I'll lay my snares well. James Cormack, I swore I'd have blood for blood, and I will; I will, by heaven, I will, even if I should be damned for it."

"Waal, waal, that'll do now. Let us look to business, bide a weel; we can speak mair another time."

They did speak more about it, and the artful web was woven that was to bring one man—and that man an uncle to the arch plotter—to a sudden and unprovided death; that was to send a wronged girl adrift upon the wide world, and to bring two innocent men to the gallows. We loathe to follow their hellish plotting, but we will show forth its fruits.

It was evening before Mr. Ellis returned. He had prejudiced the mind of Lord Clearall against the unfortunate O'Donnells. He told him that the old man was a reckless swindler, that had collected the

people's money into his bank and now had closed.
In order to screen himself from the law, he got his
stock and things seized upon. As to the son, he
was the leader of secret societies and Ribbonmen;
the sooner he could be got rid of the better. Mr.
Ellis found the O'Donnells waiting for him in the
office. The careworn, haggard appearance of Mr.
O'Donnell would have made an impression upon the
heart of a man made of less stern stuff than Mr.
Ellis; but Mr. Ellis's heart was long since closed
against the softer feelings of humanity.

"I'm sorry, Mr. O'Donnell, to put you to the
trouble of coming, for you don't appear well," said
Mr. Ellis, in his usual bland manner.

"Indeed, I'm not, sir; for besides the trouble
caused by the ruinous state of my affairs, I have domestic afflictions. I have a darling child dying fast,"
and the old man wiped his eyes.

"Bad enough, Mr. O'Donnell—but to business.
Your lease is out; there is a year and a half's rent
due, while the sale of your stock scarcely covers the
half year."

"But, sir, there is a year of it a running gale that
is due time immemorial. Since the first of my ancestors took the place it was never looked for. It
was due on the whole estate."

"That may be, sir; but, then, we can't allow it
to run any longer. I had better give you a receipt
for the half year, which the price of your stock
covers."

"The price of my stock! Why aren't you going
to give them to my son, as you promised?"

"Yes, if he pays for them."

"Good heaven, do I hear him right!" exclaimed
Mr. O'Donnell, as he raised his eyes.

"Mr. O'Donnell, I am sorry to say that my orders
are to keep the stock to meet your rent. You know
they were sold by fair auction."

"Didn't you tell me that you'd befriend me, and
that you'd give them back to my son again?"

"I think I have befriended you in putting to meet
your rent what might go for nothing ; and as to the
stock, I'll return them if your son pays the selling
price of them."

"You know well that we couldn't do it, and that
the stock were sold for one-third of their value,"
groaned Mr. O'Donnell.

"I can't help it; it was a fair open auction ; I
must obey orders ; and more than that, I must tell
you that his lordship has ordered me to clear the
estate, now that it's out of lease."

"Good God, we are ruined, beggared — beggared forever!" groaned Mr. O'Donnell, clasping his
hands.

"Sir," said Frank, "can you reconcile it with your
conscience or duty to entrap us this way, to sell our
stock for half nothing, under pretence of protecting
us, and then keep them yourself. I tell you it is a
robbery, sir, it is——" Frank stopped, choked with
passion and indignation.

"Well," said Mr. Ellis, calmly, "go on, my young man."

"Don't, don't, Frank," said the father. "Oh, Mr. Ellis, have pity on us; deal fair with us, and God will bless you. I'll go to his lordship and tell him all. I once saved his father's life. Sure he can't forget it. He won't ruin myself and my darling family; he won't bring these grey hairs to a pauper's grave. Oh! no, he won't do it, Mr. Ellis; he won't; I'll go to him."

"I'm acting by his orders," said Mr. Ellis, unmoved.

"No, no, it can't be; he don't know all, all I'm suffering! Poverty staring me in the face—my sweet, darling child dying. "O God! O God!" and the old man bent his head, and the tears streamed down his furrowed cheeks.

"Let us be done with this fooling," said Mr. Ellis, sternly—"Splane."

"Here, sir."

"Give that paper to Mr. O'Donnell."

"What's this?" said Mr. O'Donnell, as he took the paper.

"A notice to quit," replied Mr. Ellis.

"Have pity on me! have pity on my grey hairs and dying child. See, I throw myself upon my knees before you."

"No, father, recollect you are an O'Donnell," said Frank, stopping him, and his eyes glared, and his breast heaved with passion.

"You're right, boy, you're right. But sure he won't do it; sure you won't, Mr. Ellis. But what's this? I feel dizzy," and he raised his hand to his head, and then fell upon the floor.

"Is he dead?" said Mr. Ellis, pushing over to feel his pulse.

"Robber! murderer! keep off; his blood be upon you," said Frank, as he struck Mr. Ellis a fierce blow, that sent him reeling against the table, until he fell at the other side.

"Father, father dear, speak to me," said he, tenderly, leaning over him. "He breathes; he's not dead, thank God, thank God!"

"Frank, where are we?" said the old man, recovering himself.

"Here, sir, here."

"Tell me, is it a dream, Frank? Was I dreaming?"

"You're better, father, aren't you?" said Frank, avoiding the question.

"Yes, Frank, yes; let us go home. There is no mercy in his heart," said he, looking about, and recalling his interview with Mr. Ellis. "No, he has no mercy—God forgive him; but God will judge him!"

Mr. Pembert thought it prudent to get away from the fiery wrath of Frank's arm; so he hastily bore Mr. Ellis into the drawing-room.

Frank helped his father to the car which some of the servants, through compassion, got ready for him. Though weak and faint, Mr. O'Donnell would not rest until he went to Lord Clearall's, for he expected his lordship would see justice done him. Again he was doomed to disappointment, for his lordship refused seeing him ; and when he sent up his message, his answer was that he did not meddle in the management of his property ; he left it all to Mr. Ellis. He got a sheet of paper and stated his case, and reminded his lordship of how he saved his father's life. The note was returned with the remark that " he had nothing to do for him ; Mr. Ellis wouldn't wrong him."

With heavy hearts they returned to their once happy home, but now miserable indeed. Not only was poverty staring them in the face, but death, too, seemed to triumph in their wretchedness.

Mrs. O'Donnell and Kate were anxiously awaiting their arrival ; they read the tale of their disaster in their faces. Mr. O'Donnell seemed years older since he left that room a few hours before. So ghastly and feeble did he look that Mrs. O'Donnell ran to support him.

"You're sick, my love. What's the matter? Has the journey injured you?"

"Oh, no, no. I'm sick, indeed. How is Bessy, poor child?"

"Something better. You had better go to bed."

"No, love, no ; I can't bear it!"

"Bear what? tell us all," said Mrs. O'Donnell.

"Come here"—and he took her by the hand— "we are old now, sinking into the grave ; we were lately rich and happy, dispensing blessings around us ; we hoped to leave a nice inheritance to our children ; but now we are ruined, we are beggars, beggars! He has robbed us ; yes, it is robbery; who says it's not? Our stock and effects were valued at nearly five hundred pounds, and because he promised to return them, no one bid against him. Now he has given me a receipt for one hundred and fifty pounds—half a year's rent for five hundred pounds worth—is not this robbery? But the law protects him in his robbery of us ; and the law will transport a poor man for stealing a sheep to keep himself and his family from starving, as it did to Ned Curren, who lived for days upon grass and turnip-tops ; but, then, when one of his family died of hunger, he stole a sheep from Mr. Ellis, and he got him transported, though he now robs us of over three hundred pounds. O God! O God! is Thy justice sleeping? We would kill the highwayman, and here is this robber living and glorying in his robbery. There was a time—but, no, God forgive me—I don't know what I'm saying. Let us leave him to God !"

Mrs. O'Donnell sank into a chair beside her husband, and Kate bent her beautiful head upon her hands. Frank stood looking out of the window, his arms crossed upon his breast, his teeth clenched.

"Father," said he, turning to the old man as he concluded, "you're right, death is too good for such a demon. He has brought ruin and misery upon us. He's a robber, and he shall die—death, death to him ; the robber shall die !" he muttered between his teeth.

"Who speaks of death !" said the old man, awakening from his reverie—" who speaks of death, Frank ? No, no, boy, you would not kill any one, you would not ; you would not sully the name of O'Donnell. No, no ; leave him to God ! He's a robber, though ; then God will punish him ! No, God forgive him, have mercy upon him !" and the old man sank into his reverie once more.

Mrs. O'Donnell looked at her son ; there was a stern determination in that fierce look and that glaring eye. She went over to him and embraced him.

" Frank, my child !" said she, taking his hand, " promise your poor heart-broken mother that you will not injure Mr. Ellis, or have him injured."

" He's a robber, mother—a robber and a murderer !"

"Even so ; leave him to God, my child. Though God's vengeance sleepeth, it is sure. Leave him to God."

" He has shown mercy to us, hasn't he, mother ?" sneered Frank. " The mercy he has given he'll get !"

"Come here, Kate, come here, for I fear evil has taken possession of your brother's heart."

Kate went over and put her arm about his neck and kissed him. " O Frank, Frank ! do as mother asks you."

"Do, boy," resumed his mother. "I have never asked a request of you before. I have borne and suckled you; I love you as my first-born; I'd rather see you in your grave—see Bessy and Kate and that poor man there—all in one grave, than have you called a murderer. I have not long to live, I fear; but were your hand stained with blood, I would not live one week; so now promise me that you will not touch him. O God Almighty, soften his heart!"

The tears began to flow from Frank's dry eyes at this pathetic appeal; he stooped down, and, raising his mother, said—

"I promise you, mother, that while you live I will not bring dishonor upon you. I will not touch him —I leave him to God."

"O God! I thank Thee—Thou hast heard my prayer!" exclaimed his mother.

Day after day little Bessy was sinking slowly and softly to the grave.

It was May, and the soft rays of the morning's sun came floating through the windows of Bessy's room. The little birds were singing and chiriping in the garden without, filling the apartment with their sweet music.

Bessy lay still upon her little bed, her eyes intently fixed upon a large crucifix that hung at her feet. The sun shone upon the crucifix, and seemed to surround it with a halo of heavenly glory.

A celestial joy seemed to illumine Bessy's calm features.

The priest heard her last confession, and then administered to her the Holy Sacrament. He then knelt and prayed a considerable time beside her. Bessy all this time lay still wrapt in prayer.

"Now, my child," said the priest, "resign yourself into the hands of God, and trust His mercy, for He is good and merciful, indeed."

"I do, Father. 'Into Thy hands, O Lord! I commit my spirit : Lord Jesus, receive my soul,'" she murmured.

The priest then read the prayers for a departing soul, which were responded to by the family.

Oh, there is hope in this inspiring prayer. When the soul is trembling upon the verge of eternity, how sweet to hear the consoling words—

"No one hath hoped in the Lord, and hath been confounded.

"The Lord is my light and my salvation ; whom shall I fear?

"In Thee, O Lord, have I hoped ; may I not be confounded forever.

"Into Thy hands, O Lord, I commit my spirit : Thou hast redeemed me, O Lord, Thou God of truth."

The priest took his departure, promising to call in the evening. Her mother and Kate sat beside the bed all day.

"Dear Kate, will you read out of Father Faber's 'All for Jesus ?' There are some beautiful passages in it."

"Yes, Bessy, dear!" and Kate brought the book and read the following beautiful passage:—

"All this goes to the salvation of a soul. To be saved it has to be God's child, God's brother, and to participate in God's nature. Now, see what is involved in being saved. Look at that soul yonder, that has just been judged: Jesus has this instant spoken; the sound of his sweet words has hardly died away; they that mourn have scarcely yet closed the eyes of the deserted body. Yet the judgment has come and gone—all is over. It was swift, but merciful—more than merciful; there is no word to say what it was—it must be imagined. One day, please God, we shall experience it. The soul must be very strong to bear what it is feeling now; God must support it, or it will fall back into nothingness. Life is over. How short it has been."

"It has, indeed; it has, indeed; it is vanity," said Bessy. "Read some of Liguori's 'Preparation for Death.'" Kate read:—

"I accept with joy, death, and the pains I shall have to suffer until my last breath; give me strength to bear them with perfect conformity to Thy will; I offer them all to Thy glory, uniting them with the pains which Thou didst endure in Thy passion. Eternal Father, I sacrifice to Thee my life and my entire being; I entreat Thee to accept this my sacrifice, through the merits of the great sacrifice of Himself, which Jesus, Thy Son, offered to Thee on the cross."

"That will do, Kate; that will do."

Thus did this bright May day pass away in the chamber of death. The sun had now sank in the west, and the light was fast fading in the room.

"Papa," said Bessy, as the old man entered the room, supported by a servant; with bursting heart he clung to his darling child, her on whom he doated and felt so proud of—"papa, don't fret for me; I'm going to heaven, and I'll watch over you, and pray for you."

"God, help me! my heart is breaking," he exclaimed, as he was borne from the room.

The moonbeams now played through the open window, and a flood of golden light danced around the papered walls. Bessy's head was heavy, her cheeks were ashy pale, and the light was fast fading from her eyes. She, sweet child! was dying.

Her little hand was clasped in Kate's, and her head rested upon her mother's lap; her golden ringlets, damp with the dews of death, fell heavily down. Her blue eyes closed, and her lips moved as if in prayer; she clasped her hands and seemed to sleep; but no, she was but communing with the angels, for a sweet smile played around her mouth, and she said:—"O mamma, I have seen so lovely a sight. Look at these golden-winged angels floating about; they are beckoning me away. Oh, how bright heaven must be"—and she smiled, as if it were open before her.

"Kiss me, mamma, darling; and Kate, sister

18

sweet; and Frank, dear; poor dear papa, where is he? God comfort him. Do not weep; sure you don't grudge me to God?"

"No, darling, no."

"We shall meet again. Farewell, mamma; kiss me again. That will do—lay me down. How sweet that music."

They laid her back; she stretched out her little hands and closed her eyes, and angels sealed them and bore her pure spirit away.

There she lay, pale, pale as alabaster, and a sweet angelic smile seemed to play upon her lips, as if her gentle spirit yet hovered around its earthly prison. She looked beautiful in death—so beautiful, indeed, that one might exclaim—

> "How sweet, how calm she sleeps,
> —— can this be death?"

The moonbeams floated again with a dim and shadowy light, casting gloomy shadows around, for there were wet eyes and sorrowing hearts in the chamber of death; but a pure spirit had forsaken its earthly tenement and fled to the bosom of its God.

CHAPTER XXV.

HOW MR. SLY TURNS THINGS TO HIS ADVANTAGE—ATTACK
UPON THE MILLS—MR. ELLIS AND LORD CLEARALL'S
RECEIPT FOR DISPERSING A MOB.

LIFE is one system of cold, stern realities. Though
it has lost all interest and hope for us, still we must
move on with the current; we must eat, drink, buy
and sell, when shadowed by its darkest frowns, as
well as when basking in its brightest sunshine. We
still pursue the gilded shadows that dazzle our im-
aginations, as if their enjoyment could bring peace to
the weary spirit. There is something in our natures
that solemnly and significantly make us feel that
there is another life, where the meeting of friends
shall be a happy union   This supports many a
weary heart when oppressed with the heavy leth-
argy of care and sorrow.   Though stern necessities,
or mechanical observances, may urge us on with the
rapid current, still there is hope in the religious
sentiments and aspirations that yearn after a happy
future.

If we could but understand the wise dispensations
of Providence, death, and all its gloomy attributes,
often come for our good. The death of those we
love stirs up our moral perceptions to a true sense
of our religious obligations.

As the furnace purifies gold, so sorrow chastens and purifies us, giving a softened, gentle tone to our lives.

The cares and sorrows of life pressed heavily upon the O'Donnells. That strength of mind and resolution that gained an honorable position in life for Mr. O'Donnell now forsook him. Unable to sustain his ruined affairs, he hopelessly sank with them, and from an active man of business, became an imbecile paralytic. Mrs. O'Donnell, too, sank under the double affliction ; naturally of a delicate frame and constitution, all her hope and joy seemed centered in her darling child ; and now, unable to bear her loss, and the world's vicissitudes, she gave way to a sad melancholy, and pined away.

It now devolved upon Frank and Kate to tend and console their parents, and to try and make the best of their shattered fortunes. They could expect but little assistance from their neighbors or friends, for in general they were not much better off than themselves.

Few knew how soon the pestilence would call at their own doors ; so even those who were comparatively rich trembled for the future. The country had become one vast lazaretto. Living skeletons stalked about, with barely the semblance of life. These poor, emaciated-looking beings, covered with wretched, patched rags, that breathed forth a living miasma, everywhere met one's gaze. Women and children, and men too, often died of want and fever

in their cabins, and there lay unseen, uncared-for,
until the putrid corpses sent forth such a stench,
that some charitable people collected to level in the
cabin, or burn it over them.

Let us turn from these sickening details and see
how our friend, the Rev. Bob Sly, was progressing
in his evangelical career. Armed with the authority
of Lord Clearall and Mr. Ellis, the reverend gentleman spared neither trouble nor expense in enlighten-
ing the benighted tenantry. His school, or soup-
house, as it was called, was pretty well attended by
the children of dependents, who were forced to put
on the semblance of apostacy in order to keep from
starvation. I must confess that these were few, for
the majority, with a heroism that would ennoble
martyrdom, spurned their bribes and threats alike,
and perished sooner than barter their faith. Father
O'Donnell's receipt, of throwing themselves upon
their knees, and marking themselves with the sign
of the cross, frightened away many of the preachers,
for they were unable to bear, from almost every one
they met, this marked expression of public detestation. The Rev. Mr. Sly bore it meekly, and only
raised his eyes to heaven to supplicate mercy upon
the erring ones. Miss Ellis, who generally accompanied "her dear pious Bob," took this as an act
of homage to his extraordinary zeal and devotion.

He encouraged her in this belief.

"Look," he would say, "look at that poor creature how she flings herself in the puddle to thank

me for some little favors I have done her, and for
leading her from the darkness of Popery. These
poor people are grateful indeed."

" Yes, dear Bob. What a source of consolation
it must be to you to see the heavenly seed you have
shaken upon the highway bring forth such fruit."

" It is, indeed, dear Lizzy; but then, I am but
an humble instrument in the hands of God, who
uses all things, great and small, according to His
will, and often uses the meanest to work out great
designs."

He who bears in mind the immense revenue
arising out of church property in Ireland, and
pocketed by idle, wealthy ecclesiastics, will certainly
wonder why such men as the Rev. Mr. Sly should
be countenanced even by Protestants themselves.*
It is true, there are some liberal Protestants who
look upon such men with as much detestation as the
most rigid Catholics. When again we consider that
of this large revenue that goes to the maintenance of
the Protestant Church in Ireland, the greater part
is paid by Catholics, one should expect that they
would leave us in peace, and pocket their livings in
quiet gratitude. Many of them do so, it is true, and
many of them are models of true charity and Christian forbearance. There are others who do not wish
to deprive us of all value for our money ; so they
join the Exeter Hall saints in their vile slanders

* This was written before the disendowment of the Church Establishment in Ireland.—AUTHOR.

upon Catholicity and its priests. It is useless for
any band of men, particularly illiterate men, as the
Exeter Hall missioners generally are, to try to upset
the popular religion, as Catholicity undoubtedly is,
in the eyes and hearts of the people of Ireland. In
vain they go about with the Bible in one hand and
bribes in the other, to upset a faith which withstood
the fiery ordeals of persecution and the sword.
They are but breeding dissension and disunion, and
might be much better employed at home in instructing the ignorant, besotted masses that swarm in
England's large towns. In a country like Ireland,
where the spiritual wants of the people are attended
to by a zealous, numerous priesthood, where there
are ministers without congregations, one would naturally think there would be no need of a supply of
preachers who only engender religious animosities.
They oftentimes reviled the rites and sacraments of
the religion of the people, called opprobrious names
to things held sacred. Is it to be wondered at, then,
if some of them met with abuse and ill-treatment
from persons so jealous of the proper respect due
to their religious forms and ceremonies? We calmly
ask our English readers how would they receive
a crusade of Irish priests, who would go to their
homesteads reviling their religion, and trying to
corrupt their families with tracts and pamphlets reflecting upon their religious feelings, and holding up
to ridicule the very things that they (the English)
held most sacred? We need not require an answer,

for there is spirit and manliness enough in England
to prevent any violation of the rites of their Church,
and of that Christian charity and forbearance that
one sect should observe towards another.

Lizzie Ellis had now become so attached to Mr.
Sly that she did not feel herself happy unless when
in his company. She had seen little of the world;
her affections were fresh and warm. It is not surprising, therefore, that one so artful as Mr. Sly—one
who affected such sanctity—one who, in her estimation, was perfection exemplified—should, with his
opportunities, win the love of her young heart. He
did his utmost to cultivate this growing feeling. He
did not alarm her at first by too hasty advances.
By his piety, his zeal and his goodness, he fast gained
her esteem ; then, by his cunning, insinuating ways
he won her affections.

She loved him with all the gushing warmth of
a first love. He—though he knew nothing of love
in its holiest and purest sense—looked upon her,
with her immense fortune, as a most desirable
match.

It is strange that Mr. Ellis should be blind to this
growing affection of his child. But, then, he was so
hardened by the cares of the world and his own
sensual enjoyments—for he was, in every way, a
sensualist—that he never loved with that deep,
yearning love of a parent. He had provided for all
her wants ; she had plenty of money, and servants
to attend her ; she should, or ought, therefore, be

happy. He did not consider that the heart requires something besides external enjoyments to make it happy—he did not consider that the young affections, like the ivy, must cling to something for support, and that when its tendrils are not clasped in the embrace of domestic love, they are apt to stray elsewhere.

Mr. Ellis was, as I have said, a sensualist; he was also a man of no religion. He went to church because it was most respectable, and because Lord Clearall went there. He countenanced Protestantism, partly for the same reasons. He entertained Mr. Sly in his house because he was recommended to him, and because such devotion to the cause looked well in the eyes of his Protestant neighbors. He thought if it were necessary for the maintenance of Church and State to have a religion, that that should be Protestant, as being the most fashionable and aristocratic.

Again, he looked upon Mr. Sly in the light of a guide to Lizzie. He knew that her education, both religious and secular, was grossly neglected. To whose guidance could he more safely entrust her?

We must take our readers to the Mills, as they were called. Mr. Sly's school was in full operation; soup and stirabout were liberally bestowed upon the young neophytes, so that their souls and bodies were kept in proper order. Hymns and prayers were chanted in the same breath in which Popish rites were mocked. Miss Ellis became a most zealous teacher, and delighted in instructing her young catechumens.

The works on Knockcorrig were stopped, the public money was squandered, and the people were dying in thousands.   In many places they had risen in open revolt, and had broken into stores and shops, and plundered them, to appease the cravings of hunger.   Additional bodies of police were quartered in the country—the expense of their support to be borne by the people.

There was a large committee meeting at the Mill on this occasion, for it was felt that something should be done for the people ; that relief should be given more extensively, or that more police should be quartered in the locality.

The people were collected outside in anxious groups.   Their lives, the lives of their families, were staked upon the issue of this meeting.

There they were, displaying all the ragged misery of extreme poverty.   Men, women, and children, shivering with cold and hunger, squatted upon stones and logs of timber, living, emaciated skeletons, frightful to behold.

With eager, anxious look, the hungry crowd awaited the result of the debate within.

There were some humane men there, who were for relieving the poor at all costs and risks.

Lord Clearall and his party prevailed ; they carried a resolution that the quarter-acre clause should be strictly adhered to ; that no more than half a pound of Indian meal, daily, should be given to each pauper, and this only to a limited number in each family. It might be necessary to explain the quarter-acre clause. It provided that any one holding a quarter or more land with his house should not get relief. Now, this was a powerful lever of extermination in the hands of the landlord. Many, through dire necessity, sooner than starve, were forced to resign their little farms. Oftentimes the landlord refused taking the land without getting possession of the house with it ; he then shortly hurled the poor wretch adrift upon the world. As soon as the decision of the committee was made known to the anxious crowd, which awaited it with the same breathless anxiety that a culprit in the dock might that verdict that was to consign him to death or liberty—and no wonder, for to them, indeed, it was a matter of life or death—no sooner had they heard it, than they raised a loud wail of bitter disappointment. Excited and phrenzied men, driven to desperation by hunger, rushed up to the door ; poor, emaciated women and helpless children joined the choruses of human voices.

"They will break in the house, my lord," said a member, pale with fear, to Lord Clearall.

"Never fear, never fear !" replied his lordship, " we have a strong body of police, and I have ordered the inspector to send for the military.'

Meanwhile the fury of the crowd outside became intense. Cries arose of, "Break it in "—''D——n

them, are we to starve like dogs? his lordships'
dogs are well fed, and we Christians are left to die
of hunger in our own country."

"Let us tear down the house and kill the bloody
crew ; betther to be shot or hung than to die in this
way."

"My good people," said Mr. Ellis, from a window,
"keep yourselves quiet, and we will do all we can
for you; if not, as a magistrate, I will order the
police to fire upon you."

"Bah! Ellis, you dog, dare you do it! We will
tear you limb from limb, you sneaking robber.
Where is the poor O'Donnell's property, you dirty
lickplate—you house-leveller? You order them to
fire upon us. Oh, thry it, though."

Mr. Ellis drew in his head, for he knew that he
would hear things that he would not wish to reach
Lord Clearall's ears.

"Brethren!" drawled the Rev. Mr. Sly, "brethren,
you are going the road to perdition ; you—"

"My curse upon your impudence, you ould swaddling ranther ; 'tis you look sleek and well in com-
parisment when you come cadging to Ellis's."

"Arragh, do ye hear the sly chat of him. Faith
it was no nickname to call him Sly."

"How is Miss Ellis? Does ye be singing the
psalms together yet? Faith it would be betther for
that ould fool, Ellis, to be looking afther ye than
tumbling houses."

"Musha, let the dacent man alone. Who'd blame

him? Shure he's only taking patthern by Mr. Ellis himself," said an old withered crone that squatted upon a log of timber.

"Thrue for you, Peg aroon!" said another.

"Oh, the ould sinner, the ould reprobate that ought to be thinkin' of his sowl."

"Sowl, inagh! Musha it is a gizzard he has. Shure it would be well for him if he had no sowl, for that's the sowl that will get the crispin'."

Mr. Ellis and Mr. Sly, under the impression that they would hear a good many things not to their advantage, withdrew.

"Arragh, bad luck to ye, hould yer tongue!" said a fierce, gaunt-looking fellow elbowing his way through the crowd. "Shut yer mouths, and let us make smiderheens of the door. There is meal and flour enuff widin for the soupers."

"That's true, Jem ; let us smash it."

"I will order the police to fire at you, if you do," shouted Mr. Ellis.

"To the divil wid you! Where yers goin' every day? Put out your mug, until you see what you'll get ?"

About ten of the strongest bore over a large log and forced it against the door.

The door shook and creaked upon its hinges.

They struck it again and again. The door was giving way. Mr. Ellis read the Riot Act from the inside of a window, as well as he could, with the shower of stones and dirt that was flying at him.

" Fire on them !" said he to the police, as soon as he read it.

" Stop !" said their officer. " Mr. Ellis, it would be throwing away the lives of my handful of men. All I can do until the military come, is to protect you."

" You're a coward, sir !" said Mr. Ellis, vehemently. " If you fire at them, the dogs will run for their lives."

" Coward, sir !" said the officer, indignantly " Coward ! you shall answer for that, Mr. Ellis."

" I repeat it, sir. If the men were under my command, I'd have every dog of them either dead or scampering away in a minute."

" Heaven knows," said the officer, " you have a surer method for killing them."

" The door is giving way," said Lord Clearall, as he heard the crash of its timbers. " Could you get the men in by the back way ?" said he to the officer.

The officer went round to the back door and got in his men, whom he placed to protect the room where they were assembled. The door had given way, and the crowd burst in with loud yells. In a moment, sacks, bins, and everything that contained flour, meal, or corn, were broken open. Some of the rioters forced their way into the school-room, and tore the tracts and broke the boilers.

It was amusing to see women with their petticoats converted into sacks, and men with their old coats performing the same office, while they marched off, almost naked, with their booty. The flour and meal were either removed or scattered about when the military arrived. Mr. Ellis and his party read the Riot Act, and wanted the commanding officer to fire on them. He, with a sneer of contempt, replied that it was "not the duty of soldiers to shoot poor, starving wretches like these," and he pointed to some hungry-looking women and children who were ravenously devouring the raw meal.

"But, sir, it is their duty to fire upon robbers and house-breakers," replied Lord Clearall.

"If they had enough to eat, my lord, I think they would not be house-breakers or robbers," said this human Englishman. "God help the country," he muttered, as he turned away, "where the rich thirst for the blood of the poor."

CHAPTER XXVI.

WINTER had now come around again; Christmas had passed, marked by no festive greetings or celebrations.

It was a day in February; the snow was heavy upon the ground, and a thick sleet drifted fiercely with the wind, as Mr. Ellis and a large military and police force came to evict the O'Donnells. Man is a selfish animal, and when he becomes hardened with power he seldom makes allowance for the feelings and wants of his fellow-men. Mr. Ellis was now all-powerful. He was a magistrate and sub-sheriff. So onerous were his duties as sheriff in ejecting the unfortunate peasantry, that he had invented and constructed a machine for pulling down their houses. The grapple-chain was fixed to some of the rafters, and then a few turns brought down the roof over the unfortunate inmates, if they were foolish enough to remain inside, which was often the case, for they clung to their homes to the last.

" Come, come," said Mr. Ellis, " clear the house quick. I have more to eject, and I want to be back to dine with Lord Clearall."

His men rushed into the house and flung out the furniture.

A large crowd of people had collected, and looked on menacingly.

"The old lady isn't able to get up, your honor. I think she's dying. What will we do?" said one of the bailiffs.

"All a sham, Horan—all a sham—pull her out. She'll come to in the air."

The fellow went in and approached the bed— "Get up, ma'am, or we must pull you out," and he shook her.

Mrs. O'Donnell essayed to rise.

"I'll help you, ma'am," said the fellow, taking her in his arms.

"Ruffian! touch her not!" shouted a voice, hoarse with emotion, behind him; and with a fierce blow, that sent the blood welling from his mouth and nose, Frank levelled him on the floor. "Dog!" said he, kicking the fellow from him, and then, turning to his mother, said, "Mother, dear, I'll carry you."

"Do, Frank, do. God bless you, my darling boy, and keep quiet. Our Divine Lord suffered more, Frank, and see how He bore it. As for me, it matters little."

Frank took her tenderly, and wrapped the covering around her; he bore her in his arms, and as her head rested upon his bosom, his heart swelled with emotion, and the tears rushed from his eyes. He laid her down softly in a sheltered corner.

"Frank," said she, " my heart is breaking. Bring me your father."

"Yes, mother, yes ;" and as he looked upon her features he saw that the hand of death was already overshadowing them. Frank went, and shortly returned, leading the old man. His body was bent, and his grey hair was now almost white from the effects of sorrow. Uncle Corny followed, with his regimentals thrown upon his only arm. The crowd fell back in reverence.

"Mother," said Frank, " here he is."

"John," said she, " I'm dying !"

The old man looked up with surprise.

"It's cold here, Frank ; come home to your mother," said he.

"John, John, don't you know me? Say you do, before I die ?"

He pressed his hands to his head, and seemed to collect himself ; he looked around with surprise ; he looked at the soldiers and at Mr. Ellis ; he then knelt down, exclaiming—

"My love, my love, is it come to this? O God, help us—God, help us !" and he bent down and passionately kissed her. There was not a dry eye there except Mr. Ellis's, and those used to such scenes.

"If I but had the priest now, I'd be content. O God, hear my prayer !"

Just then Father O'Donnell rode into the yard. Frank ran to him and told him all. He hurried over to Mrs. O'Donnell.

Father O'Donnell heard her confession, and administered the holy sacraments. He then knelt and prayed beside her.

Oh, what a scene in a civilized country! To see that poor old priest, his hair floating in the breeze, and covered with sleet and snow, and that gentle woman dying beside a wall, her wailing friends around her!

Father O'Donnell stopped reading ; he took her hand, and looked into her face.

"My God," he exclaimed, "she's dead!"

Mr. O'Donnell took her hand, exclaiming, "How cold you are. Won't you come in, love ; do, and we'll warm you. Sure it's very cold here." And when she stirred not, he sank down beside her and rested his head upon Kate's bosom, who was all this time supporting her mother, herself more dead than alive.

"It is a melancholy sight indeed," said Father O'Donnell, turning away.

Frank was phrenzied. He ran over and seized Mr. Ellis's horse. "Look, look," said he, pointing to the group. "You have murdered her. You robbed us first, and now you have murdered her. But I'll have revenge, revenge! Yes, her blood is crying to Heaven for vengeance, and vengeance will it have. Murderer and robber, you shall die like the beast of the field. God, I call upon you for vengeance!"

"Seize him," said Mr. Ellis, trembling with fear.

"They dare not, they dare not!" shouted Frank; and the people took up stones and sticks, and rushed around him.

"Can we make no defence?" said Uncle Corny, leaning his hand gently upon Frank's shoulder; "if not, let us march." He then turned around, talking to some neighbors, who were asking him to their houses. This was set down at a large discount as so much treason.

"Look at the ould Croppy thrying to stir them up," said one of the bailiffs to Mr. Ellis.

Frank let go the bridle of Mr. Ellis's horse, and fell back to the crowd.

"I see him, I see him! I'm d——d but I'm a magistrate to no purpose if I leave him his pension!" And Mr. Ellis kept his word.

The people were intensely excited. Some stones were flung at Mr. Ellis; the soldiers and police had collected around him, with their guns loaded and bayonets screwed.

Shemus-a-Clough wept and shouted for a time beside Mrs. O'Donnell. He then jumped up and rushed through the crowd, and hit Mr. Ellis with a stone that sent him reeling from his horse. A wild shout ran through the crowd, and they rushed at the military.

"Ready, present——" shouted their officer.

"Stop, stop, for God's sake stop!" said Father O'Donnell, throwing himself between them. "Are you Christians at all? Here, in the face of death, you're going to shed each other's blood!" and he pointed to the corpse. " Oh! you savages! But God help you! it's hard to blame you. But leave them to God—to God, who will judge them according to their doings. I'd rather be the poorest man here than that guilty man," and he pointed to Mr. Ellis, who, foaming with rage and covered with blood, had remounted his horse. " So, thank God, that though you are poor, your souls are not black like his ; and now go home in peace."

Most of the people went away, except the immediate friends, who remained to carry the body somewhere, for none of Lord Clearall's tenants dare shelter it.

The Rev. Mr. Smith chanced to be driving by at the time ; he left his car upon the road, and went in. After Father O'Donnell told him how things stood—

"My God! my God!" said he, "how man abuses his power."

Father O'Donnell told him that they could not get a house to convey the body to, so great was their dread of the landlord.

" It's fortunate that I have come this way," said Mr. Smith. " I have a snug farm-house a few miles off; let Mr. O'Donnell's family remove there, and I'll see that this decent woman shall get proper burial. They can occupy the house as long as it suits their convenience. Nor shall they want, either. But they had better remove this furniture. Will

one of you," said he to some men near, "run over
to my farm and tell the men to bring over the cars
to remove this furniture ?"

"Yes, your riverence, and God bless you !"

"Stop !" said Mr. Ellis, who overheard the order.
"That furniture is mine ; I canted it with the other
effects, so don't touch it at your peril !"

Father O'Donnell and Mr. Smith looked at each
other.

"I thought, Mr. Ellis, that you got more than
your rent then, besides this little furniture," said
the minister.

"No, Mr. Smith ; it's no business of yours ; all
this was fairly auctioned, so it is my property."

"I beg your pardon, Mr. Ellis ; it is business of
mine ; it is the duty every Christian man to try and
protect a poor honest man from scoundrelism and
tyranny," and Mr. Smith walked away.

The body was carefully removed, followed by the
mourning relatives and a crowd of people ; Father
O'Donnell and Mr. Smith also accompanying
them.

Irish wakes and funerals are very much alike in
general, so we need not describe them. This, indeed, was a peculiarly sad one, on account of Mrs.
O'Donnell's tragic death, and the former high standing of the family.

Father O'Donnell read the funeral service outside
the little gate of the churchyard. Mr. Ellis carried
his hostility so far as to prevent him from reading it

inside, moreover, as the church was on Lord Clearall's property.

Mr. Sly offered to read the service, but would
have been torn in pieces but for Father O'Donnell.

The people now left for their homes. The little
church was silent; but one returned to weep over
that newly covered grave. Frank knelt and prayed
by times. Kate would be there too, but she was
not able to rise from her bed, poor girl.

"O mother! mother!" said Frank, in the depth
of his anguish; "mother! you have left lonely,
breaking hearts after you; but, then, I should not
weep for you, for you are happy with your God;
but for us, want and affliction are our portion.
Better, mother, to sleep beside you in that cold
grave, than live on a worthless life! Oh! what is
life to me! Once, I hoped that it would be a life of
joy and happiness; but no, no, it is to be one of
dark bitterness. I have no object now to live for;
no occupation to call forth my energies. Death,
indeed, would be a blessing now. Men boast that
the laws of England protect the poor and weak
from the rich and strong. How little do they know
of these laws. Like the fabled fruit, they are fair
without and foul within. A tyrant landlord and
agent, under protection of these boasted laws, have
robbed us of our property, have murdered you, my
dear, fond mother! and yet they live, and are re-
spected and feared. O God! O God! how long
will this continue? Was not the land intended for

the support of man ? Have not we, therefore, an inherent right to the soil, and are we to be thus crushed and trampled and hunted from it ? O mother ! I'll have revenge upon your murderers, and then I'll fly the country. Yes, Ellis, the murderer of my mother, shall die by my hand ; but, Alice ! Alice ! girl of my heart ! how can I leave you ?"

In his excitement his eyes glared, he clenched his hands, and ground his teeth, and spoke in a hurried, audible manner.

The ruins of an old abbey stood near the grave.

After Alice Maher had left the churchyard, she missed Frank, and while her father and Father O'Donnell were in earnest conversation, she returned, knowing that she would find him at the grave.

Seeing Frank speaking to himself in an excited manner, she stood to listen, and overheard his wild soliloquy. She went over and gently laid her hand upon his shoulder.

"Who's this ?" said he, rudely flinging the hand from him and turning round. "O Alice !" said he, gently taking her hand, "forgive my rudeness ; I was in a strange mood."

" I forgive and pity you, Frank ; but I must tell you that I overheard you. Frank, could you think of being a murderer without horror ?"

"Yet, Alice, he has murdered her," and he pointed to the grave.

" Even so, Frank. Vengeance belongs to God,
and He will deal with every one according to his
works. Leave him to God ; He is just."

" Alice, love ! if you were a man you'd feel as I
do. The very reptile will recoil upon the foot that
crushes it; and can I, a man, see my means plundered from me, my mother murdered, and yet
calmly look on ? Look at my poor father, Alice.
See what a wreck he is ! He was beloved and admired, and now he's a poor paralytic. Look at my
fine, noble sister, once the pride of the parish—the
toast of many a festive scene—and now ! and now !
she's a pauper, dependent upon the charity of others.
Think of my darling mother, Alice. Was she not
murdered, dragged from her warm bed to die upon
the cold ground, with the home of her early joys and
affections knocked in ruins beside her ? And myself, Alice. Oh ! I had hopes and yearnings of enjoying peace, and love, and happiness in that old
home. I thought, Alice, love ! that there, with you,
my own sweet wife, nestling upon my bosom, after
the toils and anxiety of the day, or cheering me
through the world's strife, I could, indeed, be happy
—happy as mortal man could be. Often, Alice, have
I pictured to myself a happy home, hallowed by all
the gushing warmth of loving hearts, all the holy
influence of domestic bliss—a home made cheerful
by your loving, greeting smiles. Often have I imagined ourselves seated by our own fireside, foster-
ing our little plots and plans of life, until my heart

19

expanded with joy and happiness. But, oh! all this, this was but a dream! I, who long so much for domestic repose—I, who have a heart so susceptible of love and all the finer feelings of man's nature—must wander an outcast upon the world. And can it be a sin to murder him who has caused all this ruin and misery?"

Frank placed his head between his hands and wept. Alice gently took his hand from his face and said—

"You must promise me, Frank, to give up this horrid thought. You know I love you ; love you! oh, yes, next to my God, I love you!"

Frank pressed her hand.

"And think, Frank, how I would feel if you, whom I love so dearly, were branded with a murderer's shame. O my God! I would not survive it. You, who are so noble and generous, to pollute your hands and soul! If it were so, I would soon sleep in my grave. Promise me now—here, upon your mother's grave I ask it, and her pure spirit is looking down from heaven upon us—here," and she knelt upon the grave—"here I ask of you that you'll not be guilty of the blood of Mr. Ellis or Lord Clearall ; that you'll not injure them, but leave them to God, who will bring them to an account in His own wise time ; here, do kneel beside me—that's it ; now promise me," and she looked up into his face with such pure sweetness that one might fancy her an angel pleading for erring man.

Though Frank knelt beside her, he kept his hands pressed over his face.

"Speak, Frank ; say you do."

"O Alice! don't ask me ; I can't do it."

"Can't do it! Go from me! You're not the noble, generous youth you were at all. Oh! have I given my heart to a murderer?—to one who could bear to see me pine and sink into an early grave? O God! help me, and soften his callous heart."

Alice burst into tears. Frank looked on for a time ; his heart was full ; at length tears came from his eyes, and he wept.

"Frank! Frank! say you'll do it. I know you will, for now you weep. Oh! those blessed tears!"

"Yes, Alice, love. Here on my mother's grave, before Heaven, I promise you I'll leave them to God. May He have mercy upon them."

"O Frank! thank God!" and her little head rested upon his bosom.

"That will do, Frank. Let us be going now."

"Come, love ;" and they left the churchyard.

"Alice," said Frank, as they walked along, "I must tell you."

"What, Frank?"

"You know, love, I can do nothing here ; I'm young and strong ; I love enterprise ; many are making wealth in California in a few years ; I intend going there, and return home again, I trust, a wealthy man."

"O Frank! what will I do?"

"Under present circumstances I would not ask
your father's consent, even if he were willing to
give it, which he's not.   I could not think of marrying you, my own sweet love, to bring you into a
struggle with the world.   Now, we are young; let
us remain single for five years; be true to me as I
will be to you, and, believe me, I will return with
boundless wealth to claim my darling wife."

"But, Frank, if you should fail, or——"

"Stop, Alice, I cannot fail. Cheered by the hope
of your love, I will strive, and toil, and grow rich. If
riches are to be gained at all, I must win them for
my own sweet one.   Alice, I know that I must
make riches to get you. I love you deeply, wildly,
and this love will strengthen my arm in the strife."

"Oh, cursed riches! cannot we be happy without
them, Frank?"

"No, Alice, no.   But here is your father and my
uncle."

Alice looked fondly on him, and whispered—

"Come to see me soon, Frank."

"Yes, love."

"Where have you been, Alice?" said Mr. Maher,
looking rather displeased as he saw her leaning upon
Frank's arm.

"She was with me at my mother's grave, sir,"
said Frank.   "I am just telling her that I have resolved on going to America to try my fortune."

"Going to America! Frank," said Father O'Donnell. "No, boy. What would your poor father do,

and Alice, and I, poor old man that I am, now to lose my fine boy? No, Frank, don't go," and the old man put his handkerchief to his eyes.

"It is hard enough, no doubt," said Mr. Maher, evidently well pleased at the matter; "but, after all, what can the boy do here? Many a man made a fortune there in a little time. If you want money, Frank, I'll help you."

" No, sir," said Frank, proudly, " I have enough."

" Well, perhaps you're right, perhaps you're right. But what will I do? Won't you try and keep him, Alice?"

This appeal was too much for Alice.

"There now, there now, don't cry, child, and he won't go; though maybe it's better, maybe it's better. Let him go, Alice, let him go."

"Uncle," said Frank, firmly, "I have resolved upon going; I cannot be a pauper here; and you, Mr. Maher, I have one request to ask of you—that is, you know that this darling girl and I love one another; I could not think of asking her now, even if I thought I would get your consent; but do not ask her to marry until I return. I will return with wealth, or never return. If living and rich, I'll be back in five years. She and I are pledged for that time. If I don't return then with wealth, she's free."

" Do promise them, promise them. Sure they are fond of one another, God bless them. He'll be rich yet. Promise them," said Father O'Donnell.

"Give me your hand, Frank," said Mr. Maher. "I do promise; and if you return with wealth, there is not a young man in the county I'd sooner give her to; but then, in your present circumstances, it would be your ruin to marry. I have a good many sons, Frank, so I could not give her a farm, and, you know, the money soon goes."

"God bless you God bless you!" said Frank, grasping him by the hand; "you are right; but I'll win wealth for her sake, for i could die to gain her."

CHAPTER XXVII.

A SHORT ACCOUNT OF THE WORKING OF THE POOR LAWS
—HOW THE POOR ARE TREATED—A HUMANE BOARD—
THE FRUIT OF EVICTIONS.

I INTENDED to devote some chapters to the working and management of the poor laws in Ireland,
and also to the sophistry of political economists,
who assert that Ireland is rapidly increasing in
material wealth; but as my work is extending
beyond the limits I had prescribed, I must confine
myself to a few remarks.

In the first place, I fearlessly assert that the poor
laws have destroyed the happiness and independence of the very poor for whose benefit they were
created.

Since the introduction of poor rates, pauperism
has increased, and poverty has become more pre-
dominant.

The law has provided the indigent against absolute
starvation. This protection destroys every principle
of energy in the sinking man's heart; it also checks
the unforced sympathies of our nature, which, at all
times, have been found a surer protection against
misery than any legal enactments.

The best legal enactments for providing for the maintenance of the poor seem somehow to clash against the wise dispensations of Providence; for even a casual observer must see that the best safeguards against extreme poverty lie in that charitable feeling planted by the hand of Nature in our bosoms. The poor laws close up the many fountains of charity, and fling over the poor to the merciless protection of paid officials, whose hearts become steeled to misery, and whose only study is to please their superiors, and to make the most they possibly can of their own situations. They possess not one feeling of sympathy for the poor wretches thrown on their care. They stand to each other in grim hostility—the one party thankless and dissatisfied, and claiming as their due what the others niggardly administer. In fact, the system has transformed the whole nature of charity. It has closed up those sacred fountains which are the poor man's best protection—namely, the kindness of friends and relatives, the sympathy and charity of the wealthy, and these acts of mutual help and kindness which the poor render each other, and which are of more importance than a casual observer could conceive. Again, the poor laws are an encouragement to vice; they support the unfortunate and her offspring; they take in the forsaken mother and her children, whom the husband and father would never desert, only that he knew he was thereby affording them legal protection. On the whole, it gives a respectable maintenance to paupered officials, who consume over a third of the rates levied for the ostensible purpose of maintaining the poor, but in reality to maintain blundering officials in princely lazar-houses. We see what good is effected in towns by pious communities. We see foundling hospitals, penitentiaries, reformatories, and houses of orphan-age all admirably conducted by the pious zeal of some humble religious, and supported by voluntary charity. Had these at their command the princely revenues that are extorted from the people for the maintenance of poorhouses, what would they not effect. It would be for the good of society at large that poorhouses were abolished altogether ; that these abodes of wretchedness were converted to some useful purpose, and leave the poor to that fountain of human sympathy which God has planted in our nature, and from which flows those streams of charity that amalgamate the various classes of society, and that afford a more abundant, or, at least, a more effective and generous tide of charity to relieve the wants of the suffering poor.

There is another matter, too, of equal importance, which is taking deeper root every day among the landocracy of Ireland—I refer to the principle of amalgamating small farms. This appears now to be the favorite panacea for Ireland's grievances. A notion has gone abroad that small farms are in-jurious to the material wealth of the country. This, to a certain extent, might be true of a great commercial country like England, but, if persisted in, will prove the ruin of Ireland.

The landlords unthinkingly follow the advice and example of political economists, without reflecting how far this will benefit the country at large. The poet was wiser than these writers when he asserted—

"Where wealth accumulates, men decay."

Large farms are unfavorable to the increase of population ; but increase of population is favorable to the growth of liberty, intelligence, and prosperity.

In England it has been found that the poor have increased in misery as farms have increased in size. If this be true of a commercial country like England, how much more so must it be of an agricultural one like Ireland.

The smaller the farms, the more food must be raised, and consequently the more employment given. The humble agriculturist of a few acres— if he be but protected by law—might be as happy and independent as the man with hundreds.

The increase of farms tend to convert arable land into pasture, and thereby diminish the means of employment and the increase of wholesome food, for be it known that the complement of land required to grow corn for six or eight men would not grow animal food for more than one man.

The quantity and quality of food has great influence on the increase of the peasantry and their physical development. This accounts for the appearance and comparative independence of the Irish peasant previous to the famine years.

Until the failure of the potatoe crop, a wholesome and nutricious food was easily procured ; population naturally increased, and a certain prosperity reigned among the peasantry, despite the many cruel evictions and extortions practised by the landlords.

I say to you, landlords of Ireland, if you favor the increase of farms, you are ruining your country, you are ruining the peasantry—debaring him from any right or enjoyment in the soil which gave him birth. Are there no philanthropists among you to come forth in defence of the poor man's rights? It is not in human nature to seek misery. We all strive for happiness ; yet the Irish peasant, the most laborious and patient under God's sun, pines in misery in his own native soil—a soil teeming with abundance, fruitful as God's Eden. His existence, indeed, is miserable. He meets no love, no sympathy from those bound to protect him. Suckled and nursed amidst filth and poverty, embrowned with the constant smoke that reeks around his chimneyless cabin, covered over with rags, and fed sparingly, and often with unwholesome food, he still grows to manhood, strong, stalworth, and impulsive. What would he be if he were nurtured and reared as he should be? But no, he is looked upon as an incumbrance in the land which he loves so dearly. Better for him, poor fellow! that he had no existence at all than to live on to see his life one bitter strife of unrequited toil, with hope and energy crushed in his breast—his wife, with love and joy torn from her heart, droop and pine, and his babes, born to their father's inheritance of strife and misery, mere objects of sufferance; for the will of the landlord or agent may hurl them from their wretched home to a more wretched fate still, namely, to die beside some ditch, or to prolong this miserable life amidst the moral leprosy and contagion of a poorhouse.

Landlords of Ireland, will you do nothing for the poor? Aristocracy of Ireland, will you do nothing for them? Think of their patience, their virtues, their wants, and their fruitless toils—think of all these—think how the love and tenderness of their lives are chilled and overborne by a system of neglect and exclusiveness—I was going to say oppression—that is fast exterminating the hapless peasantry. Landlords! encourage small farms; give the poor man his little garden to till; give him an interest in the soil that will give him wholesome remunerative employment for his wife and children; make him feel that he is a man, that you and the laws are his protectors, that he can safely enjoy all these domestic hopes, enjoyments, and gushing affections that ennoble our nature. Do all this, and you not only render a moral benefit to society at large, but you make your fellow-creature happy and independent, thereby discharging your duty both to God and man. Leave aside all sectarian feelings, look

upon the peasant as an unfortunate brother, reach
to him the hand of friendship and fellowship, and,
believe me, he will repay you with gratitude and
esteem.

We beg our readers to accompany us to a select
little party given by the amiable Mrs. Thrifty, mis-
tress of the —— poorhouse.

Mrs. Thrifty was a plump, tidy, good-looking little
woman. She always had a smile on her pouting
lips for her superiors in office, though the poor
devils under her charge asserted that to them she
was the essence of vinegar. She was particularly
gracious to the master of the house, who was a
good-looking young man of about thirty, who had
replaced her dear husband, who was master before
him, but who had taken it into his head to take too
much spiritual comfort, and to make his exit from
the scene of his useful labors. Some say that Mrs.
Thrifty did not bestow all her gracious smiles upon
him, that she treated him to more of the acid than
the honey of matrimony, and that in order to kill
care he killed himself. Mrs. Thrifty fretted and
fumed a good deal after his death. She was continually crying and bemoaning the good man for a
time. Perhaps her conscience smote her. However, she became wonderfully reconciled to her fate
after the appointment of the new master.

A bright fire blazed in Mrs. Thrifty's comfortable
little room ; the round table glistened with glasses
and decanters, and four wax candles burned brightly,

Mrs. Thrifty sat at the fire in an easy-chair; she continually smoothed down her nice lace collar and her new bombazine; she then cast a wistful look at the door, as if anxiously expecting some one. A pretty little child of about two years old twaddled about. The child fell upon the carpet and began to cry. "Hold your tongue, or I'll throw you into the fire," said she, rudely snatching up the child. "Hush, pet, darling, love; don't cry; that's it; there's a lump of sugar," said she in soothing tones, but loud enough to reach the ears of Mr. Tomkins, the master, whom she heard opening the door.

"Ah! Mrs. Thrifty," said Mr. Tomkins, "what ails the poor dear?"

"She just got a fall, Mr. Tomkins. Pray, sit down. It's nothing, for it was only upon the carpet; but then I'm so alarmed lest anything should happen to this only pledge of affection left by my dear, dear husband." Here Mrs. Thrifty put her handkerchief to her eyes.

"What a loving, affectionate body she is," thought Mr. Tomkins.

"Poor pet—that's it; be quiet now. There's a darling. Mix a glass of punch, Mr. Tomkins."

Mr. Tomkins did so, and mixed one for Mrs. Thrifty, too."

"Ah, I won't take it, Tomkins; it sickens me."

"Do, please, ma'am, for me. It is the first I have ever asked you;" and Mr. Tomkins pushed his chair over near the widow, I suppose to urge her

Mrs. Thrifty at length consented.

"Do you know, Mr. Tomkins," said the widow, "I don't know, have I acted prudently in asking a few friends here to-night? for my dear man is dead no more than six months; but then you and I were so long under the same roof, discharging similar duties, that I thought it too bad without inviting you to a cup of tea. Fill another glass, Mr. Tomkins. Besides, it is so lonely to be alone, without any one to speak to only this dear little pet," and she fell to kissing the slumbering child. "Only for her I couldn't live at all."

"It is, indeed, too bad," said Mr. Tomkins, tossing off his punch, and edging his chair nearer to the widow. "I am often tempted to spend an evening with you in this nice quiet room. Isn't it comfortable?" and Mr. Tomkins looked, evidently well pleased, about the cheerful room. "I'll tell you what, Mrs. Thrifty, it would be agreeable to spend an evening here, and we such near neighbors, only the voice of slander, the voice of slander, Mrs. Thrifty."

Mr. Tomkins was waxing eloquent, for he had emptied his third glass.

"The people are very talkative, Mr. Tomkins; but who'd mind their talk, who'd mind their talk? Mustn't people live and enjoy themselves, Mr. Tomkins?"

"That's true, ma'am," said Mr. Tomkins, and he gave something that resounded like a kiss to Mrs. Thrifty, which made her blush and toss her head.

" Oh, fie, Mr. Tomkins, don't do that again ; see, you have wakened the child.   Hush, my darling; sleep now, pet."

" Isn't it lovely," said Mr. Tomkins, running his hand through the silken hair of the child.

" Ah! no, Mr. Tomkins, it's not fashionable, you know—it's rude."

" What, curly hair not fashionable? Why, I never saw anything so beautiful."

" Ah! but I meant—no matter. It is indeed lovely.   Are you fond of children?"

" Passionately, passionately, ma'am.   I'd give the world to be the father of that lovely child, to have her nestle confidingly in my breast, to have her little silken head resting against my bosom, to have her call me father, to have her prattling about me like a little cherub.   Ah! Mrs. Thrifty, that, indeed, would be living in love and happiness."

" Stop, stop," said she, " there is some one coming."   In fact Mrs. Thrifty's guests were assembling.

Mrs. Thrifty's guests were highly pleased with everything.   They were delighted ; so much so, indeed, that they did not quit until about twelve o'clock.   They were all gone except Mr. Tomkins, who seemed as if bent on saying something, for he had one arm around Mrs. Thrifty's waist, and the other resting upon the table.

" Who's there?" said Mrs. Thrifty, as a rap came to the door.

" I, ma'am ; I want to see you."

"Come in, then. Well, what do you want?"

"Nothing, ma'am, only that Nelly Sullivan's son is dying, and she's making such an uproar to get to him, and he says 'he'd die asy if he saw her.'"

"Well, did any one ever hear the like," said Mrs. Thrifty, raising her eyes in surprise, "to think that I could go admit her now, and into the men's ward, too? it is provoking."

"It's scandalous!" said Mr. Tomkins, sympathetically.

"Well, ma'am, what will I do?" said the nurse, hesitatingly.

"Go about your business, and if she persist, let her be locked up. Why, there are so many dying now, if we were to mind them we couldn't get a moment's sleep."

"Why don't you go?"

"Please, sir, there is another man dying, and he's calling for the priest."

"Priest, now, indeed. What a nice hour it would be to rattle up a priest. Let him hold till morning if he likes."

"I'm sure the priest would come if sent for; I'd go myself, sir."

"Do as you're bid, woman; and, mind you, to-morrow will be board day. Let the stirabout be made thick and strong."

"Yes, sir. Can't we do anything for them, sir."

"You have got your answer, woman; go about your business."

" How will we stand them?   Aren't they a pest?"
said Mrs. Thrifty, as she emptied a glass of wine to
compose her nerves.

" They are provoking; they are sure to take it
into their heads to die at night, as if to vex people,"
said Mr. Tomkins, as if the poor wretches had a
choice of dying when they liked ; and Mr. Tomkins
drank off a glass of punch to keep Mrs. Thrifty company.

As I am about taking leave of Mr. Tomkins and
Mrs. Thrifty, I might as well state that Mr. Tomkins,
in his warmth of feeling and deep admiration of
the child, popped the question, which Mrs. Thrifty,
after some bashful objections, accepted, to the great
joy of Mr. Tomkins, who swore he was the happiest
man in Christendom, but had sufficient time to regret his rashness afterwards.

The following day was board day.   Lord Clearall
was in the chair, and Mr. Ellis sat beside him.   There
was a good sprinkling of guardians, most of whom
seemed there for no other earthly purpose but to
nod an assent to everything Lord Clearall said and
did.   The clerk read the minutes; the deaths for
the week were sixty-three.

" I declare," whispered Lord Clearall to Mr. Ellis,
" that's a grand thing.   At that rate the house will
be soon empty, and the rates down to a trifle."

" True, my lord, true," replied Mr. Ellis.

" How do you provide coffins, Mr. Tomkins?" said
his lordship.

" Can't get them, my lord. We had to get a ninged bottom put to a strong coffin, and drop them into the grave."

" Well, there's a saving in that. Now for the clerk's estimate of the rates."

" Here it is, my lord," said the clerk.

" Ah! by this I see that the rate on my property is twelve shillings in the pound, and we are after paying four. How is this ?"

" Why, my lord, the influx of poor from your division is very large; within the last fortnight it has been over a hundred ; and you know the rate is struck according to the number in the house."

" It is enormous," said Mr. Ellis.

" It's confiscation. See, it's but one shilling upon the earl's property," said Lord Clearall, flinging down the sheet.

" It is the fruit of your evictions," thought many a guardian there, but had not the courage to express it.

CHAPTER XXVIII.

FRANK BIDS FAREWELL TO THE OLD HOUSE AND HIS
MOTHER'S GRAVE—A SCENE—NELLY SULLIVAN GIVES
HER BENEDICTION TO MR. ELLIS—THE SEPARATION—
THE EMIGRANT SHIP.

AFTER the eviction of their family, Frank made
his sister acquainted with his resolution of going
to America. Though she keenly felt the separation,
still, she saw that there was no other course open
for him, and, like a noble girl that she was, she
sacrificed her own feelings to his interest. She
could not bear to see him, the educated, high-
minded youth, become a laborer in a land where
there was no reward for toil; it was better that
he should go.

Mary Cahill accompanied the O'Donnells to their
poor home ; she vowed that she'd never leave them,
and to their remonstrances that they couldn't give
her hire, she indignantly replied that she did not
want it. She even refused to marry James Cormack until the O'Donnells would be somehow settled
in the world.

"Do you think, James," said she to him, "that I
would leave the old gentleman that was always so

kind to me, and the dear young lady, in trouble.
No, James, if I'm worth havin' you must wait for
me."

Frank had made his little preparations. He engaged a steerage passage in a ship bound from
Cork, in order to leave all the means he could to
his father and sister. A few days before his departure he went to visit the old house. It looked
desolate indeed; the gates and doors were all torn
away, and that home, that so often resounded with
mirth and festive greeting—that home of his childhood, where himself and his sisters often played,
where he often nestled in love upon his father and
mother's knees, where he hoped to spend his manhood and his declining years in peace—was now
one heap of ruins.

He wept like a child on the spot where his
mother died. He went from house to house taking
leave of each as he would with an old familiar friend.
He then went to see his mother's grave.

" O mother! mother!" he passionately exclaimed,
as he stood over her grave, "I am going to leave you
forever, forever; and who will mind your grave?
Perhaps it may be desecrated like those around me.
O mother! I wish I were with you, for my heart is
full of grief, and my life of bitterness. Good, kind
mother, look down upon me with pity, and watch
over your unfortunate child! O mother! mother!"
and in his wild paroxysm of grief he threw himself
upon the grave, and wept bitter tears. He remained

thus half unconscious for some time, until roused by
a voice behind.

" Please sthand up, Misther Frank," said the voice.
" Shure there is people have leave to weep as well
as you."

" Who are you ?"

" Musha, then you ought to know me; but people
are so changed they don't know one another at all,
at all."

" Oh ! is this Mrs. Sullivan ? Poor woman ! what
has brought you here ?"

" Oh ! not much. Shure it is no difference about
the poor. The Lord be praised, we are kicked and
buffeted about like dogs. Do you know, Misther
Frank, but I often think is there a God at all to
allow the poor to be trampled on ?"

" Don't say that, don't say that. See all the Lord
Himself suffered, and did not murmur."

" That's true, sir ; but then misery—and God
knows we have enough of it—makes persons beside
themselves ; but come and I'll show you what
brought me here."

Frank followed her to the end of the old abbey,
and there he saw an old tattered cloak thrown over
some object. Frank stood beside her while she
stooped down and raised up the covering, revealing
the ghastly features of a corpse.

Frank stepped back and shuddered.

" No wonder that you should start, Misther
Frank ; no wonder at all, for my colleen-bawn is

much changed. Och! och! mavrone! they kilt,
they kilt him. They would not let his mother that
suckled him near him to close his eyes or hear his
dying prayer! and they feasting and eating all the
time. So, alanna, you were the darling boy; but
they murthered you, and they'd throw you in a
hole like a dog. Oh! they would, they would, the
savages; but I stole him away to lay him in holy
ground," and she knelt at the head of the corpse
and swayed her body to and fro.

"God, help us!" said Frank, covering his eyes
with his hands.

"O God, help us! Asthore machree, shure you're
in heaven; but they kilt you. They hunted us out
of the cabin, and then refused us work since we
wouldn't sell our souls. But you are in heaven,
alanna; they can't touch you now."

"I had better get a spade to make a grave for
him," said Frank, leaning his hand upon her shoulder.

"Do, and God bless you! But sthop, I'll send
the gaffers for one."

Two emaciated, wretched-looking children soon
returned tottering under the weight of a spade and
shovel. Frank stripped off and dug a grave, and
then helped the mother to lay the body in it. Frank
commenced to shovel in the earth.

"Leave these big stones aside, Misther Frank;
they might hurt him; and let me settle the cloak
about him, for fear of his eyes. Shure, after bring-

ing him seven miles upon my back, the laste I'd
bury him tinderly."

Frank closed up and nicely sodded the grave, and
while the widow was shedding bitter tears over her
only son, he went over to take leave of his mother's
grave.

"Farewell, mother!" said he; "farewell, and
watch over me and protect me."

"Well," said he to Mrs. Sullivan, on his return,
"where do you mean to go now?"

"I am shure I dunna where—any place at all.
God's will be done."

"Come with me then."

Frank took them to his old home. There was a
small out-house, with the door on, and the roof
partly up. He lit a fire in a corner, and drew
some of the dry thatch and made a bed; he then
brought in a bundle of sticks.

"That's all I can do now, ma'am," said Frank,
"and here is a shilling; I have no more about me
so go and get something to eat."

"God bless you! I hadn't a bit since morning."

The children crouched around the fire, and the
mother went to the next village, a distance of two
miles or more, for bread.

• The day was sharp and cold, and the evening set
in with sleet and snow, as Nelly Sullivan proceeded
upon her errand. On her return, her way lay partly by Mr. Ellis's. As she was passing through a
grove, near the house, which was a kind of pleasure-

ground, and specially reserved for the family, Mr. Ellis crossed her path.

"How dare you come this way?" said he, shaking her by the shoulder.

"Ha! ha! ha!" she exclaimed; "how dare I indeed. How dare I trespass upon Mr. Ellis's land, that came here a pauper himself; that evicted half the country, and sent them to die in the poorhouse, or the ditch-side; that murthered Mrs. O'Donnell. Ha! ha! ha! that's not bad."

"Woman, begone!" shouted Mr. Ellis, foaming with rage, "or I'll let this dog tear you to pieces," and he pointed to a large mastiff that was near him.

"Och! mavrone, that's little to what you could do. Shure you tossed me out of my cabin, because I wouldn't send my children to Mr. Sly's school. Och! what a minister he is. Faith, it's he that's tachin' Miss Lizzie nicely. The devil take the whole lot of ye; ye have brought ruin and misery and starvation upon us. Shure it is only to-day I buried my darling boy, that ye murthered."

"Wretch," said Mr. Ellis, "be off!" and he shoved her violently; she fell, and in his passion he raised his foot to kick her.

"That's it, do it," she exclaimed, as she threw herself upon her knees. "May the curse of the widow and orphan follow you! may the blood of the murthered cry to Heaven for vengeance! may your death be sudden, without one to pity you or close

· 20

your eyes! may you die with curses upon your lips!
and may the dogs lick up your blood! may——"

"Stop, you old beldame, your d——d croaking,"
said Mr. Ellis, furious with passion.

"You have shown little mercy to man; may God
show you as little. May the curse——"

"Well, this might stop you," and he struck her
with his clenched fist.

The blood flowed from her nose and mouth, and
she fell insensible. When she recovered she was
alone, and the darkness of the night was setting in.

"I'm cowld and dry," said she; "if I could get
some water," and the poor creature crept to a stream
near her.

After drinking some, she tried to eat a morsel of
the bread she was carrying to her orphans. The
snow and sleet were falling fast, and she crept under
the shelter of a tree.

"It's very cowld—cowld, so it is, and I'm gettin'
so weak and my eyes are gettin' dim," and she
wrapped her tattered garments around her and fell
into a kind of stupor. It commenced snowing and
freezing by times, and so intense was the cold, and
so weak was she from fatigue and hunger, that she
never awoke from that stupor. Some days afterwards her body was discovered in a crouching position by Mr. Ellis himself. If he had a conscience at
all, how must he have felt then?

The children remained at the fire wondering what
was keeping "mammy."

" Mary," said the youngest, " I'm so weak I can't see ; I don't know what's keeping mammy," and she began to cry.

"Don't cry," said the other, " but come near me," and they crouched together and clasped their arms around their necks, and shortly fell asleep The dry thatch around them shortly took fire, their clothes lit up, and they awoke screaming with pain and terror. Their cries and shrieks were drowned by the hissing flames, for the bed and roof were now all on fire. The cabin shortly fell in, burying them in its ruins ; even their charred remains could scarcely be recognized.

Frank having finished his little arrangements, went to pay a parting visit to his uncle and to Alice. The old man seemed bewildered ; at one time imploring him not .to leave him ; again, advising him to go. Frank feared his parting with Alice more than any other. Though he resolved to appear calm, still it was not easy for him to school himself into a resigned kind of indifference, when the heart was overflowing, when he was to part from one he loved so well, perhaps forever. It was a soft, calm evening for the season—one of those evenings that seem to herald in the spring. As Frank, thoughtful and gloomy enough, approached Mr. Maher's, he passed by the little summer-house where they spent many a happy hour together. There, in that old trysting spot, sat Alice ; she looked pale, and her eyes were red from weeping. They were alone, and

Frank was seated beside her, clasping her little soft hand in his own. Though their hearts were full, they were silent. She rested her head upon his bosom; her breath and her silky hair fanned his cheek; their hearts beat and throbbed in unison.

"Alice, love!" said he, "how wildly your little heart throbs."

"Does it, Frank, does it? Oh! I'm sure it does."

"Yes, love. Will it beat this way for me when I'm far away?"

She looked softly into his face, as much as to say, "Do you doubt it?"

"Oh! it will, it will, love. Alice, do you know that, next to my God, I love you. Sweet girl, I could almost adore you. Oh! life, indeed, would be so burdensome to me now, that I fear I would be reckless of it, indeed, were I not cheered with the hope of one day clasping you to my bosom, my own darling wife. For you I'll toil and win wealth and fame—all, all for you; for, oh! your love will be a powerful talisman to cheer me through life's battle. Yes, while supported by it, I must win—I must succeed."

Alice sobbed and looked into his face, and her peachy cheek pressed against his.

"Ah! Alice! Alice!" said he again, "how can I leave you?"

"Frank, I don't know. Couldn't you stay? Wouldn't we be happy together anyway?"

"It can't be, it can't be, Alice. Oh, let me be a man again. Oh, love, I would almost as soon lose the chance of heaven as lose the hope of one day calling you mine ; and yet I must go, for I could not bring you into poverty or a struggle with the world. No, I'll go and win wealth ; and if I live, in five years I will return. Be faithful, Alice. Let not any false rumors shake your confidence in me ; for if I were to return and find you the bride of another, oh ! what would wealth or fame be to me then ? No, I would seek a grave in some foreign land."

"Frank," said she, mildly, "do you doubt my love ? If not your bride, I will be the bride of heaven."

"God bless you. You know love is suspicious. We fear to part a costly gem when once we possess it."

"Well, well," said she, trying to smile, "I promise you will find the gem as pure as when you parted with it. Now let us go in. You must see my father, and I and my brother will go over as far as your uncle's with you."

"Yes, love. But wait a moment. Here is a little song I composed expressive of our feelings. When you sing it, it will recall your absent lover."

"No need of such, Frank, to make me remember you. This throbbing heart can never forget you."

"I know that, love ; and now I'll sing it before we part."

He sung in a low, plaintive voice :—

ALICE A R'UIN.

My heart's full of love and light,
  Alice a r'uin ;
Your bosom fair as blossom white,
  Alice a r'uin.
Your cheeks are of the roses hue,
Your sparkling eye of heaven's blue,
And your heart is real and true,
  Alice a r'uin.

But, oh ! the world's cold and dark,
  Alice a r'uin ;
Cursed wealth is all the mark,
  Alice a r'uin.
Men's hearts are growin' cold ;
Where, where's the love of old ?
Fled away to gems and gold,
  Alice a r'uin.

My love, awhile I must forego,
  Alice a r'uin ;
Away to golden lands I'll go,
  Alice a r'uin.
Weep not, for, some future day,
True love shall guide my way
To thee, o'er the ocean's spray,
  Alice a r'uin.

I'll win an honored name,
  Alice a r'uin ;
I'll win both wealth and fame,
  Alice a r'uin.
I'll win thee, gems and gold,
Then, with fond love untold,
To my longing breast I'll fold
  Alice a r'uin.

Then, I ne'er again shall roam,
   Alice a r'uin;
For happy in our cottage home,
   Alice a r'uin,
With you, my fond love, my pride!
Life shall be one gushing tide
Of happiness, my own sweet bride!
   Alice a r'uin

"God grant that fortune may be as propitious as you describe it, Frank."

"Well, well, let us hope in God, Alice. He never filled our hearts with such deep love to make us miserable."

"I hope not; and now, Frank, let us go in, and be sure this will be my favorite song."

There is no need of describing to our Irish readers Frank's separation from his family, for there are few but have met with such bereavements. To his dear sister he promised to write regularly, and to send her money if he could. Nothing affected him so much as the childish imbecility of his father. As he kissed him and wept in his arms, the old man said—

"Where are you going, Frank? Won't you come back soon, and bring your mother. Sure Mr. Ellis won't turn us out of the house."

"I'm going away, father, for good."

"Are you? God bless you, boy! but come back soon, and mind bring your mother; it's time for her to come home."

Frank and his fellow-passengers were carried down on a steamer from Cork to where the ship lay

at anchor in the bay. The scene on board the emigrant ship was new to him. Every one was busily
engaged hauling on board his luggage or stowing it
away in some safe corner. The cabin passengers
sauntered about with their hands stuffed in their
pockets and with an air of no small consequence.
The young were fast making acquaintances with the
fair *belles* that accompanied them, and were—or what
amounts to the same thing—affected to be smitten
with their laughing eyes and ruby lips. Some of
the deck passengers were keeping watch over their
bundles, that looked, with their winding sheets
around them, as if waiting for interment; whilst
others that had no earthly goods to trouble them,
were sauntering about listlessly watching the scene.

Here sat a poor old man, with his wife and three
or four children clinging around him—the latest
victims of Irish landlordism. In another place a
crazed mother is giving her blessing and parting
advice to her only son or daughter. Here is a poor
man with an oak stick in his hand and a small box
of earth with a few shamrocks in it, taken from behind the old house at home. He closely presses
them under his arm as a mother would her af-
frighted child. Huddled in groups were poor infirm men, with their hearts too seared to cry, and
weeping women and wondering children. They all
look fondly towards that land they loved so well—
that land that gave them birth, but denied them
bread.

I tell you what, you can read the history of Ireland's wrongs in the stern necessity that urges on her children, and the deep love that binds them to the soil in the groups that throng the deck of an emigrant ship. Indeed, it is Ireland in miniature.

The steamer that brought down the passengers and their friends now leaves. What a parting! There is weeping, and sobs, and wild cries of agony. Promises are made never to be fulfilled, hopes entertained never to be realized. Fond parents are torn from their children. Friends shed mutual tears in each other's embrace; they know they part to meet no more, except beyond the grave. Lovers are separated. The steamer now moves off, hats and handkerchiefs wave, friends leaning over the side of the departing vessel converse for the last time. At last their views are lost in the distance, and parents, children, and friends part to meet no more on earth.

CHAPTER XXIX.

MR. ELLIS and Hugh Pembert were alone in the office.

"So this young hot-headed O'Donnell has left the country? That's an ease, anyway," said Mr. Ellis.

"I dinna ken that makes things the safer. You see, people canna stop speaking; but I'm na going to tell all they say."

"Why, Hugh, what are they saying?"

"Weel, it's na concern of mine. I often told you that you dinna look to your ain family. Why, maun, it's on every one's tongue that Mr. Sly is fond of Lizzie. I'm telling you so this good spell, but you dinna believe me. Now, it's as weel get them married at once."

"Can it be that he thus presumes upon my friendship to steal the affections of my child? No, it cannot be, and if even so, Hugh, she might meet a worse match. I don't want riches; I have enough."

"Weel, as you like, sir But you dinna ken that

he is no minister at all, but a Bible-reader, and
Mister Steen is his own brother."

"Impossible, Hugh, impossible! If I thought so,
I'd hunt him out of the house. No doubt, himself
and Lizzie have been thrown at me this time back
Any letters?" This was addressed to a servant
with the post-bag.

"Yes, sir."

After reading one letter, his brows knit together
and a dark scowl crossed his face.

"Read that," said he, flinging the letter to Hugh.
Hugh read:—

"Priory, March 1st.
"Dear Sir,

"I have reason to believe that Mr. Sly, who
is, I fear, bringing your name into disrepute by his
uncharitable interference with the rights of his poor
fellow-Christians, is not a minister; he's merely a
Bible-reader, and was expelled from C—— on account of some acts not consistent with the calling
of an expounder of the word of God. It is currently reported that he's about forming an alliance with
your family. As a Christian minister, I mention
this that you may make all due inquiries about him.
Begging that you'll keep this communication private,
"I am, dear sir,
"C. SMITH."

"Weel," said Hugh, handing back the letter, "just
as I said."

"Damnation! but he shall leave my house this instant."

Mr. Ellis arose in a boiling passion and passed to the drawing-room, where Mr. Sly and Lizzie were seated together enjoying a pleasant chat.

"Viper! wretch!" shouted Mr. Ellis, shaking his hand at Mr. Sly, "have you come into my house to rob me of my child; but no—be off at once!"

I will not detail the stormy scene that ensued. Despite of Lizzie's tears and entreaties, Mr. Sly got but that day to make arrangements for his departure.

Lizzie was beside herself. How could she part from her dear, gentle Mr. Sly? She went to Hugh, who was her confident of late. She told him that Mr. Sly wanted her to elope. Hugh encouraged her, telling her that her father would relent after a few days; and as she was an only child, he could not part with her. In fact, he took such an interest in her, that he made all the arrangements for their elopement.

Next morning, when Mr. Ellis was apprised of Lizzie's elopement, he stormed and raved; for notwithstanding all his wickedness, he was deeply attached to her.

He upbraided himself with his precipitancy, and ordered his car to follow them to Dublin, for he learned that they had taken the train from the next town for Dublin.

Hugh Pembert now saw all his plans crowned

with success. He knew that Lizzie and Mr. Sly were gone direct to Scotland, for so it was concocted. If Mr. Ellis were out of the way, he was in possession of his large property, and who could dispute his right? He would take good care that Lizzie would not. Nelly Cormack had been expelled from Mr. Ellis's, and was living with some charitable neighbors. The Cormacks were often heard to vow revenge upon Mr. Ellis for the eviction of the O'Donnells and the seduction of their sister; everything combined to throw the murder upon them.

Blinded as he was by his avarice, he shuddered at the crime of shedding his uncle's blood; it was a frightful deed; but then, property was at stake; now was his time or never; no, he couldn't recede. Since his uncle's departure he drank deeply, as if to smother his conscience with deep potations.

On the fourth day, he got a letter from his uncle, saying that he would return the next day; to have the car meet him, for he would go home by the evening train; that he got no account of the fugitives. Each time he read this letter he drank off a glass of spirits, until his eyes glared and his brain reeled.

He rang the bell.

"Tell Burkem to come up to me," said he to the servant.

"Weel, Burkem," said he, as the latter made his appearance, "read that, maun."

" I see," said Burkem, coolly returning the letter.

" Weel, maun, what do you say?"

" Whatever you like, Mr. Hugh."

" I dinna, maun, to say anything; but here's twenty pounds," and he flung him the note.

" I understand," said Burkem, putting the money into his pocket. " These fools the Cormacks got a loan of my long gun to shoot rabbits; they might want it for some other business; however, I'll watch them."

" Do, do. Ye canna say I told you to do anything. Na, na! Here, drink," and he shoved the glass towards him.

Burkem drank off the liquor.

" That's a maun," said the other, filling out a tumbler full of the raw liquid and drinking it off.

" That'll do, Burkem, that'll do. Go. I wish the devil had him. If the job were done, I'll manage him," muttered Hugh, as Burkem closed the door after him.

" Ha, ha, ha! I'll have my revenge upon the Cormacks, and I'll keep a screw upon Hughy, and make him fork out for the job. Not a bad beginning this," said he, looking at the twenty-pound note.

In the evening, Hugh Pembert went over to Mrs. Cormack's, for he had managed to keep upon friendly terms with them; not only that, but to be looked upon as a benefactor; for when Nelly Cormack was driven from Mr. Ellis's, he got her comfortable lodgings, and supplied her with money, for she indignantly refused taking any from Mr. Ellis.

Had the Cormacks known that Burkem was the agent of Mr. Ellis, in giving money to Nelly, and that he paid himself well for his trouble, they would not have esteemed him so highly. Mr. Ellis had some love for her, and now that she was discarded by her friends, he did not wish that she should want.

" God save all here," said Burkem, as he entered the cottage.

" God save you kindly, Mr. Burkem; take a seat; and what news have you ?" said Mrs. Cormack, placing a seat before him.

" Musha! not much, ma'am. Sorra a tidings the master got of Miss Lizzie or that other sly chap. I know he was never any great things; he was always putting the master up to badness. Mr. Hugh didn't like him at all either."

" Sorra a loss he is but for the colleen, God help her. I fear she has made a thorny bed for herself; and they say she wasn't the worst, iv let alone."

" True for you, ma'am. The worst of them would be better but for bad advisers."

" That's true for you, Mr. Burkem. But tell me," and she whispered into his ear, though there was no one present but a little girl, for the two Cormacks were out—" tell me, when did you see Nelly ?" and the poor mother rubbed her eyes.

" Only a few days ago, ma'am. She's brave and strong; and do you know, now as Miss Lizzie is gone, for she was the worst against her, I think the master will marry her."

" Whist ; God send it."

" Not a lie in it. Says he to me the other morning before he went, ' Burkem, I know sorrow and trouble now, and I will try and recompense any one I have caused them to.' Faix, ma'am, I shouldn't be surprised if you all got back your places again."

" God send it ! God send it !" said Mrs. Cormack, piously raising her eyes towards heaven.

" Where are the boys, ma'am ?" said he, after a pause.

" I think they went over in the evening to see poor Mr. O'Donnell. He's very ill since Frank went."

Burkem knit his brows, and a dark cloud passed over his face.

" Will you tell them, ma'am, that I have good news for them. Mr. Pembert sent them word that he would increase their wages to one-and-sixpence, or give them the herding of Croaghbee, with a good living, if they choose. I think, as I always tell them, there is no use in keeping in enmity. I'm sure they'll find Mr. Ellis changed, if they return to his employment. He's resolved to make them comfortable, for he told me so."

" I think so, Mr. Burkem. God bless you for the good news, for indeed our means are out ; and sure it could do no good to the O'Donnells now to have us starve. The poor people, they were good and kind. Heaven knows, I couldn't cry more for my own child than I did for Masther Frank when he came to take his lave of me."

"No wonder, ma'am. But tell the boys not to fail meeting me at Ned Short's to-morrow night, as I want to go there ; and tell James to bring the old gun I gave him to shoot rabbits ; Mr. Hugh was looking for it. I'll give it back again when I show it."

"I will, Mr. Burkem."

"Good-night, ma'am, and don't forget."

"Never fear, Mr. Burkem."

"Ha, ha, ha!" thought Burkem, "I have thrown out the bait for them now. I know the poor devils are in want, and will take it. I'm too many for them. Blood for blood! Ha, ha!"

The following evening the two Cormacks went over to Short's. They found Burkem waiting for them.

"Welcome, boys," said Burkem ; "I see you've brought the gun ?"

"Faith I have," said James Cormack, "and deuce a much I shot with it either."

"I hope you'll bring in the losses to-night ; it's a fine night for fowling."

"Ay, iv you had cats' eyes," said Ned Short.

"Let us go," whispered Burkem into James Cormack's ear. "I don't want to tell you anything before Short ; he's looking for the herding himself."

" Very well," said the Cormacks.

" Is the gun loaded before we go ?" said Burkem.

" No."

" Oh ! I'll load it," and he pulled a paper of slugs out of his pocket and loaded it, tearing some of the paper off the slugs for wadding. " Here are these," and he handed the rest to one of the Cormacks.

Burkem promised a living to the Cormacks. He, by the most plausible arguments, reconciled them to Mr. Ellis's employment. He went into the house with them to smoke on his return, and he then asked them to accompany him home, as the night was dark. They, unsuspectingly, went with him, until they left him near Mr. Ellis's place, and then returned home.

The night was pitchy dark. As Mr. Ellis neared a narrow part of the road leading to his own place, the horse stopped suddenly and shied. The driver came down, and found a tree drawn across the road.

" Begor, there's a tree across the road, sir," said Splane.

" Pull it away—quick. Hold, who——"

But ere the sentence was finished, the report of a gun was heard, and Mr. Ellis fell dead from the car. The horse turned back and ran, and Splane had to go nearly half a mile to the next house for assistance. He then went to Mr. Ellis's house, and when he returned with assistance, Mr. Ellis was found dead. Blood was flowing from a wound, and a dog was actually lapping it up. His death must have béen instantaneous, as several slugs passed through his heart.

The body was removed; an inquest was held, and the two Cormacks were empanneled upon the jury. Splane swore that he didn't know who fired the shot, for the night was dark, and he was engaged removing the tree. The jury returned a verdict of wilful murder against some person or persons unknown. A few days passed over, the slavish journals rang out with the report of this cold-blooded murder, this diabolical crime, that disgraced civilization. A good, a great man, a kind, bereaved father, returning from the search of his deluded child, is foully murdered. He was called an amiable victim, a kind landlord, and a good agent, and all those pet terms in requisition on such occasions—no matter how worthless a tyrant the victim may have been. A large government reward was offered for the perpetrators of the deed.

It was remarked that Burkem and Splane were seen very much together after the reward was offered. The result was that the two Cormacks were arrested, charged with the murder. A package of slugs was found in a drawer, and the paper around them corresponded with the wadding found near the murdered man.

It is not our intention to follow them through the fearful ordeal of their trial. A special commission was called. Murder was rife in Tipperary, and victims were wanting. .

Sir William Placeman* was one of the judges sent down ; and the people hoped that justice would be done, for he had lately ascended the bench upon the shoulders of the people.

Public sympathy was strong in favor of the Cormacks. They were known to be quiet, industrious young men, who were never known to mix themselves up with any of the factions or parties that disturbed the country. Add to this the execration in which Mr. Ellis was held, and it is no wonder that the court-house was crowded to excess upon the morning of that day which was to restore the Cormacks to a loving mother or consign them to an ignominious death and an untimely grave in their early manhood.

At length the trial came on, and the prisoners were placed at the bar. There, in that fatal dock, side by side, stood the two brothers. They were two noble-looking specimens of the peasant class. They stood erect, equally free from indifference or braggadocio. Though they wore a somewhat dejected appearance, their fair symmetrical forms still retained their erect positions : their eyes had lost nothing of their lustre, nor their cheeks the bloom of health.

The attorney-general opened the proceedings by a long and able statement, and by a recapitulation of the evidence to be brought forth. He dwelt upon each point minutely—upon their sister's disgrace,

* Help me God Keogh

and they being in Mr. Ellis's employment. The first witness called was Bill Burkem. He gave a minute account of how the Cormacks inveigled him to join in shooting his master, after the eviction of the O'Donnells; how he gave them his master's gun and the slugs; how he met' them the night of the murder at Ned Short's house.

Though ably cross-examined, his testimony could not be shaken. Then he took the rod to identify the prisoners. He looked for a moment at his victims; his usual dark scowl passed over his brow, and a sneer of deadly vengeance distorted his guilty face. His victims stood erect, their eyes met his, and, even hardened as he was, his soul of crime and villainy could not withstand that innocent, fearless gaze. The next witness was Splane. He swore positively that he knew the Cormacks, and that it was James that fired the shot. When asked why he did not swear this upon the inquest, he said "he was afraid, and was so alarmed that he did not know what he was doing." Ned Short corroborated Burkem's evidence about meeting the Cormacks at his house, about loading the gun, and the remarks about the fowling.

A constable swore to comparing the wadding and the paper around the slugs, and found them to agree with those found on the Cormacks; also to the slugs found in the body and those in the paper, which also agreed.

The doctor swore as to the cause of his death.

There was only one other witness, and a deep
silence reigned in court as the crier called—

"Mrs. Cormack!"

She had to be helped to the witness-box, and a
seat given her; as she sat down, she wiped the
tears from her eyes.

"Oh! my boys! my darlin' boys! is it there ye
are?" said she, looking earnestly towards the dock.

The prisoners' lips quivered, and they rubbed
their eyes.

The question was put to her— "Do you recollect
the night Mr. Ellis was murdered?"

"Oh! sure I do; and that's the sorrowful night
to me."

"Did you see your sons, the prisoners at the
bar, with Bill Burkem that night at your house?"

"Oh! the murtherer, the murtherer! Shure, my
lord, he pretended to be our friend; and he came
that night to get back the work for the boys. Oh!
the murtherer! it was to enthrap them."

"Had they a gun, ma'am?"

"Och, I'll say no more; maybe it's to injure them
I'd do."

"You must answer the question."

"Oh, my lord, don't ask me; don't ask the
mother that suckled these boys, that bore them in
thrial and throuble, to swear against them—the
mother they never vexed nor crossed. Oh! if you
knew them, my lord—they were like two children.
No, my lord, I can't say anything aginst them; no,

acushla ogo machree," and she stretched her hands towards the prisoners. "No, avourneen, yer poor ould mother won't swear aginst you !"

There was scarcely a dry eye in court at this pathetic appeal, and the two young men in the dock wept like children. The judge appeared perplexed at her refusal, and threatened to commit her for contempt of court.

" Mother," said James, "it can't do us any harm. Speak the truth. We are innocent, and God will protect us."

"I will, alanna, if you ask me."

" Do, mother."

The question being put, if she saw a gun with them.

" I did, my lord. Shure that foul-hearted villain gave it to them to shoot rabbits."

" Did they go out with Burkem when leaving ?"

"Yes, my lord. He asked them part of the way wid him, as the night was dark."

" And how long were they out, ma'am ?"

"I dunna how long, my lord."

"No matter. That will do. Go down, ma'am."

" Stop. Had they the gun when they returned ?" srid the counsellor.

"No, sir. My lord, my lord !" she exclaimed, stretching her hands towards the judge, " have pity upon my boys. They are innocent, I know they are, God knows they are. I couldn't live without them ! Have pity upon them, and God will have pity upon you."

The counsellor for the defence dwelt upon the characters of the witnesses, one of whom was a perjurer, as he swore at the inquest that he did not see who fired the shot. The other, a man that, according to his own evidence, joined in a conspiracy to murder his own master, was not to be believed upon his oath. As to the evidence of Short. Was it likely that they would meet at his house to go and commit a murder? that is, to get up a witness against them; besides the house was out of their way. It is not possible that, with such intentions in their heart, they would go into their mother's house, knowing that she would be brought forth in evidence against them. Is it likely that they would retain the slugs in the house? Again, the mother swore that they had not the gun when they returned, and the gun was Burkem's. Now, my lord, is it not evident that it was all a conspiracy of Burkem's, to weave a network of evidence against these men; perhaps to do the deed himself, and then reap the fruit by earning the blood-money? What was his motive in bringing them to Short's house, in giving them the slugs there, and loading the gun with some of the paper that covered the slugs, but to fix them in his meshes? I call upon you, gentlemen of the jury, to recollect all these, to weigh them minutely, and to give the prisoners at the bar the benefit of any doubts that may occur to your minds.

This is but a mere outline of the long and able defence of their counsel. Indeed, so telling was it that many a heart began to throb with hope—a hope which the judge's charge shortly dissipated. He recapitulated the evidence, dwelling with fearful minuteness upon any point that could tell against the prisoners. As to their oversight in having the slugs and going into Short's, he said that murder will always come out somehow. Then he spoke of the agitated state of the country—the many agrarian murders that disgraced it—that, in fact, unless such murders were put down by the strong arm of the law, there would be no safety for life or property. His charge was so strong and pointed, that the jury, after leaving the box, shortly returned, and amidst the most breathless excitement of the vast crowd that thronged the court, handed in the fearful verdict of "Guilty."*

Then the judge assumed the black cap, and, after exhorting the prisoners to repentance for their sins —to look to God for that mercy which they refused their fellow-creature—he pronounced the sentence " That you be taken, on the 10th of next month, at the hour of ten o'clock, from the prison from whence you came to the front of the jail, and there be hanged by the neck until you be dead. May God have mercy upon your souls !"

A wail and cry of grief ran through the court as the fearful sentence was pronounced. The deadly

* The first jury that tried the Cormacks disagreed, and Judge Keogh immediately empanneled a jury that he felt sure would bring a verdict to crder.

word had gone forth and stricken many a heart with the fearful announcement. A wild and piercing shriek rose high above the sobs of the women and the strong grief of the men. The prisoners turned around and recognized their mother's insensible form borne by a crowd of women. Mary Cahill, pale and weeping, stood beside her. Her glance met her lover's, and he bent his head and sobbed, and she wildly wept and wrung her hands.

"My lord," said James Cormack, as they were leaving the dock, "before God, I solemnly declare that we are as innocent as the child unborn. Our lives are sworn away. But may God forgive our murderers."

Another murmur ran through the court.

CHAPTER XXX.

THE SEPARATION—THE EXECUTION.

Our tale is fast drawing to a close. It is melancholy, indeed, to dwell upon the fate of two strong young men consigned to an ignominious death for a crime of which they had not the slightest knowledge.

The Cormacks clung to life with a hope; but there was no hope for them. Notwithstanding their conviction, still there was a general feeling abroad that they were innocent. A petition, numerously and respectively signed by the leading gentry and clergy of the county—even by the archbishop—was got up in their favor; but offended law should take its course, and two innocent men should die to strike terror into the guilty. It was even said that this petition was submitted to the consideration of the judge that tried them, but he saw no reason why the law shouldn't take its course. Afterwards, when one of the witnesses felt some remorse of conscience, and began to make some unpleasant disclosures, it is thought that the same judge besought the viceroy to grant a reprieve; but the fiat had gone forth and

could not bo revo'/ed In fact, a special commission
seems called to strice terror into the people, and
this can never be effective without victims. But to
return to the poo/: doomed Cormacks.

After the reply to the petition, all hope of life was
shut out from them. They gave all their thoughts
to God, and joined their spiritual guide in devotion
and prayer. There was a melancholy kind of resignation abor.t them, more saddening than the most
callous indifference. Poor fellows, it was no wonder
that they should fret. The bright world was about
closing on them ; they were sinking into a dishon-
ored grave for the crime of others. But the dreadful day drew near, and the parting time had come.
The day previous to that on which they were to give
up their young lives upon the scaffold, the mother
and discarded sister entered their cell. The old
woman was supported by one of the turnkeys. So
thin, so emaciated, and worn was she, that she
seemed as if risen from the grave. She cast a
vacant, unmeaning look about the cell, but as her
sons approached to embrace her for the last time,
she exclaimed—

"My darlin', my darlin' boys! shure they can't
murther you. Oh, no ; shure ye never hurt or injured any one, ye that were so thender-hearted and
kind to your poor old mother. O God! O God!"
Silently she sat down between them upon the seat,
and took their hands in hers and bathed them with
kisses and tears.

Nelly Cormack stood aside weeping at this scene. At length she exclaimed—

" My God, won't they forgive me? My own poor brothers won't forgive me! Oh! miserable, miserable girl that I am!"

" They will forgive you, Nelly. Come here. Won't ye forgive her, my darlin' boys? You know she is the only one I have now."

" Yis, mother, yis. And when we are gone we trust she'll bo kind and faithful to you," and the brothers kissed and embraced their erring sister.

" Thank God! thank God!" she exclaimed. " I will devote my life to our poor mother, boys."

As the old woman sat between them, she was again in her humble but happy cottage, with her darling sunny-haired children playing about or nestling their cherub little cheeks against her bosom. She was caroling to them a little soft song to lull them to rest, and angel voices and dreamy music seemed to float around their little cottage. She went back to the happy days, when, a fond young mother, she dandled her first-born in her lap or covered him with kisses, whilst the doting father looked proudly on. But this was but a dream, and the fearful reality recurred to her mind, and she clung to them, exclaiming—

" My boys, my boys! shure ye won't lave your poor ould mother alone and helpless—alone in the world, no one to care for her? No matter, iv they kill ye, I'll shortly find ye in heaven. I feel it here,

here; my heart is breaking," and she pressed her hand against her bosom.

The brothers pressed their hands against their faces, and the boiling tears gushed forth, and then they fixed their despairing gaze upon that stricken woman, and in a touching tone exclaimed—

"Ah! mother, mother, God pity you!"

At length the jailer came to separate them; she wildly clung to them, screaming "Spare them!" As she was torn away from their embrace, she stretched out her thin hands to them in an agony of despair, and then fell senseless upon the floor. She was borne into a house near the jail, but the crimson tide gushed from her pale lips; ere the following morning broke, that poor bruised, bleeding heart was at rest. The condemned men had scarcely recovered their composure after that sad interview when Kate O'Donnell and Mary Cahill were admitted into the cell.

We will not attempt to paint that last and awful meeting, when two fond young hearts, that were united by the sacred ties of love, were stricken forever. All their bright dreams and hopes of happiness had vanished with that wild phrenzied embrace. All were gone, and they were left to commune with the God before whose awful tribunal they were to appear on the morrow.

An execution in Ireland does not attract those large crowds of curious spectators that witness the like scenes in England. No; here while the culprit's soul is passing into eternity, the chapels are open, the people join in offering up the Holy Sacrifice, supplicating the Almighty God to grant them mercy. Thus were they employed upon the morning of the execution. With the exception of the police and military, there were few present.

At the appointed hour the prisoners were led to the fatal drop. They appeared calm and reconciled. They joined the priest in prayer and supplication. James Cormack looked down at the crowd for a moment, and then, in a firm voice, said—

"Good people, before God, who is shortly to judge us, we declare that we are as innocent of the murder of Mr. Ellis as the child unborn. We had neither hand, act, nor part in it. May God forgive our prosecutors."

An exclamation of sympathy arose from the people, and at a sign from the priest they fell upon their knees in fervent prayer.

The executioner had now adjusted the rope, and as he settled the knot about James Cormack's neck, he hissed into his ear—

"Blood for blood! I have sworn it. You crossed my love for Mary Cahill, you spilt my blood, and now I have yours."

James Cormack turned upon him a withering look, but then his awful position recurred to him, and he bent his head in prayer, and muttered, "God forgive you." A few moments and they had passed into eternity.

They were laid to rest in the same grave with their poor mother.   May they rest in peace!   Their sister Nelly soon followed; for, unable to bear up against her heavy grief, she heart-broken, soon went to the happy land where, the weary are at rest and sin no more.

CHAPTER XXXI.

THE WRECK—MEETING OF OLD FRIENDS—TRUE LOVE
REWARDED.

IT is a fearful sight to see a noble ship, crowded
with human beings, drifting helplessly upon an
angry sea. The good ship *Mary Jane* sailed proudly
with her freight of passengers.

Over three hundred emigrants were upon her—
some going to meet old friends—some going to try
their fortunes in foreign lands; but all full of hope
and spirit.

For a few days the noble vessel sped merrily
along, like a thing of life. A storm set in, and the
angry seas hissed, and boiled, and foamed, tossing
her about like a plaything, as if to mock the powers
of man. Her sails and rigging were torn, and her
masts were gone, leaving her absolutely helpless.
The sea swept over her deck, and on she went before the relentless storm, until she fiercely dashed
against some projecting rocks. She bumped and
tossed about.

The shouts and screams and cries for mercy that
rose from that fated ship were fearful; but there
was no one to hear them but God and his angels,
for the tossing waves and roaring elements had

drowned them to the ears of men. In the stern of that ill-fated vessel two men clung to a rope ; they clung for life—but in vain.

"O God! O God! we'll be lost ; lost here and hereafter ; damned, damned forever !" shrieked the perjured Splane. "The blood of the Cormacks is rising up in judgment against us now — to be damned, to be damned forever—ever in hell's fire ! Isn't it fearful? What use is our blood-money to us now, Burkem ? Yes, it will help to drag us down deeper into the pits of hell. May my curse light upon you ; but for you I'd never have their blood to answer for. No, you——"

A fierce sea swept over the vessel ; the rope they clung to snapped asunder ; and ere the recording angel had registered the oath, they were swept into eternity.

We must take our readers for a moment to a thriving town in the Western States of America. Look at that pretty shop beyond ; the windows well filled with green and blue and yellow bottles, full of leeches and the like, tell us plainly as words that it is a doctor's establishment. What name is this over the door? "William Shea, M. D."

In a snug little parlor that bespoke comfort sat Willy Shea. We cannot bring ourselves to call him doctor : there is something formal in it, and we like to be on the most intimate terms with old friends.

Willy sat near the fire reading a paper. He looked much fleshier and manlier than when we last saw him. The china cups and saucers, and the fresh rolls and the golden butter, all stood ready upon the tea-table, waiting for the kettle, which seemed to boil very leisurely.

Willy had on his slippers, and he looked so happy and contented in his easy-chair that one might envy him.

Near him sat his wife, a fine blooming-looking young woman. She had a prattling little baby of about a year old in her lap.

The little thing kicked and crowed lustily, to the great delight of the doting mother and fond father, for the latter occasionally raised his eyes from the paper he was reading to reward the little prattler with a smile.

" I declare, Willy, but she knows you. The little ducky tries to go to you," said the mother, as the baby stretched her hands to her father.

" She does, the darling. Come, little pet. I'll take her while you're getting the tea, Kate."

" Do, love ;" and the mother, after kissing her, handed her to her father.

Sitting at the other side of the fire was a young man of about thirty. His face was covered with beard, and he looked sunburnt, as if he were after coming from some warm clime. He, too, played with a little boy of about two years, that he nursed upon his knee.

Tea being ready, they sat around the table, and began to converse upon various subjects.

"I declare, Frank," said Mrs. Shea, "you ought to remain with us. You could buy a nice property here, and have us all settle together."

"You know, Kate, there is a talisman in old Ireland for me yet; besides, despite all her wrongs and miseries, the love of native land has become strong with me while toiling for wealth in the golden fields of California. No, Kate, I long to meet old friends; to ramble through the old haunts, where you and I, and others that are now in heaven, chased the butterfly and pulled the wild flowers, or listlessly sat upon some mossy bank, listening to the rippling of the stream or the merry notes of the birds. No, Kate, somehow I could not live from that old land where my fathers' and mothers' bones are laid to rest."

"But, Frank, so few of us have escaped the fatal ruin of our family, we ought to try and live near one another."

"I should like it very much. I'll tell you what you might do: I have more wealth than I can well want; now, come to Ireland with me; I'll set you up, and buy a small property for you. What do you say to that, sister mine?"

Mrs. Shea looked enquiringly at her husband.

"Really, Frank," said he, "I have seen so much misery and wretchedness and oppression in Ireland that my heart grows sick at the thought of encoun-

tering it again. Since I set up here I have a good
lucrative practice, and would not like to change, if
it's the same to my dear Kate. There is a field here,
Frank, for an active man that cannot be found in
Ireland."

" Willy, do as you think best," said Kate, like a
dutiful wife.

" Did my father ever get his reason rightly ?" said
Frank, changing the conversation.

"Yes ; he had a lucid interval before his death ;
and when he learned our sad history, and how we
were scattered, he wept like a child, and then sunk
again into his childish ways, until he died."

" And poor Uncle Corny ?"

"Poor man ! he was always raving about battles
and sieges, and other things of the kind, until he
died, exactly six months after you left."

" And our good, kind uncle, Father O'Donnell,
how did he bear up ?"

" Poorly, Frank. After our father's death he
sank rapidly ; he was always speaking of you. You
know I went to live with him after father's death.
That noble girl, Alice Maher—you cannot esteem
her too highly, Frank—spent many an evening with
us. We often wept over old times, and breathed
many a sigh to Heaven for your safe return. Father
O'Donnell was like a child near Alice. At length
we found that he was getting childish ; for he used
to ask Alice where you were, and when did she see
you, and the like."

Frank held down his head and wept.

"He then sank rapidly," continued Kate; "and about a month before his death Willy, here, returned; the old man was just able to perform the marriage ceremony, but it was his last, for he was soon after laid to rest in his own little chapel. We sold his effects; they were barely able to cover his debts; then, with what money Willy had, and the last check I got from you, we came and established ourselves here."

Frank held his sister's hand in his and wept, as the thoughts of home and old friends rose to his memory.

"Come, come, don't be childish," said Willy. "You must come with me to-morrow, Frank, to see an old friend."

"Who is it, Willy?" said Frank.

"You recollect Mary Cahill; she's now Sister Mary Joseph. She never raised her head, poor girl, after the execution—murder, I ought to call it—of the two young Cormacks; so she's now a sister of charity."

"The Cormacks, poor fellows, and faithful Mary. I will go, Willy; and her convent will not regret my visit. Do you know what became of Parson Sly and Hugh Pembert?"

"Really I couldn't say, Frank. After squandering the property between them, they went—nobody knew nor cared where—it is thought, to a foreign land."

We must now return to the old country. Though times went hard with many a wealthy man in Ireland, still Mr. Maher, owing to his good, kind landlord, throve and increased in wealth. He is much changed since we saw him last; the gray hair is fast thinning over his brow. Alice, too, looks thin and pale. Instead of that old gay, sprightly appearance, she looks rather sad and more spiritual.

"Alice," said her father, as she poured out the tea at the breakfast-table, "I see that Mr. Ellis's place, including the O'Donnell's old farm, has been bought upon trust. I should like to know who is the purchaser. Tell me, Alice," and Mr. Maher put down his cup, after imbibing about half its contents—"tell me, Alice, isn't it strange that we have had no letter this long time from Frank. Why, the five years will be up in a month. If he doesn't keep his word, I think you oughtn't refuse Mr. —— any longer. You know he's a rich man."

Alice sighed, and the tears started to her eyes.

"Ah! I might as well let you alone. What strange beings you girls are!" and Mr. Maher drank off his tea, as if it were the aggressor, and then walked over to the window.

"Alice!" said he, looking out, "come here. Who the deuce is this strange-looking fellow? He might cut off some of his beard anyway."

The stranger drove up and jumped off the car. Mr. Maher, in answer to his knock, went to open the hall door.

" You don't know me, sir," said the visitor, as
Mr. Maher looked at him in perfect bewilderment.

Alice was standing at the parlor door, her little
heart beating violently, she couldn't tell why; but
as soon as she heard the stranger's voice she ran
out.

" Alice! Alice!" said the stranger, extending his
hands towards her.

" Frank! Frank!" she replied, and sank swoon-
ing into his arms.

" I declare!" said Mr. Maher. " Frank, my boy—
Bring here something to recover her—a cup of
water; run, Mrs. Moran."

Alice quickly recovered, for joy seldom kills.

" Alice! my own fond, faithful Alice!" said Frank,
pressing her to his bosom. "I have returned with
means beyond your father's conception; I strove
and toiled for wealth for you, love. In that rich
land everything I touched seemed to turn into
gold, for I became a regular Fortunatus, and
seemed to have possessed the gift of Midas; but it
was all the fruits of love."

" God bless you, children!" said Mr. Maher, wiping his eyes with a big red handkerchief, and giving
his nose a few great blows that made it resound
like a horn.

" Didn't I always tell you," said Mrs. Moran, with
her apron to her eyes, *"that God never made two
such loving hearts to be unhappy."*

" I would wish," said Frank, next morning, to Mr.

Maher, to take a drive to see where the old house stood, and to shed a tear over the grave of my parents.'

Mr. Maher consented, and Alice and he and Frank set out together. Frank, after visiting the graves of the household, expressed a wish to see Glen Cottage, as it was uninhabited but by a keeper.

"As to that," said Mr. Maher, "it has been bought in the Incumbered Estates' Court; it has gone to the hammer like all Lord Clearall's property. So, I'm sure who ever bought so sweet a place will shortly come to live in it."

Having reached the cottage, they walked from room to room. It was richly furnished with Turkey carpets, rich papers, costly furniture, and splendid drawings and paintings.

"How very civil the servants are," said Mr. Maher.

"It's a little paradise of a place," said Alice, looking out of a window that commanded a magnificent view, and then resting her eyes upon the costly furniture and works of art.

"Would you like to live here, Alice?" said Frank, with a smile.

"Oh! yes, Frank dear, how happy one could be here with those they loved."

"Alice," said Frank, pressing her to him, "you have been true and faithful to me in all my trials and troubles. Sweet love, this is your home; I am the purchaser of it!"

Alice turned her tearful, loving eyes upon Frank's and Mr. Maher again used the red handkerchief, exclaiming—

"God bless you! God bless you! my darling children!"

A few years have passed over, and the place is different from what it was in Mr. Ellis's time. Peace and plenty, love and happiness, now reign around Glen Cottage.

THE END.